HTML5 Guidelines for Web Developers

Klaus Förster
Bernd Öggl

Addison-Wesley

Upper Saddle River, NJ • Boston • Indianapolis • San Francisco
New York • Toronto • Montreal • London • Munich • Paris • Madrid
Capetown • Sydney • Tokyo • Singapore • Mexico City

Figure 4.9 © 2008 Blender Foundation / www.bigbuckbunny.org

Cover design: Marco Lindenbeck, webwo GmbH, mlindenbeck@webwo.de

Many of the designations used by manufacturers and sellers to distinguish their products are claimed as trademarks. Where those designations appear in this book, and the publisher was aware of a trademark claim, the designations have been printed with initial capital letters or in all capitals.

The authors and publisher have taken care in the preparation of this book, but make no expressed or implied warranty of any kind and assume no responsibility for errors or omissions. No liability is assumed for incidental or consequential damages in connection with or arising out of the use of the information or programs contained herein.

The publisher offers excellent discounts on this book when ordered in quantity for bulk purchases or special sales, which may include electronic versions and/or custom covers and content particular to your business, training goals, marketing focus, and branding interests. For more information, please contact:

>   U.S. Corporate and Government Sales
>   (800) 382-3419
>   corpsales@pearsontechgroup.com

For sales outside the United States, please contact:

>   International Sales
>   international@pearson.com

Visit us on the Web: informit.com/aw

Library of Congress Cataloging-in-Publication Data

Förster, Klaus, 1964-
   [HTML 5. English]
   HTML5 guidelines for Web developers / Klaus Förster, Bernd Öggl.
      p.   cm.
   Includes bibliographical references and index.
   ISBN 978-0-321-77274-9 (pbk. : alk. paper)
   1. HTML (Document markup language) 2. Internet programming. 3.
   Web site development. I. Öggl, Bernd. II. Title. III. Title: HTML 5
   guidelines for Web developers.
QA76.625.F6713 2012
006.7'4—dc23

                                     2011014135

ISBN-13: 978-0-321-77274-9
ISBN-10:   0-321-77274-1

Text printed in the United States on recycled paper at RR Donnelley in Crawfordsville, Indiana.
First printing, June 2011

Editor-in-Chief
Mark L. Taub

Senior Acquisitions Editor
Trina MacDonald

Development Editor
Susan Brown Zahn

Translator
Almut Dworak

Managing Editor
John Fuller

Full-Service Production Manager
Julie B. Nahil

Project Editor and Compositor
Mary Sudul, Fastpages

Copy Editor
Anne Marie Walker

Indexer
Jack Lewis

Proofreader
Linda Seifert

HTML5

> GUIDELINES for **WEB DEVELOPERS**

Klaus Förster
Bernd Öggl

Thanks to Andrea and Sabine—you are wonderful!

Contents

Preface

In 2010, HTML5 became *the buzzword* on the web developer scene. Large companies, such as Google, Apple, and Microsoft, began to use the new technology. The popularity of the catchword HTML5 grew, not least of all because of the heated debate between Apple and Adobe over whether this would mean the end of Flash.

In this book, we give you extensive insight into the new possibilities of HTML5. In addition to the classic specification components, such as video, audio, canvas, intelligent forms, offline applications, and microdata (to name but a few), this overview also includes topics in the immediate context of HTML5—for example, geolocation, web storage, WebSockets, and web workers.

Numerous compact, clear, and practical examples illustrate the new elements and techniques in HTML5. There is something here for everyone, whether you decide you want to construct a web log, program your own video and audio player, use the browser as a graphics program, work with geographical data, test to the limit the capacity of your browser, or prefer to live out your playful nature by trying a quiz with drag and drop or playing *Battleships!* with WebSockets. We also give you plenty of tips and tricks regarding JavaScript and the DOM.

It is to be expected that sooner or later all browsers, in order to remain competitive in the future, will accommodate HTML5. We therefore decided not to include workarounds and compatibility libraries in most cases. In this book you will find *pure* HTML5, supported in our examples by at least *one* browser, but in most cases supported already by several manufacturers. For an up-to-date and complete reference of the new HTML elements, we refer you to the Internet. You will find the relevant links in the appropriate text passages of this book.

How to Read This Book

How you decide to explore this book is entirely up to you. The individual chapters do not necessarily have to be read consecutively and are designed to be easily understandable, even if you have not yet read the other chapters. So, you can read the book in the traditional way, from front to back; alternatively, you can read it from back to front or in any order, letting your curiosity guide you.

Who This Book Is for

You should definitely have a basic knowledge of HTML, JavaScript, and CSS; a willingness to work with a different browser for a change, not just the one you are used to; and above all, a desire to discover something new. Try new ideas, such as those in this book, or have a look at the companion website where you can see all the examples in color. Decide what you want to do and, most important, have fun!

The companion website can be found at http://html5.komplett.cc/welcome.

About the Authors

The authors of this book are as versatile and multifaceted as the new web standard they were brave enough to write about while it was still in development.

Klaus Förster, an open source enthusiast, works at the Department of Geography of the University of Innsbruck, Austria. He has attended numerous SVG Open conferences as speaker, reviewer, and workshop leader, and contributed SVG modules to the free software projects PostGIS, GRASS GIS, and SpatiaLite.

Bernd Öggl, lecturer and system administrator at the University of Innsbruck, is the coauthor of a book on PHP and MySQL and has many years of experience programming web applications.

Overview of the New Web Standard

As is appropriate for a web standard, the story of HTML5 starts with the World Wide Web Consortium (W3C), or more precisely, with the W3C Workshop on Web Applications and Compound Documents in June 2004. But rather unusually, the development of HTML5 initially took place outside of the W3C, because the W3C was not at all thrilled with the idea of HTML5 to start with. What had happened?

1.1 How It All Started

In a joint position paper, Mozilla and Opera demanded that the W3C should ensure the continued development of HTML, DOM, and CSS as the basis of web applications of the future. Given the fact that the W3C had already sidelined

HTML4 six years before and had instead elected to back XHTML, XForms, SVG, and SMIL, it was hardly surprising that this suggestion was rejected. The result was very close, with 8 votes in favor and 11 votes against, but the decision still had far-reaching consequences. In the following years, the development of HTML5 was to take place in direct competition with the W3C.

Ian Hickson, who at the time supported the position paper, together with the second Opera representative Håkon Wium Lie and Mozilla's David Baron, reviewed the events in his web log and came to the conclusion:

> *The issues have been discussed, the positions have been given, everyone knows where everyone else stands, now it's time to get down and actually start doing work.*

Referring to recent events, he finishes with these words:

> *What working group is going to work on extending HTML...*

He is referring to the Web Hypertext Applications Technology Working Group (WHATWG), which was created on June 4, 2004, just two days after the end of the workshop. The WHATWG describes itself as a *loose, unofficial, and open collaboration* of the browser manufacturers Safari, Opera, and Mozilla, as well as interested parties. Its aim is to continue development of the HTML standard and to submit the results of this process to a standards organization to achieve standardization.

The founding members of the WHATWG include Anne van Kesteren, Brendan Eich, David Baron, David Hyatt, Dean Edwards, Håkon Wium Lie, Ian Hickson, Johnny Stenbäck, and Maciej Stachowiak. This select circle of developers from the browser and HTML community was to shape the fate of HTML5 from then on, together with the active WHATWG community.

Three specifications were initially on the agenda of Ian Hickson, who took on a central role as editor: *Web Forms 2.0* as advancement of HTML forms; *Web Apps 1.0*, which focused on application development within HTML; and *Web Controls 1.0*, a specification centered around interactive widgets. The latter project was soon abandoned, and *Web Forms* was integrated into *Web Apps* at a later time. The working method of the WHATWG has always been geared toward collaboration with the community; if you look at the homepage (see Figure 1.1), you can see this very clearly.

Figure 1.1   WHATWG homepage at http://www.whatwg.org

Anyone looking for help with learning or using HTML5 will find answers under FAQ, Help, and Forums. The Wiki, hidden behind the Volunteer button, is not quite as helpful yet, because it is geared more toward development issues and contains little documentation on the HTML5 language. The blog, accessible via the News button, seemed a little neglected in 2010 too, which was perhaps due to the fact that the main author, Mark Pilgrim of Google, was at that time busy writing his own online book, which is freely available at http://diveintohtml5.org in case you want to take a look. Fortunately, Anne van Kesteren resurrected the blog in 2011 with reports on developments of the standard—a valuable source for keeping track of recent changes.

One of the most active areas is the Chat at irc://irc.freenode.org/whatwg, linked via the IRC button. Here, the WHATWG community meets up with browser developers and works with them to implement the specification. This is also the place to have heated debates on matters concerning HTML5, make political statements, or tell critics exactly what you think. An imaginary character, Mr. LastWeek, comments on the events with sometimes hefty blog entries at http://lastweekinhtml5.blogspot.com in reaction to the publicly accessible IRC protocols at http://krijnhoetmer.nl/irc-logs, which anyone can not only read, but also actively comment on. Just click on the yellow box at the end of a line you deem relevant, exciting, or important to color the line yellow. To scan the most recent topics, marking entries works quite well.

Three public mailing lists, linked via the Contribute section, are the main instruments of communication—one for user questions, one for contributions to the specification, and one for all those working on implementing the specification. If you do not want to subscribe to the mailing list, you can also access the public archives where all news items are filed and can be searched or downloaded:

- help@whatwg.org
  http://lists.whatwg.org/listinfo.cgi/help-whatwg.org

- whatwg@whatwg.org
  http://lists.whatwg.org/listinfo.cgi/whatwg-whatwg.org

- implementors@whatwg.org
  http://lists.whatwg.org/listinfo.cgi/implementors-whatwg.org

The specification is also being developed in a public and transparent manner—more on this topic in a moment; it is not as straightforward as it sounds. In reality, there is not just one specification but several versions of it. But for now, let's get back to the history of HTML5.

While the WHATWG was working on renewing HTML, the W3C's XHTML2 Working Group set about creating a completely new web. Unlike the WHATWG, which was aiming to achieve backward compatibility, the XHTML2 Working Group, led by Steven Pemberton, tried to further develop HTML in a different way.

Instead of FORMS, XFORMS would be used; FRAMES would be replaced by XFRAMES; and new XML Events would take the place of DOM Events. Each element could have both a src and an href attribute, and the headers h1, h2, h3, h4, h5, h6 would be obsolete and be replaced by h in combination with a new section element. Manual line breaks with br would be realized with l elements; hr would be called separator; the new nl element would allow navigation lists; and to improve semantic options, you could assign a role attribute with predefined or namespace-extensible keywords to each element.

A drop of bitterness and the final nail in the coffin of the XHTML2 project was the lack of support from the browser vendors. The attempted changes were too radical and did not take existing web content into consideration. Soon, the W3C also came to realize that this development would not get far. In October 2006, Tim Berners-Lee, the director of W3C and inventor of the World Wide Web, finally relented and wrote in his blog:

> *Some things are clearer with hindsight of several years. It is necessary to evolve HTML incrementally. The attempt to get the world to switch to XML, including quotes around attribute values and slashes in empty tags and namespaces all at once didn't work.*

Admitting that XHTML2 had failed to become the new web language, he announced the creation of a new HTML working group—on a wider scale this time. The group would involve the browser vendors and would aim at further developing both HTML and XHTML step by step. In the last paragraph of his blog entry he emphasizes his conviction that this is the right way to go:

> *This is going to be a very major collaboration on a very important spec, one of the crown jewels of web technology. Even though hundreds of people will be involved, we are evolving the technology which millions going on billions will use in the future. There won't seem like enough thankyous to go around some days. But we will be maintaining something very important and creating something even better.*

In March 2007, the time had come: The new HTML Working Group was formed. Shortly after it had been announced to the W3C, all members of the WHATWG were invited to participate in the HTML WG—an offer the WHATWG gratefully accepted.

A few months later, a vote was taken to decide if the specification drawn up by the WHATWG should become the basis of the new, joint HTML5 specification. In contrast to the vote taken during the Workshop in 2004, the result was in favor, with 43 voting for, 5 voting against, 4 people abstaining, and 1 explicitly rejecting. After a delay of three years, the original idea of further developing HTML had prevailed.

But this was just the beginning: New ways of cooperating had to be found—a task that proved to be anything but easy because the philosophies of WHATWG and W3C were only compatible to a limited extent. The fact that the two camps were not always in agreement was reflected not only in extensive discussion threads in the W3C's own archived and publicly accessible *public-html* mailing list (http://lists.w3.org/Archives/Public/public-html), but was also evident in the assessment of the HTML5 project's road map.

Although the W3C assumed in its Charter that HTML5 would reach Recommendation in Q3 of 2010, Ian Hickson of the WHATWG anticipated a much longer period. The year 2022 has often been suggested, but such a long time span is considered completely unacceptable by many critics. Yet this time frame may seem more realistic if you take into account the ambitious aim of HTML5 to replace the three specifications—HTML4, DOM2 HTML, and XHTML1—and to expand them significantly, to create a test suite with thousands of tests, and to prescribe two faultless implementations of the standard as *proof of concept*.

One look at the decision-policy rules of the HTML WG gives you an inkling of how complicated the decision-making process of the two groups involved in further developing the specification is (http://dev.w3.org/html5/decision-policy/decision-policy.html). After the XHTML2 Working Group was disbanded in late 2009, the number of critics willing to fully exploit this decision policy increased.

As a result, a constantly growing list of so-called *Issues* is being tracked by the W3C's HTML WG (http://www.w3.org/html/wg/tracker/issues). These issues need to be resolved before declaring Last Call under moderation of the chairs Sam Ruby, Paul Cotton, and Maciej Stachowiak. On the part of the WHATWG, Ian Hickson took advantage of a calmer period and was able to temporarily reduce his issues list (http://www.whatwg.org/issues/data.html) down to *zero*, leading him to announce *HTML5 in Last Call* to the WHATWG in October 2009.

A visible sign of the complexity of the events is the status of the specification. With the WHATWG, the main specification is a compact document, whereas in early 2011 the W3C had eight parts, all counting as part of the HTML5 package. Two of them are generated directly from the WHATWG version and are marked with an asterisk; the others are supplements and are in turn not contained in the WHATWG version.

WHATWG Specification:

- **HTML—Living Standard:** http://whatwg.org/html

W3C HTML WG Specifications:

- **HTML5 - A vocabulary and associated APIs for HTML and XHTML *:** http://www.w3.org/TR/html5
- **HTML5 differences from HTML4:** http://www.w3.org/TR/html5-diff
- **HTML: The Markup Language Reference:** http://www.w3.org/TR/html-markup
- **HTML+RDFa 1.1:** http://www.w3.org/TR/rdfa-in-html
- **HTML Microdata:** http://www.w3.org/TR/microdata
- **HTML Canvas 2D Context *:** http://www.w3.org/TR/2dcontext
- **HTML5: Techniques for providing useful text alternatives:** http://www.w3.org/TR/html-alt-techniques
- **Polyglot Markup HTML-Compatible XHTML Documents:** http://www.w3.org/TR/html-polyglot

Another WHATWG document exists in which all the WHATWG sections are combined with additional specs for *Web Workers*, *Web Storage*, and the *Web Sockets API*. This document, *Web Applications 1.0—Living Standard*, is well suited to serve as an endurance test for HTML rendering: With more than 5MB of source code and JavaScript to display the implementation stage of each section, plus the option of adding direct comments to individual sections, it will stretch any browser to its limit:

http://www.whatwg.org/specs/web-apps/current-work/complete.html

> **TIP**
>
> If you want to go easy on your browser, you could either use the multipage version of that document at http://www.whatwg.org/C or add ?slow-browser at the end of the URL. That way, dynamic components will be skipped and you end up with a static, faster-loading version without interactive elements.

If you want to keep track of the changes made to the specification, you have several options. The WHATWG offers a *Subversion repository* of the complete specification of which you can create a local copy:

- svn co http://svn.whatwg.org/webapps webapps

You can also access Commit messages of the individual revisions via Twitter, a mailing list, or the web interface, the so-called *web-apps-tracker*:

- http://twitter.com/WHATWG

- http://lists.whatwg.org/listinfo.cgi/commit-watchers-whatwg.org

- http://html5.org/tools/web-apps-tracker

Whereas the WHATWG specification changes continuously with each revision, the W3C drafts are subject to the so-called *Heartbeat requirement*, which means that new versions of the W3C specification must be published at regular intervals of three to four months as Working Drafts. By the time this book is published, the next heartbeat will probably have occurred, and who knows, maybe even a *Last Call Working Draft* will have been announced by the W3C.

If you want to explore the history of HTML5, the Time Travel section offers a selection of links as portals to milestones and historic events. The article "Why Apple is betting on HTML 5: a web history" offers a very good summary of the entire HTML history. It is available at *AppleInsider* under the shortened URL, http://bit.ly/2qvA7s.

1.2 Time Travel through Historic Events

Milestones in the development of HTML in selected links include the following:

- **W3C Workshop on Web Applications and Compound Documents (June 2004):** http://www.w3.org/2004/04/webapps-cdf-ws/index

- **Position paper by Opera and Mozilla on further development of HTML:** http://www.w3.org/2004/04/webapps-cdf-ws/papers/opera.html

- **Ian Hickson's assessment of the workshop in three blog posts:** http://ln.hixie.ch/?start=1086387609&order=1&count=3

- **Creation of the WHATWG is announced two days after the workshop:** http://www.whatwg.org/news/start

- **Blog entry "Reinventing HTML" by Tim Berners-Lee (October 2006):** http://dig.csail.mit.edu/breadcrumbs/node/166

- **Relaunch of the W3C HTML Working Group (March 2007):** http://www.w3.org/2007/03/html-pressrelease

- **Ian Hickson informs the WHATWG community of the relaunch:** http://lists.whatwg.org/htdig.cgi/whatwg-whatwg.org/2007-March/009887.html

- **Official invitation to the WHATWG to sign up for the HTML WG:** http://lists.whatwg.org/htdig.cgi/whatwg-whatwg.org/2007-March/009908.html

- **Ian Hickson congratulates the W3C on the initiative on behalf of the WHATWG:** http://lists.whatwg.org/htdig.cgi/whatwg-whatwg.org/2007-March/009909.html

- **HTML Design Principles as basis of HTML5 (November 2007):** http://www.w3.org/TR/html-design-principles/

- **First official HTML5 Working Draft at W3C (January 2008):** http://www.w3.org/2008/02/html5-pressrelease

- **Announcement that the XHTML2 Working Group will be disbanded (July 2009):** http://www.w3.org/News/2009#entry-6601

- **WHATWG declares HTML5 at Last Call (October 2009):** http://blog.whatwg.org/html5-at-last-call

- **W3C publishes eight Working Drafts, two of them new (June 2010):** http://www.w3.org/News/2010#entry-8843

- **W3C announces Timeline to Last Call, expecting to reach Last Call end of May 2011 (September 2010):** http://lists.w3.org/Archives/Public/public-html/2010Sep/0074.html

- **W3C Introduces an HTML5 Logo (January 2011), causing controversy:** http://www.w3.org/News/2011#entry-8992

- **Ian Hickson declares that the WHATWG HTML specification will henceforth just be known as "HTML" and can be considered a "living standard" (January 2011):** http://blog.whatwg.org/html-is-the-new-html5

1.3   In Medias Res

After the preceding brief trip through the history of HTML5, the time has come to finally tackle the elements and attributes of HTML5 directly. What could be more appropriate than the classic *Hello world!* example? This is what it looks like in HTML5:

```
<!DOCTYPE html>
<html>
  <head>
    <meta charset="UTF-8">
    <title>Hello world! in HTML5</title>
  </head>
  <body>
    <p>Hello world!</p>
  </body>
</html>
```

Every HTML5 document begins with the document type declaration `<!DOCTYPE html>`, and it does not matter if you write it in uppercase or lowercase. The second innovation you will notice is the shortened way of specifying the encoding—`<meta charset="UTF-8">`. The rest, like `html`, `head`, `title`, or `body`, you will be familiar with from HTML4, which leads us to the question: *What is really new in HTML5?*

1.3.1   What Is New?

The W3C provides the answer with the specification *HTML5 differences from HTML4*, moderated by Anne van Kesteren. In addition to lists of new and obsolete elements and attributes, we can also find tips on new or changed APIs, external parts of the specification, and finally the *HTML5 Changelog*, which logs in chronological order how and when individual features have found their way into or out of the specification: http://www.w3.org/TR/html5-diff/.

The tables contain a lot of detail, but do not give us a very clear overview. Four *wordles* are therefore going to guide us through this chapter. They were all created using Jonathan Feinberg's Wordle Applet, which is available free of charge at http://www.wordle.net. The frequency of the relevant terms is reflected by the size of the letters for new elements and attributes, and determined by the number of cross-references connected to the relevant feature in the HTML5 specification. For obsolete elements and attributes, the font size corresponds to the frequency of online use, as researched by Opera within the *MAMA* project *What is the Web made of?* (http://dev.opera.com/articles/view/mama).

Let's first take a look at the new elements in the wordle in Figure 1.2. Highlights are definitely the media types `video`, `audio`, and `canvas`—the latter is, simply put, a picture you can program with JavaScript. Many innovations concern structuring elements, for example, article, section, header, hgroup, footer, nav, or aside. For figures, you have figure with figcaption, and you can show or hide additional information with details in combination with summary. You can indicate progress with progress, any kind of measurements with meter, and time and date with time.

We are not likely to come across the elements ruby, rt, and rp in English-speaking countries very often; they are a typographical annotation system used mainly in Chinese and Japanese to give guidance on pronunciation. More useful for us is mark for emphasizing terms or wbr to show that a line break could be inserted at a certain point if necessary.

Some elements tend toward web applications, such as keygen for generating key pairs for encryption or digital signatures, command for executing commands, or output as a result of calculations in forms or other parts of a document. As a container for option elements, datalist offers nonvisible select lists for form fields. For listing alternative resources for video and audio elements, there is source— the browser picks the first known format from this list to play the file. And last but not least is the frequently used embed element introduced by Netscape, now in an amended version.

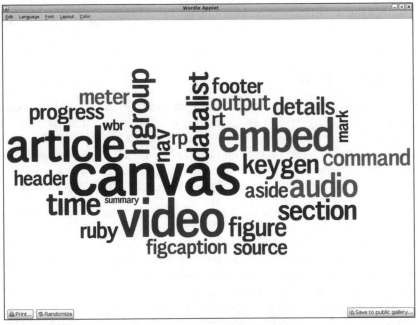

Figure 1.2 New HTML5 elements

The input element also entails many changes. Here is a brief summary of new types: You now have several new input types for specifying the date with date-time, date, month, week, time, and datetime-local. Also, there are types for search fields (search) and for entering URLs (url), e-mail addresses (email), telephone numbers (tel), numbers (number) or numeric ranges (range), or colors (color). As you can see in Figure 1.3, many of the new attributes relate to forms. Thanks to the form attribute, input elements can be external to the form in question and be, as it were, linked to the desired form. Attributes, such as min, max, step, required, pattern, multiple, or autocomplete determine restrictions or conditions for input elements, influence the validation of the entered data with formnovalidate and novalidate, and offer practical help for filling in forms with placeholder or autofocus. What happens when the form is submitted can be overwritten in input and button elements with formmethod, formenctype, formtarget, and formaction. The list attribute serves to assign selection lists created with datalist to the relevant input component.

As security features for iframes, we have sandbox, srcdoc, and seamless. These isolate the embedded content from the rest of the document. If you want to load scripts asynchronously, you can use async, and ping opens the list of URLs specified in the ping attribute in the background whenever you click on a hyperlink.

Figure 1.3   New HTML5 attributes

The manifest attribute of the html element seems inconspicuous but has far-reaching consequences: It paves the way for offline web applications by referring to the configuration file determining which parts of the page should be made available offline. The style elements with the attribute scoped can also be useful, limiting the validity of the specified styles to the area of the superordinate DOM node and all its child elements. For menu elements, type and label determine the type of menu (for example, context menu or toolbar), plus its label.

Small but sweet improvements include using the charset attribute in the meta tag to simplify specifying the encoding; having the option of using li elements via value to assign explicit list values; specifying a starting point for ol with start; and finally being able to sort lists in reverse order with reversed.

Some of the global attributes that are valid for all elements have been changed significantly. This does not apply so much to class, dir, id, lang, style, tab-index, and title, which are now global in contrast to HTML4, but mainly to the new attributes that have been added. With contenteditable you can now edit elements directly; contextmenu enables assigning your own menus, defined as menu; draggable marks the relevant element as a potential candidate for drag-and-drop actions; and spellcheck prepares for checking the relevant section for spelling errors.

Contents that are not or no longer relevant at the time of display can be hidden; the attribute role or aria-* can be used to offer additional help for assistive technologies, such as Screenreader; and the reserved prefix data-* enables you to define as many of your own attributes as you like.

Another important part of HTML5 is that of new programming APIs, for example, the canvas element API, an API for playing audio and video contents, and an interface for programming offline web applications. Further APIs are devoted to the topics drag-and-drop, editing documents, or governing the browser history. The specification even contains some initially exotic-seeming APIs for registering and applying your own protocols or MIME types.

We should also mention that in HTML5 all event handlers are global attributes and that certain changes were made to the objects HTMLDocument and HTMLElement. With getElementsByClassName(), you can find all elements with a particular class attribute; you can manipulate class attributes with the classList API; and you can now use the method innerHTML with XML documents, too. You can determine which element in the document is currently in focus with activeElement and hasFocus—both as attributes of the HTMLDocument object, just as with the method getSelection(), which returns the text currently selected by the user.

1.3.2   What Has Become Obsolete?

When discussing the innovations in HTML5, we should also determine which features we should no longer use. The term *deprecated* is frequently used in other W3C specifications in this context, but this term is not appropriate in the case of HTML5. Because HTML5 is backward compatible, such features also have to be displayed correctly by the browser. For the author of a web page, however, the specification of differences from HTML4 offers a list of elements and attributes that should or may no longer be used. The term *absent* now replaces the term *deprecated*.

If you look at the wordle in Figure 1.4, you can see that the elements font and center are definitely *out*. They are replaced by more up-to-date CSS solutions, and the same applies to the elements u, big, strike, basefont, and tt. Now, iframes replaces frame, frameset, and noframes; instead of acronym you should now use abbr, instead of dir you should use ul, and isindex is abandoned in favor of the better options offered by forms. If you are wondering why some of the elements mentioned do not appear in the wordle, this is due to the fact that they were used very infrequently and are therefore no longer part of HTML5.

For obsolete attributes, the picture is equally clear. Dominant in the wordle in Figure 1.5 are width, height, alignment (align, valign), spacing (cellpadding, cellspacing) , and coloration (bgcolor). They appear mostly in combination with table, td, or body and are now replaced by CSS, like many of the obsolete elements.

Figure 1.4   Elements no longer used in HTML5

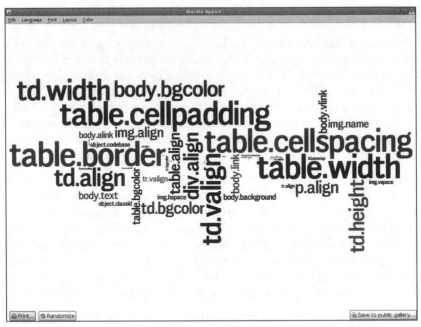

Figure 1.5   Attributes no longer used in HTML5

How do we know in detail which elements and attributes should no longer be used? It would be very time-consuming to have to keep searching through the HTML5 differences. A better solution is offered by the HTML5 validator at http://html5.validator.nu: The validator knows exactly what is right and wrong. Let's give it a try: We select *Text Field* as input mode and replace the line <p></p> in the preset HTML basic frame with the following wrong markup:

```
<center>
  <acronym>WHATWG</acronym>
</center>
```

The error messages this returns look like this—at least at the time of this writing:

1. Error: The center element is obsolete. Use CSS instead.
2. Error: The acronym element is obsolete. Use the abbr element instead.

The link in *Use CSS instead* leads us directly to the WHATWG Wiki, to the page *Presentational elements and attributes*, where we can read details regarding correct use. The validator also shows syntax errors directly, as you can see in the next test. Let's try the following source code:

```
<!DOCTYPE html><title>
```

We get another error message in answer—this time with the comment that the document is not yet complete and therefore invalid:

1.   Error: End of file seen when expecting text or an end tag.

If we fix this error by adding the end tag `</title>`, this error message disappears as well and we have created the shortest possible HTML5 document:

```
<!DOCTYPE html><title></title>
```

Error recognition in the validator is based on one of the key features of HTML5, the HTML parser. Unlike all previous specifications, it was formulated to the last detail, and with its 90 pages is about as exciting to read as the local phone book. From a technical point of view, however, this chapter is essential, because it defines how the HTML5 markup should be parsed and how the document's DOM tree should be structured.

Our preceding mini example generates in reality a complete HTML5 DOM tree, including `html`, `head`, and `body` elements. You can prove this with another tool, the *HTML5 Live DOM Viewer*, at http://livedom.validator.nu. Give it a go!

1.3.3   And What About XHTML?

The HTML5 specification basically defines an abstract language for describing documents and web applications with APIs for interaction, which are representable in an *in-memory* DOM tree. It does not matter which syntax is used as the basis for creating this DOM tree—HTML is one of them, and XHTML is another. What matters is always the result after parsing, which is a valid DOM-HTML tree in both cases.

So the decision whether to use HTML or XHTML when creating documents is up to the author. HTML is more widely used, easier to write, more forgiving with small syntax errors, and requires the MIME type `text/html` for output. XHTML follows the strict XML rules (keyword *well-formedness*) and always has to use an XML MIME type, such as `text/xml` or `application/xhtml+xml`, which was not the case previously with XHTML 1.1.

The *Hello world!* example in XHTML5 manages without `DOCTYPE` but does require a valid XML declaration instead, which can be wrapped up in the encoding, and of course it has to be *well-formed*:

```
<?xml version="1.0" encoding="UTF-8"?>
<html xmlns="http://www.w3.org/1999/xhtml">
  <head>
    <title>Hello world! in HTML5</title>
  </head>
```

```
<body>
  <p>Hello world!</p>
</body>
</html>
```

You probably cannot see much difference between this and the HTML version. That is due to the fact that we have not made full use of the permitted level of simplification in HTML code for the first *Hello world!* example. In *lazy* HTML5, this markup would have been sufficient:

```
<!DOCTYPE html>
<meta charset=utf-8>
<title>Hello World! in HTML5</title>
<P>Hello world!
```

We can leave out quotation marks for attributes if the attribute value does not contain any spaces or any of the symbols " ' > / =. Tags can be written in uppercase or lowercase; sometimes they can even be omitted as in the preceding example. If you are not sure, the validator can once again help you out. Regarding implementation of the new HTML5 parser, Mozilla has taken the lead. Henri Sivonen's Parser, which is also the basis of http://validator.nu, is included with Firefox 4.

1.4   Can I Start Using HTML5 Now?

Yes and no. HTML5 is not finished yet by any stretch of the imagination, but unlike previous practice, the development of the HTML5 standard is taking place hand in hand with its implementation. Who would have thought that Internet Explorer 9 (IE9) would offer SVG and Canvas, or that Google would start offering HTML5 videos on YouTube? Many of the new features can be used now, provided you can choose your browser. HTML5 can be used in a company's internal intranet as well as on your private homepage that only selected friends can access.

With Firefox, Chrome, Opera, and Safari, four great browsers are already supporting a wide range of HTML5, and IE9 has finally ended Microsoft's long hesitation in supporting web standards in 2011. Browser manufacturers and their developers are now actively participating in forming the standard. They implement new specification drafts first in test versions as *proof of concept* and then post their feedback and suggestions for improvements in the WHATWG or the W3C. This makes them important parts of the development cycle. Anything that cannot be implemented is removed from the specification, whereas other components are adapted and finally implemented.

Early adopters of HTML5 are well advised to familiarize themselves with the individual browser's release notes, as trends in response to the question *What will come next?* will most likely emerge here:

- https://developer.mozilla.org/en/HTML/HTML5
- http://www.opera.com/docs/changelogs
- http://webkit.org/blog
- http://googlechromereleases.blogspot.com
- http://ie.microsoft.com/testdrive/info/ReleaseNotes

The timeline of the development of HTML5-relevant specifications in combination with the milestones of browser releases indicate with their shorter and shorter release intervals that standardization and implementation are closely linked (see Figure 1.6).

It will be interesting to see how the two areas continue to develop. You can find an up-to-date version of the timeline at the following URL:

http://html5.komplett.cc/code/chap_intro/timeline.html?lang=en

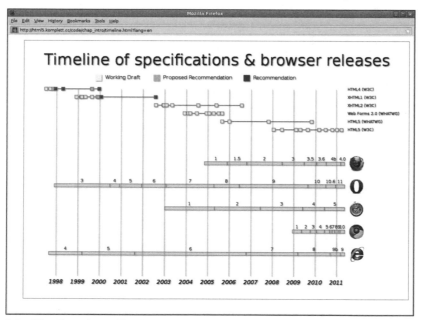

Figure 1.6 Timeline of specifications and browser releases

Summary

This chapter begins with a bit of historical background and then provides a high-level overview of the changes the HTML5 specification brings to web development. In addition to a look behind the scenes of the specification development, our main focus is on the long list of new elements, attributes, and APIs. Two brief *Hello world!* examples demonstrate the basic frame of a website encoded in HTML5 and XHTML5, and last but not least we address the question: Can I start using HTML5 now? The answer is yes, albeit with minor reservations. But now we will move on to the practical application of HTML5. Let's first start with a big chunk of innovations: more structure and semantics for documents!

2

Structure and Semantics for Documents

Both the previously mentioned *MAMA* survey conducted by Opera and Google's study of *Web Authoring Statistics* of 2005 (http://code.google.com/webstats) conclude that it was common practice at that time to determine the page structure of web sites with the class or id attribute. Frequently used attribute values were footer, content, menu, title, header, top, main, and nav, and it therefore made sense to factor the current practice into the new HTML5 specification and to create new elements for structuring pages.

The result is a compact set of new structural elements—for example, header, hgroup, article, section, aside, footer, and nav—that facilitate a clear page structure without detours via class or id. To illustrate this, we will use a fictitious and not entirely serious HTML5 blog entry to risk a look ahead to the year 2022 (see Figure 2.1). But please concentrate less on the content of the post and focus instead on the document structure.

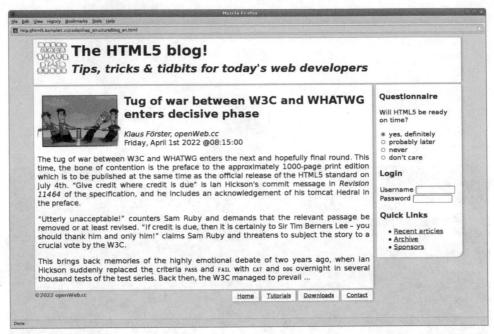

Figure 2.1   The fictitious HTML5 blog

Before analyzing the source code of the HTML5 blog in detail, here are a few important links, for example, to the specification *HTML: The Markup Language Reference*—subsequently shortened and referred to as *markup specification* at http://www.w3.org/TR/html-markup.

Here, Mike Smith, the editor and team contact of W3C HTML WG, lists each element's definition, any existing limitations, valid attributes or DOM interfaces, plus formatting rules in CSS notation (if to be applied)—a valuable help that we will use repeatedly. The HTML5 specification also contains the new structural elements in the following chapter: http://www.whatwg.org/specs/web-apps/current-work/multipage/sections.html

The `.html` and `.css` files to go with the HTML5 blog are of course also available online at:

- http://html5.komplett.cc/code/chap_structure/blog_en.html
- http://html5.komplett.cc/code/chap_structure/blog.css

At first glance, you can see four different sections in Figure 2.1—a header, the article, the footer, and a sidebar. All the new structural elements are used in these four sections. In combination with short CSS instructions in the stylesheet `blog.css`, they determine the page structure and layout.

2.1   Header with "header" and "hgroup"

In the header we encounter the first two new elements: header and hgroup. Figure 2.2 shows the markup and the presentation of the header:

```
<header>
   <img>
   <hgroup>
      <h1>
      <h2>
   </hgroup>
</header>
```

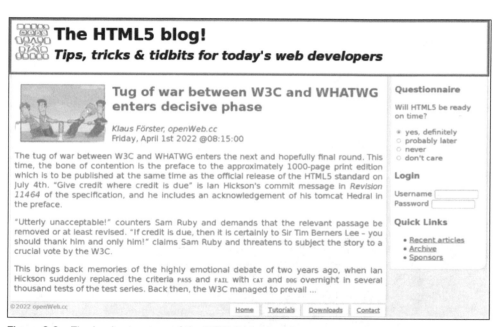

Figure 2.2   The basic structure of the HTML5 blog header

The term header as used in the markup specification refers to a container for headlines and additional introductory contents or navigational aids. Headers are not only the headers at the top of the page, but can also be used elsewhere in the document. Not allowed are nested headers or a header within an address or footer element.

In our case the headline of the HTML5 blog is defined by header in combination with the logo as an img element and two headings (h1 and h2) surrounded by an hgroup element containing the blog title and a subtitle.

Whereas it was common practice until now to write the h1 and h2 elements directly below one another to indicate title and subtitle, this is no longer allowed in HTML5. We now have to use hgroup for grouping such elements. The overall position of the hgroup element is determined by the topmost heading. Other elements can occur within hgroup, but as a general rule, we usually have a combination of tags from h1 to h6.

We can glimpse a small but important detail from the markup specification: The guideline is to format header elements as display: block in CSS, like all other structural elements. This ensures that even browsers that do not know what to do with the new tags can be *persuaded* to display the element concerned correctly. We only need a few lines of code to teach Internet Explorer 8 our new header element, for example:

```
<!--[if lt IE 9]>
  <script>
    document.createElement("<header");
  </script>
  <style>
    header { display: block; }
  </style>
<![endif]-->
```

Of course there is also a detailed JavaScript library on this workaround, and it contains not only header, but also many other new HTML5 elements. Remy Sharp makes it available for Internet Explorer at http://code.google.com/p/html5shim.

NOTE

In computer language, the term shim describes a compatibility workaround for an application. Often, the term shiv is wrongly used instead. The word shiv was coined by John Resig, the creator of *jQuery*, in a post of that title (http://ejohn.org/blog/html5-shiv). It remains unknown whether he may in fact have meant shim.

As far as CSS is concerned, the header does not contain anything special. The logo is integrated with float:left, the vertical distance between the two headings h1 and h2 is shortened slightly, and the subtitle is italicized.

2.2   Content with "article"

The article element represents an independent area within a web page, for example, news, blog entries, or similar content. In our case the content of the blog entry consists of such an article element combined with an img element to liven things up, an h2 heading for the headline, a time and address element for the date it was created and the copyright, plus three paragraphs in which you can also see q and cite elements for quotations of the protagonists.

Because the content element is now lacking, although it ranked right at the top in web page analyses by Google and Opera, it did not make it into HTML5 for some reason. Our blog entry is embedded in a surrounding div (see Figure 2.3). So nothing stands in the way of adding further articles:

```
<div>
  <article>
    <img>
    <h2>
    <address>
    <time>
  </article>
</div>
```

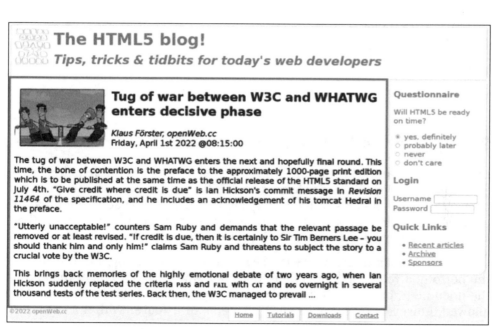

Figure 2.3   The basic structure of the HTML5 blog content

By definition, the address element contains contact information, which incidentally does not, as is often wrongly assumed, refer only to the postal address, but simply means information about the contact, such as name, company, and position. For addresses, the specification recommends using p. The address element applies to the closest article element; if there is none, it applies to the whole document. The time element behaves in a similar way in relation to its attributes pubdate and datetime, which form the timestamp for our document. You will find details on this in section 2.7.2, The "time" Element.

If article elements are nested within each other, the inner article should in principle have a theme similar to that of the outer article. One example of this kind of *nesting* would be, in our case, adding a subarticle to our blog with comments on the post concerned.

Regarding styling via CSS, we should mention that article once again requires display: block, that the content width is reduced to 79% via the surrounding div, and that this div also neutralizes the logo's float: left with clear: left. The italicized author information is the result of the default format of address and is not created via em. The picture is anchored on the left with float: left, the text is justified with align: justify, and quotations are integrated using the q element. One interesting detail is that the quotation marks are not part of the markup but are automatically added by the browser via the CSS pseudo-elements :before and :after in accordance with the style rules for the q element. The syntax in CSS notation once more reflects the markup specification:

```
/* Style rule for the q-element: */
q { display: inline; }
q:before { content: '"'; }
q:after { content: '"'; }
```

2.3   Footer with "footer" and "nav"

In the footer of our HTML blog, we find two other new structural elements: footer and nav (see Figure 2.4). The former creates the frame, and the latter provides navigation to other areas of the web page. footer contains additional info on the relevant section, such as who wrote it (as address of course); are there other, related pages; what do we need to look out for (copyright, disclaimer); and so on.

Unlike the human body, where the head is usually at the top and the foot at the bottom, a footer in a document does not always have to be at the end of the document, but can, for example, also be part of an article element. Not allowed, however, are nested footer elements or a footer within a header or address element.

If you want to create navigation blocks to allow page navigation via jump labels within a document or to external related pages, you can use nav. Just as with footer, nav can appear in other areas of the document as well, as you will see in the section 2.4, Sidebar with "aside" and "section"—the only exception being that you cannot have nav within the address element:

```
<footer>
  <p>
  <nav>
```

```
      <h3>
      <div>
         <a>
      </div>
    </nav>
  </footer>
```

Figure 2.4   The basic structure of the HTML blog footer

As for CSS, our HTML5 blog's footer has a few special features. For example, the entire footer is colored in the same light gray as the page background, and only the links are formatted with `background-color: white`. The copyright in the first p requires `float: left`, and the navigation `text-align: right` plus the h3 heading in the nav block are hidden with `display: none`. Just why there is an h3 element in there at all will become clear in section 2.5, The Outline Algorithm. To improve the style of the links, they are surrounded by `div` tags. And of course we have `display: block` for header and nav, plus a reduction of the width in the footer element to 79%.

2.4   Sidebar with "aside" and "section"

For areas of a page that are only loosely related to the main content and can therefore be seen as rather separate entities, we can use the `aside` element. In our example, it creates a classical sidebar on the right with three blocks for Questionnaire,

Login, and Quick Links. If the link list is implemented as nav, as is to be expected, the two first blocks are embedded in another new element: section.

The section element contains sections of a document that are thematically connected, for example, chapters of an essay or individual tabs of a page constructed from tabs, typically with a heading. If section is used within footer, it is usually used for appendices, indices, license agreements, or the like. Generally, it makes sense to use section if it belonged in a table of contents as well. In our example, as shown in Figure 2.5, the Questionnaire and the Login are tagged with section, and the links are tagged as nav as mentioned earlier:

```
<aside>
  <h2>
  <section>
    <h3><p><input>
  </section>
  <section>
    <h3><label><input>
  </section>
  <nav>
    <h3><ul><li><a>
  </nav>
</aside>
```

Figure 2.5 The basic structure of the HMTL5 blog sidebar

For the same reason as with the nav block in the footer (see the following section), the sidebar contains a heading h2 directly before the first Questionnaire block, hidden via CSS with display: none. The sidebar format is float: right with width: 20% and font-size: 0.9em. The striking feature of the sidebar is the rounded bottom-right corner, which means it's time to admit that the HTML5 blog also uses CSS3: The rounded corner is only one of two features used. The CSS syntax for the class rounded-bottom-right looks like this:

```
.rounded-bottom-right {
  -moz-border-radius: 0px 0px 20px 0px;
  -webkit-border-radius: 0px 0px 20px 0px;
  border-radius: 0px 0px 20px 0px;
}
```

The second feature is responsible for the subtle shadow of the four areas and is defined as follows in the CSS file:

```
.shadow {
  -moz-box-shadow: 4px 0px 10px -3px silver;
  -webkit-box-shadow: 4px 0px 10px -3px silver;
  box-shadow: 4px 0px 10px -3px silver;
}
```

The tripling of the CSS command through the prefixes -moz-* and -webkit-* is conspicuous; it is caused by the fact that CSS3 is not yet in the *Candidate Recommendation* phase. Once it enters this stage of the standardization process, only then will it be ensured that border-radius and box-shadow will no longer be changed. Until then, the prefixes are maintained to show that the implementation could still contain small deviations from the standard.

> **NOTE**
>
> If you want to learn more about these two eagerly awaited features of the CSS3 specification, you will find further information here:
>
> - http://www.w3.org/TR/css3-background/#the-border-radius
> - http://www.w3.org/TR/css3-background/#box-shadow

2.5 The Outline Algorithm

Even if the details for *outlining* a document sound rather complicated in the specification, there is a simple idea behind *outlining*, which is a machine-readable summary of the underlying document structure. This structure is determined by a combination of so-called *sectioning content*—for example, body, article, aside, nav, and section—and *heading content*, such as h1 to h6 or hgroup, which provides the proper entries of the outline.

If we check our HTML5 blog with Geoffrey Sneddon's online *HTML5 Outliner* (http://gsnedders.html5.org/outliner), we see the following structure:

```
1. The HLML5 blog!
    1. Link Block
        1. Questionnaire
        2. Login
        3. Quick Links
    2. Tug of war between W3C and WHATWG enters ...
    3. Navigation
```

With the italicized entries Link Block and Navigation, we get back exactly those two headings that were hidden in the layout with display: none. If we had omitted these headings completely, we would have seen the text Untitled Section in their place. But this way, the structure is complete and the outline is much easier to read.

Regarding the choice of headings h1 to h6, we should note the following: In principle, any *sectioning content* can start with the heading rank h1, but it does not have to. In our case the heading ranks reflect the hierarchy in the outline: h1 for the blog header; h2 for the article title, the link block, and the footer navigation; and h3 for the other headers. If we tagged everything with h1, we would get the same outline, but the layout would suffer somewhat and we would need to sort it out manually in the CSS file.

When using hgroup, you need to remember that the outline only includes the highest level in the hgroup. That is why you cannot see the subtitle *Tips, tricks & tidbits for today's web developers* in the outline.

Even if there is as yet no browser that directly uses the outline algorithm in any form, this does not mean that it could not play a more important role in the future. Automatically generated navigation bars would be a possibility, or the creation of short, concise summaries, or perhaps improvements for crawlers extracting relevant content for search engines. Until then it definitely does not hurt to do some serious thinking about the structure of your document. It is easy to check the structure, so why not go ahead and do it?

2.6   Figures with "figure" and "figcaption"

The elements figure and figcaption do not really count among the structural elements, but they are still a welcome addition to our options in structuring the integration of independent pictures, graphics, diagrams, and code lists. Each figure element can have only one figcaption element. It is up to the author whether this is placed before or after the figure in question. A brief example with markup and its browser implementation (see Figure 2.6) could look like this:

```
<figure>
<img src="images/tarot_0980.jpg" alt="XXI: The World">
<img src="images/tarot_0963.jpg" alt="VI: The Choice">
<img src="images/tarot_0996.jpg" alt="XVIII: The Moon">
<figcaption> Three magical sculptures in Niki de Saint
 Phalles <em>Giardino dei Tarocchi</em> near Capalbio in the
 Tuscany region of Italy. The tarot cards from left to right:
 The World (XXI), The Choice (VI), and The Moon (XVIII)</figcaption>
</figure>
```

Figure 2.6   Example of "figure" with "figcaption"

2.7   Text-Level Semantics—More New Tags

Apart from focusing on clear structures, the HTML5 specification also attaches importance to semantics and tries to assign each element a certain meaning on the text level. At the same time, the HTML5 specification determines in which context the tag concerned can be used and in which it cannot. There are some new elements and some that have disappeared completely (such as font, center, and big), and the definitions of others have changed slightly. The following chapter will introduce new and changed elements. Later, in Table 2.2 we will show you the classical applications of all elements that appear in the specification's *Text-level semantics* chapter. Let's start with the *most exotic* of the new elements—ruby.

2.7.1 The Elements "ruby," "rt," and "rp"

The term ruby refers to a *typographic annotation system,* meaning "short runs of text alongside the base text, typically used in East Asian documents to indicate pronunciation or to provide a short annotation" (www.w3.org/TR/ruby). Ruby annotation is used in Chinese and Japanese to show the pronunciation of characters, as you can see in the example on the left in Figure 2.7.

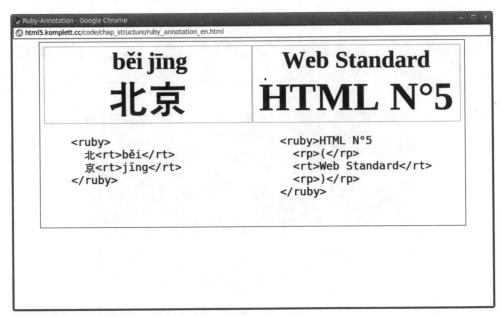

Figure 2.7 Two examples of ruby annotation

The markup for ruby annotations contains the elements ruby, rt, and rp. First, the expression that will be explained is specified within a ruby element. The explanation is then provided by the following rt element, and in browsers with ruby support the content of this rt element is positioned above the expression described. As you can see in the Beijing example, several words in a row can be annotated this way.

Browsers without ruby support (such as Firefox and Opera) display the individual components consecutively, which can make the words more difficult to read. Because it is not necessarily clear that the second word is the explanation of the first word, a visual separation of the two components is required. That is what the rp element is for: It enables adding optional parentheses that will only be displayed if a browser does not know ruby. As you can see in Figure 2.7, Google Chrome can interpret ruby and visually separate it. A browser without ruby support would display the examples as 北 *b i* 京 *j ng* and *HTML N°5 (Web Standard)*.

2.7.2 The "time" Element

The time element represents either a time in the 24-hour-format or a date in the *Gregorian calendar* with optional time and time-zone components. Its purpose is to give modern date and time specifications in a machine-readable format within an HTML5 document. Vague time references, such *in the spring of 2011* or *five minutes before the turn of the millennium*, are therefore not allowed.

To ensure machine readability, we can use the attribute datetime, and its attribute value can be specified either as time, date, or a combination of both. The syntax for specifying the time components is clearly defined in the specification and is described in Table 2.1.

Table 2.1 The Rules for Timestamps for the "time" Element's "datetime" Attribute

Component	Syntax	Example
Date	YYYY-MM-DD	2011-07-13
Time with hours	hh:mm	18:28
Time with seconds	hh:mm:ss	18:28:05
Time with milliseconds	hh:mm:ss.f	18:28:05.2318
Date and time	T to join date and time	2011-07-13T18:28
With time zone GMT	Z at the end	2011-07-13T18:28:05Z
With time zone as offset	+mm:hh / -mm:hh	2011-07-13T18:28:05+02:00

The pubdate attribute is a *boolean* attribute and indicates that the specified date applies to the next level article in the hierarchy, and—if there is none—should be understood as the publication date of the document. If you are using pubdate, there has to be a datetime element as well. If this is not the case, the section between the time element's start tag and end tag must contain a valid date.

Be careful when writing *boolean* attributes in HTML5: `true` or `false` are not valid attribute values! As soon as the parser discovers the attribute name in *boolean* attributes, it switches to `true`. So there are three valid notations for setting a *boolean* attribute to `true`:

```
<time pubdate>
<time pubdate="">
<time pubdate="pubdate"> (of course you can also omit the quotation marks)
```

To switch to `false`, you only have one option: Omit the attribute altogether!

2.7.3 The "mark" Element

The mark element represents a highlighted text segment that is regarded as relevant in a different context. That sounds a bit cumbersome, so we will illustrate it with some brief examples: If you want to highlight a certain passage of a quotation in particular, you change the original text and almost force a new meaning onto it. You can use the mark element to add significance to certain words in a document or code listing as a result of searching for them or in the course of interpreting the code.

2.7.4 The "wbr" Element

Unsurprisingly, the wbr element enables the browser to insert an optional line break in long words. For example, inserting a couple of wbr elements in a rather long word, such as *supercalifragilisticexpialidocious*, would give the browser the opportunity to break the word over two lines if the layout requires it:

```
supercali<wbr>fragilistic<wbr>expialidocious
```

It depends entirely on the layout whether and where the line break occurs. wbr only allows a line break, it does not force it. Possible applications would be long URLs or code listings. Similar to br, wbr is a so-called *void element*, which means it must not contain an end tag—a quality it shares with 14 other elements in HTML5. Here they are

area	base	br	col	command	embed
hr	img	input	keygen	link	meta
param	source	wbr			

But of course *void elements* can contain a *slash* in the start tag itself (e.g., `<br />`), which is useful with regard to meeting the requirements of valid XHTML5 documents.

2.7.5 Elements with Marginal Changes

The list of elements with marginal changes starts with b and i, two tags that no longer fit into the concept of HTML5, also because of their names: b for *bold* and i for *italic* give definite formatting instructions, and these are not popular in HTML5. The *relevance* is now essential, so we should instead use strong and em as in *emphasis* to stress the importance of a word. Unfortunately, b and i are among the most widely used tags, which is why it was impossible to prevent their use altogether. The solution was a compromise that continues to allow both but alters their meaning: b now refers to offset text in bold and i to offset text in italics. But if you want to write clean HTML5, you should avoid using b and i in the future and instead use strong and em.

Other small changes mean that cite now designates the title of a work and must explicitly not be used for citing names. small now means not only *small print*, but also represents side comments or small print in the sense of legal notices but without making statements as to their importance. hr now signals a thematic break, not just a horizontal line to break up the layout.

The specification offers a usage summary of individual tags with examples at the end of the chapter *Text-level semantics*. To save you from having to look it up, here it is in our Table 2.2.

Table 2.2 Usage of Semantic Text Elements

Element	Purpose	Example
a	Hyperlinks	Visit my <a href="drinks.html">drinks</a> page.
em	Stress emphasis	I must say I adore lemonade.
strong	Importance	This tea is very hot.
small	Side comments	These grapes are made into wine. <small>Alcohol is addictive.</small>
s	Inaccurate text	Price: <s>£4.50</s> £2.00!
cite	Titles of works	The case <cite>Hugo v. Danielle</cite> is relevant here.
q	Quotations	The judge said <q>You can drink water from the fish tank</q> but advised against it.
dfn	Defining instance	The term <dfn>organic food</dfn> refers to food produced without synthetic chemicals.
abbr	Abbreviations	Organic food in Ireland is certified by the <abbr title="Irish Organic Farmers and Growers Association">IOFGA</abbr>.

Table 2.2 Usage of Semantic Text Elements (*Contd.*)

Element	Purpose	Example
code	Computer code	The `<code>fruitdb</code>` program can be used for tracking fruit production.
var	Variables	If there are `<var>n</var>` fruit in the bowl, at least `<var>n</var>`÷2 will be ripe.
samp	Computer output	The computer said `<samp>Unknown error -3</samp>`.
kbd	User input	Hit `<kbd>F1</kbd>` to continue.
sub	Subscripts	Water is H`<sub>2</sub>`O.
sup	Superscripts	The hydrogen in heavy water is usually `<sup>2</sup>`H.
i	Alternative voice	Lemonade consists primarily of `<i>Citrus limon</i>`.
b	Keywords	Take a `<b>lemon</b>` and squeeze it with a `<b>juicer</b>`.
mark	Highlight	Elderflower cordial, with one `<mark>part</mark>` cordial to ten `<mark>part</mark>`s water, stands a`<mark>part</mark>` from the rest.
ruby, rt, rp	Ruby annotations	`<ruby> OJ <rp>(<rt>Orange Juice<rp>)</ruby>`
bdi	Text directionality isolation	The recommended restaurant is `<bdi lang="">My Juice Café (At The Beach)</bdi>`.
bdo	Text directionality formatting	The proposal is to write English but in reverse order. "Juice" would become "`<bdo dir=rtl>Juice</bdo>`»
span	Other	In French we call it `<span lang="fr">sirop de sureau</span>`.
br	Line break	Simply Orange Juice Company` `Apopka, FL 32703` `U.S.A.
wbr	Line breaking opportunity	www.simply`<wbr>`orange`<wbr>`juice.com

Summary

HTML5 offers a wealth of new structural elements, such as header, hgroup, article, section, aside, footer, and nav. The detailed example at the beginning of this chapter, the creation of a fictitious blog entry, demonstrates how easily and intuitively these elements can be used. Instead of anonymous div elements, which only make sense in combination with the class attributes, we now find speaking elements—a concept continued with figure and figcaption for integrating images and graphics. From the comprehensive list of HTML5 semantic text elements plus examples of their usage in Table 2.2, we briefly introduced the most interesting new elements, such as ruby, rt, and rp for ruby annotations; time for specifying the time; mark for marking text passages; and wbr for optional line breaks.

3

Intelligent
Forms

Whether you want to book a flight, take care of your online banking, or enter a search term in Google, without forms, none of these services would be usable. Most of the elements for interactive forms have remained unchanged since HTML 2.0 arrived in 1995. On one hand this indicates that Tim Berners-Lee's design showed great foresight; on the other hand there is now a huge need to catch up. The HTML5 specification devotes a large section to the topic of forms and will greatly facilitate any web designer's work.

Even though browser support is not yet overwhelming at the time of this writing (so far, it's only offered by Opera and the developer release of Google Chrome), the backward compatible syntax means that we can safely use the new form elements now.

3.1 New Input Types

The HTML5 specification enhances the input element by allowing several more values for the type attribute. The new types, for example, date, color, and range, enable browser manufacturers to make user-friendly input elements available and also make it possible for the browser to ensure that the input is of the desired type. If a browser does not recognize the type of the input element, it will fall back on type=text and display a text field, which is useful in any case. Even older browsers show this behavior, so there is nothing to stop us from using the new types right away.

The types for date and time will probably be the most useful. Currently, there are countless different versions of more or less successful JavaScript calendars available on the Internet. Entering a date comfortably, be it for booking a flight or a hotel room, or registering for a conference, is a problem that until now required manual work. Of course, JavaScript libraries, such as *jQuery*, offer ready-made calendars, but this function should really be supported by the browser directly.

At the time of this writing, there is only one desktop browser that includes a graphic input element for entering the date: Opera. In Figure 3.1 you can see the open calendar that will be displayed if you click on an input element with the type date. But let's tackle things in order: Table 3.1 provides an overview of the new types; then you can see what they look like in the Opera browser in Figure 3.1.

Table 3.1 New Input Types in HTML5

Type	Description	Example
tel	Text without line breaks	+1 234 567890
search	Text without line breaks	search term
url	An absolute URL	http://www.example.com
email	A valid e-mail address	user@host.com
datetime	Date and time (always in UTC time zone)	2010-08-11T11:58Z
date	Date without time zone	2010-08-11
month	Month without time zone	2010-08
week	Year and week in the year without time zone	2010-W32
time	Time without time zone	11:58:00

Type	Description	Example
datetime-local	Date and time without timezone	2010-08-11T11:58:22.5
number	Number	9999 or 99.2
range	Numerical value within a range	33 or 2.99792458E8
color	Hexadecimal representation of RGB values in sRGB color space	#eeeeee

3.1.1 The Input Types "tel" and "search"

tel and search are not significantly different from normal text fields. Both can contain character chains without line breaks. Even telephone numbers are not limited to numbers, because phone numbers often contain brackets or the plus symbol. For tel, the browser could offer suggestions from the local address book, a situation that is particularly useful with cell phones. The search type was introduced to allow the browser to make the search input consistent with the layout of the relevant platform. Mac OS X users, for example, are used to seeing search fields with rounded corners.

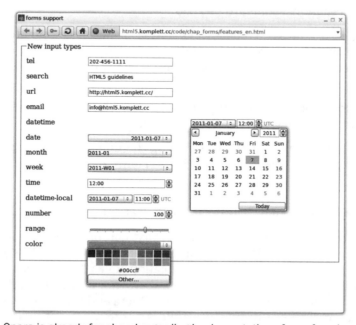

Figure 3.1 Opera is already far ahead regarding implementation of new form input types

3.1.2   The Input Types "url" and "email"

In addition to suggesting options, the browser can also check the syntax for url and email. Because there are concrete rules for e-mail addresses and Internet addresses in the form of URLs, the browser can already provide feedback on possible mistakes during input (more on this topic in section 3.4, Client-side Form Validation).

3.1.3   Date and Time with "datetime", "date", "month", "week", "time", and "datetime-local"

Let's take a closer look at the date and time formats. datetime contains date and time information; the time zone is always set to UTC. The specification states that the browser can allow the user to select another time zone, but the value of the input element has to be converted to UTC. The rules for time information in the datetime attribute of the time element, which we discussed in section 2.7.2, The "time" Element, apply here as well—with the only exception that the string always has to end in a Z, the identifier of UTC.

With date and month, the time and time zone are omitted. As defined in the specification, the date must be a valid day within the selected month, also taking into account leap years. Year, month, and day must be separated by a minus character; the year has to be at least four digits long and greater than 0. So dates before Christ (B.C.) cannot be represented in HTML5, in contrast to the somewhat more extensive international standard ISO 8601.

The type week is represented as a week in a year, and it is mandatory that the week be preceded by the year. Year and week are once again separated by a minus character. To ensure that there is no confusion with month, the week must be preceded by the character W.

datetime-local works the same way as the already described datetime; the only difference is that there is no timezone specified.

Opera uses a calendar window for selecting the date; the time can be entered manually or changed via arrow keys (refer to Figure 3.1).

3.1.4   The Input Types "number" and "range"

The types number and range require input that can be converted to a numerical value; the notation of floating-point numbers (for example, 2.99792458E8) is valid. Regarding the type range, the specification states that the exact value is not relevant; this type indicates a range of numbers, not an exact number, and the user can easily enter it with a slider bar. Both Opera and WebKit-based browsers, such as Safari or Google Chrome, use a slider bar to represent this type (refer to Figure 3.1 and see Figure 3.2).

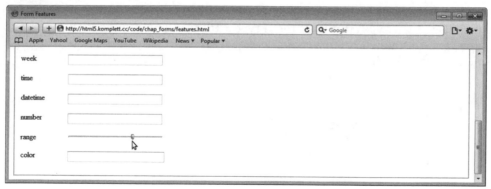

Figure 3.2   The input type "range" in Safari

3.1.5 The Input Type "color"

Once again the developers of Opera lead the way by being the first to program a graphical input option for the color element. As you can see in Figure 3.1, Opera (version 11 and later) offers a rectangular field with a choice of frequently used colors. You can also bring up a color picker along the lines of those you see in image-editing programs. Sadly, this input element is still not implemented in the other browsers.

The value of the input element must contain the 8-bit RGB values in hexadecimal notation preceded by a # character. The color blue, for example, would be written as #0000ff.

3.1.6 The New Input Types in Action

Enough with the theory: Our first example shows you the new elements, one below the other. Because that's not very challenging, we will also test each element's function. The trick is that the browser will set the type of an unknown element to text, and we can then evaluate those properties in JavaScript:

```
<script>
  window.onload = function() {
    inputs = document.getElementsByTagName("input");
    for (var i=0; i<inputs.length; i++) {
      if (inputs[i].type == "text") {
        inputs[i].value = "not available";
      }
    }
  }
</script>
```

As soon as the web page has finished loading, a loop runs over all input elements to analyze their type attributes. If the type attribute corresponds to the standard type text, its value is set to *not available*. The HTML code for the new input elements looks like this:

```
<fieldset>
  <legend>New input types</legend>
    <p><label for=tel>tel</label>
<input type=tel id=tel name=tel>
    <p><label for=search>search</label>
<input type=search id=search name=search>
    <p><label for=url>url</label>
<input type=url id=url name=url>
    <p><label for=email>email</label>
  ...
```

In Figure 3.3 you can see what the result of this test looks like on an Android cell phone. The system's WebKit-based browser (left) pretends to know the types tel, search, url, and email but does not really help when it comes to entering the telephone number via the keyboard (center). Opera Mobile in version 10.1 beta (right) supports url and email, plus the date and time types.

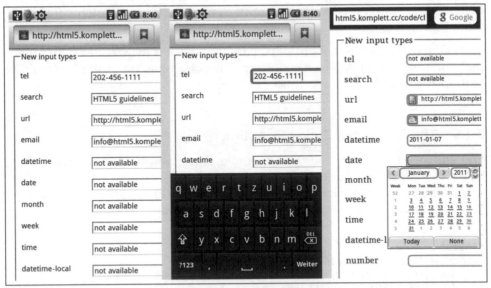

Figure 3.3 Support of new form input types on an Android 2.1 phone with browsers WebKit (left, center) and Opera (right)

That is a rather disappointing result for the otherwise so modern Android browser. Results look slightly better on the iPhone: At least the smartphone adapts the software keyboard, displaying a numeric keyboard when you try to enter a phone number and adding the @ character on the keyboard for the input type email.

This test works even better with *BlackBerry*, the operating system of the popular line of smartphones produced by the Canadian manufacturer *Research in Motion* (*RIM*). As you can see in Figure 3.4, the BlackBerry supports both `tel` and `number` plus date types, and the latter in particular are represented in very attractive graphics. Under the hood we find WebKit at work: The software was expanded to include these functions.

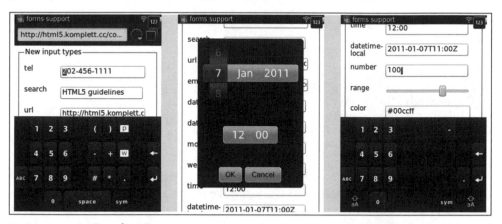

Figure 3.4   The new `input` types on a BlackBerry smartphone (BlackBerry 9800 simulator)

3.2 Useful Attributes for Forms

Apart from new elements and many new types for the `input` element, HTML5 also offers several new attributes for form elements.

3.2.1 Focusing with "autofocus"

Years ago, Google surprised many users with a simple trick that made searching much more convenient: When the page was loaded, the cursor was automatically positioned in the search field. The user was able to enter the search term directly without having to first activate the input box by clicking with the mouse. Previously, this was done with a short snippet of JavaScript; in HTML5 you can now do it with the `autofocus` attribute:

```
<input type=search name=query autofocus>
```

As with all *boolean* attributes, you can write this attribute as `autofocus="autofocus"` (see Chapter 2, section 2.7.2, The "time" Element). The specification states that only one element in a web page can contain the `autofocus` attribute.

Older browsers do not have a problem with autofocus, because they simply ignore the unknown attribute. Of course, you only get the benefit of user friendliness with new browsers.

3.2.2 Placeholder Text with "placeholder"

Usability of HTML forms can be further improved with the new placeholder attribute:

```
<p><label for=email>Your e-mail address:</label>
<input type=email name=email id=email
  placeholder="user@host.com">
<p><label for=birthday>Your date of birth</label>
<input type=date name=birthday id=birthday
  placeholder="1978-11-24">
```

The value of placeholder can give the user a quick hint about how to fill in the field, but it should not be used as an alternative to the label element. It is particularly useful for fields where a certain data entry format is expected. The browser displays the hint text within an inactive input field. As soon as the field is activated and is focused, the text is no longer displayed (see Figure 3.5).

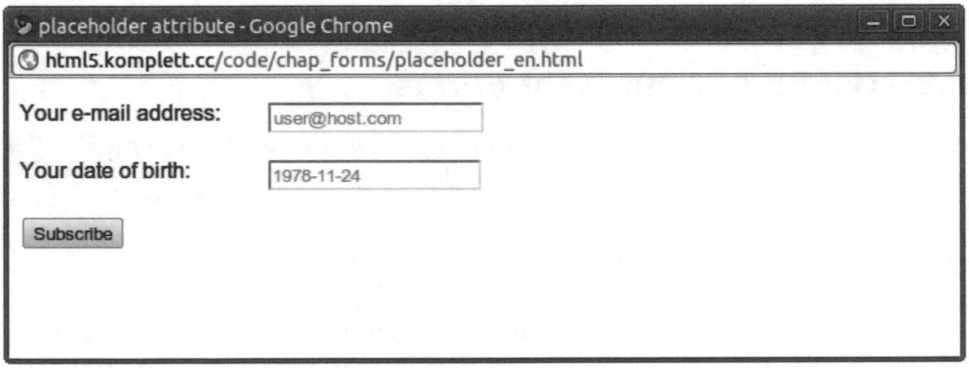

Figure 3.5   The "placeholder" attribute in Google Chrome

3.2.3 Compulsory Fields with "required"

required is a *boolean* attribute, and its name already says everything about its function: A form element that this attribute is assigned to must be filled in. If a required field remains blank when the form is sent, it does not fulfill the requirements and the browser must react accordingly. You will find more information on this in section 3.4, Client-side Form Validation.

3.2.4   Even More Attributes for the "input" Element

The input element has not only been enhanced with new types (section 3.1, New Input Types), but also with new attributes that enable easier handling of forms (see Table 3.2).

Table 3.2   New Attributes for the "input" Element

Type	Description	Attribute
liststring	Refers to the ID of a datalist element with suggestions (see section 3.3.3, Lists of options with "datalist")	list
numeric/date	Minimum value of numeric fields and date fields	min
numeric/date	Maximum value of numeric fields and date fields	max
numeric	Step size of numeric fields and date fields	step
boolean	Multiple selection possible	multiple
enumerated (on/off/default)	Automatically inserts saved data into form fields	autocomplete
string	Regular expression for validating the value	pattern

We will come across the list attribute again in section 3.3.3, Lists of Options with "datalist". It refers to the datalist element, which offers possible entries as suggestions.

min, max, and step are not only suitable for numeric fields, but these attributes can also be used for entering the date and time:

```
<p><label for=minMax>Decimal number between 0 and 1:</label>
<input type=number name=minMax id=minMax
  min=0 max=1 step=0.1>
<p><label for=minMaxDate>Date in week steps:</label>
<input type=date name=minMaxDate id=minMaxDate
  min=2010-08-01 max=2010-11-11 step=7>
<p><label for=minMaxTime>Time in hour steps:</label>
<input type=time name=minMaxTime id=minMaxTime
  min=14:30 max=19:30 step=3600>
```

In browsers that support the input type number, the first input element (id=minMax) is increased each time by a value of 0.1. This works by clicking the arrow keys at the end of the text field or by pressing the arrow keys on the keyboard. The element with the ID `minMaxDate` jumps forward seven days each time. Opera only displays those days in the calendar as active that correspond to the week cycle. For setting this element, Google Chrome offers the same navigation as with the `input type number`: two arrow keys that set the date forward or backward seven days. In the third `input` element in this example, the step size is set to `3600`; this causes the time to be set one hour forward or one hour backward. Although the specification states that the input elements for time usually work in minutes, both Opera and Google Chrome interpret this data as seconds.

We are all familiar with multiple selection from copying files; now this option exists for browsers as well. If you wanted to load several files on a website at once, you previously had to provide an `input` field for each file. The `multiple` attribute allows for the marking of several files in the file dialog. The `multiple` option was always intended for the `select` element; using it for input fields of the type `email` is new. But as yet (at the time of this writing), none of the commonly used desktop browsers can implement this function for `email` types.

Modern browsers have a function that allows them to save form data to help the user fill in forms when the form is revisited. This prefilling can be very useful but would be undesirable for security-sensitive input fields (the specification mentions the activation codes for nuclear weapons as an example). The `autocomplete` attribute was introduced to allow web developers to govern this behavior. If an element has the attribute `autocomplete="off"` assigned to it, that means the information to be entered is confidential and should not be saved in the browser. If the form element does not state if `autocomplete` should be switched on or off, the default setting is to display suggestions. The `autocomplete` attribute can also be applied to the whole form by assigning it to the `form` element.

The new `pattern` attribute allows for very flexible input verification. You can specify a *regular expression* against which the form field will be checked for a match. Regular expressions are very powerful but unfortunately not a very easy method of parsing strings. Imagine you are looking for a character string starting with an uppercase character followed by any number of lowercase letters or numbers and ending in `.txt`. Finding it is no problem at all with a *regexp* (short for *regular expression*):

```
[A-Z]{1}[a-z,0-9]+\.txt
```

NOTE

An introduction to regular expressions would be far beyond the scope of this chapter, so let's assume for now that you have basic knowledge of regular expressions when you read the following section. If you are looking for a brief online introduction to *regular expressions*, Wikipedia is a good starting point: Browse to http://en.wikipedia.org/wiki/Regular_expression. The website http://www.regexe.com gives you the chance to try regular expressions online.

When using regular expressions with the `pattern` attribute you need to remember that the search pattern always has to apply to the field's entire content. The specification also suggests using the `title` attribute to give the user a hint regarding the input format. Opera and Google Chrome display this kind of information as a tool tip as soon as the mouse pointer hovers over the field. After all this theory, here is a brief example:

```
<p><label for=pattern>Your nickname:</label>
 <input type=text pattern="[a-z]{3,32}"
  placeholder=""johnsmith" name=pattern id=pattern
  title="Only lower case, please; min. 3, max. 32!">
```

The guideline for the `pattern` attribute specifies that the character string can only contain characters between a and z (in lowercase,[a-z]) and that there are at least 3 and at most 32 characters. Special characters or umlauts are not allowed, which can be useful for a user name as in the preceding example. If you want to include certain special characters, for example, the umlauts in the German language, you need to include them in the group: [a-zäöüß]. In section 3.4, Client-side Form Validation, you can find out what happens if the validation fails.

3.3 New Elements

In addition to the new input types and the new attributes mentioned earlier, the specification also includes new elements for forms. We will discuss these in the next section. The elements `meter` and `progress` create graphical objects that previously could only be achieved with more or less complicated tricks. Suggestions for text input are offered by `datalist`, and `output` provides a placeholder for the results of calculations. The keygen element has been circulating through the World Wide Web for a long time but has only reached standardization with HTML5.

3.3.1 Displaying Measurements with "meter"

The `meter` element is used to graphically represent a scalar measurement within a known range. Think, for example, of the fuel gauge in your car: The needle shows the current level of fuel in your tank as somewhere between 0 and 100 percent. Previously, such graphic representations were usually coded in HTML with nested `div` elements, a rather inelegant solution for which the `div` element was probably not intended. A status display can also be displayed graphically, as a picture, through free web services, such as the *Google Chart API*. You can see all of these options in the example that follows.

Using the meter element is very simple: You set the desired value via the value attribute; all other attributes are optional. If you do not set a min and max value, the browser will use 0 and 1 for these attributes. So, the following meter element shows a half-full element:

```
<meter value=0.5></meter>
```

Apart from value, min, and max are also the attributes low, high, and optimum—values that the browser can incorporate into the display. Google Chrome (at the time of this writing, the only browser apart from Opera that is able to represent the meter element), for example, displays the normally green bar in yellow if the optimum value is exceeded.

In the following example you can see a graphic representation, showing the percentage of the current year that has already passed. The website presents a visualization of the output in four different ways: as text with a value in percent, using the new meter element, via nested div elements, and as graphics produced by the online service of Google's Chart API. You can see the result in Figure 3.6.

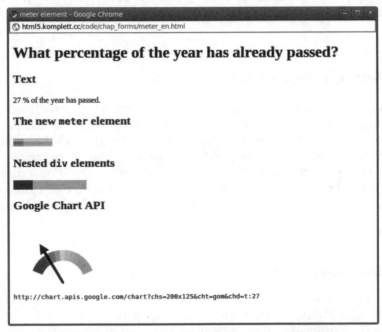

Figure 3.6   The "meter" element and similar options for representing a state

The HTML code for this example contains the still empty elements, which are filled via JavaScript:

```
<h2>Text</h2>
<p><output id=op></output>
  % of the year has passed.</p>
<h2>The new <span class=tt>meter</span> element</h2>
<meter value=0 id=m></meter>
<h2>Nested <span class=tt>div</span> elements</h2>
<div id=outer style="background:lightgray;width:150px;" >
<div id=innerDIV> </div></div>
<h2>Google Chart API</h2>
<img id=google src="">
<p id=googleSrc class=tt></p>
```

For the text output, we use the output element introduced in section 3.3.5, Calculations with "output". But first the current date is generated in JavaScript, and the meter element is initialized:

```
var today = new Date();
var m = document.getElementById("m");
m.min = new Date(today.getFullYear(), 0, 1);
m.max = new Date(today.getFullYear(), 11, 31);
// m.optimum = m.min-m.max/2;
m.value = today;
```

The variable today contains the number of milliseconds since the start of the UNIX epoch (on 1.1.1970). To make sure our meter element gets a sensible scale, we set the min value to January 1 of the current year and the max value accordingly to December 31. The value of the meter element is set in the last line of the listing; now the graphical representation is complete. If you activate the optimum value (in this case the middle of the year), which we left out, you will see the display change depending on whether you call the script in the first or second half of the year. The new element is wonderfully simple to use.

Let's now move on to the other elements on our HTML web page. We want to assign the percentage of days passed to the output element tagged with the ID op. With Math.round(), we round up the percentage to the nearest number before the comma, which is plenty accurate enough for our example:

```
var op = document.getElementById("op");
op.value =
  Math.round(100/(m.max-m.min)*(m.value-m.min));

var innerDIV = document.getElementById("innerDIV");
innerDIV.style.width=op.value+"%";
innerDIV.style.background = "green";
```

The rest of our example has nothing to do with new HTML5 techniques, but we still want to explain it for the sake of completeness. The nested div elements should also be filled with the percentage value. The idea behind this is simple: A first div area is defined in HTML with a fixed width (here, 150px). Nested into this element, another div element is displayed as filled with a green background color along the width of the calculated percentage value—a simple yet very effective trick. To round things off, we also want to include the Google Chart API. To use the online service, you have to specify the chart size (chs, in our case 200×125 pixels), the chart type (cht, here, gom, *Google-O-Meter*), and the chart data (chd, here, the percentage value op.value):

```
  var google = document.getElementById("google");
  google.src =
"http://chart.apis.google.com/chart?chs=200x125&cht=gom&chd=t:"+op.
value;
  var gSrc = document.getElementById("googleSrc");
  gSrc.innerHTML = google.src;
```

3.3.2 Displaying the Progress of a Task with "progress"

progress works in a similar way as the meter element discussed previously except that it represents the completion progress of a task. Such tasks could, for example, be file uploads by the user or downloads of external libraries required by an application.

To give you a quick example, we do not really want to upload any files or download a lot of data; it is sufficient to set ourselves a task and fulfill it 100 percent. Our following example defines ten input elements of the type checkbox, and as soon as they are all activated, we want the progress bar to show 100 %:

```
<h1>Please activate all the checkboxes</h1>
<form method=get>
  <input type=checkbox onchange=updateProgress()>
  <input type=checkbox onchange=updateProgress()>
<!-- and 8 more -->
  <p>
  Progress: <progress value=0 max=10 id=pb></progress>
</form>
```

The progress element is initialized with a value of 0 and a maximum value of 10. As soon as an input element is activated, it calls the function updateProgress(), which looks like this:

```
function updateProgress() {
  var pb = document.getElementById("pb");
  var ip = document.getElementsByTagName("input");
```

```
    var cnt = 0;
    for(var i=0; i<ip.length; i++) {
      if (ip[i].checked == true) {
        cnt++;
      }
    }
    pb.value = cnt;
}
```

The variable ip contains a *NodeList* with all input elements. Each of these elements is tested in the for loop for its condition. If it is activated (checked == true), the counter variable cnt increases by 1. To finish, the value of the progress element is set to the value of the counter variable.

3.3.3 Lists of Options with "datalist"

One long-awaited new function for forms is a drop-down menu to which you can add your own entries. Because the well-known select element is limited to the values specified as option elements, web developers used to come up with various JavaScript tricks to add expandable selection lists to text fields.

The HTML5 specification now has a very elegant solution to this problem. The new datalist element was defined to function as a container for the already familiar option element. Now we can assign to each input element a datalist element that displays the selection options when needed. Browsers that do not support the datalist element will only display the empty text field.

Listing 3.1 shows the use of the new element. The input element is defined by the type text, and the attribute list refers to the id of the datalist element (in this case, homepages). When the page is loaded, the autofocus attribute positions the cursor automatically inside the text field (see section 3.2.1, Focusing with "autofocus") and ensures, at least with the Opera browser, that the selection list appears (see Figure 3.7).

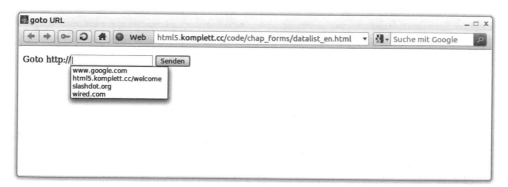

Figure 3.7 Opera, representing a "datalist" element

For the option elements within the datalist, you just need to fill the value attribute. Further attributes and a text node are possible but not required for this use. If the user clicks the Submit button, the content of the text field is prefixed with the character string http:// and the browser is redirected to the resulting URL (window.location):

Listing 3.1 The "datalist" element filled with Internet addresses

```
<form>
  <p>
  <label for=url>Goto</label>
  http://<input type=text id=url name=homepage
                 list=hompages autofocus>
  <datalist id=hompages>
    <option value=www.google.com>
    <option value=html5.komplett.cc/welcome>
    <option value=slashdot.org>
    <option value=wired.com>
  </datalist>
  <input type=submit
    onclick="window.location =
    'http://'+document.getElementById('url').value;
    return false;" >
</form>
```

If you want to equip older browsers with a selection list without duplicating the HTML code, you can fall back on the following trick. Because browsers supporting the datalist element ignore an enclosed select element, they display the new HTML5 select element. Older browsers, however, display a selection list for the text field with predefined links, which will be inserted into the text field when the selection is changed.

As you can see in Listing 3.2, we need to add a text node to the option elements because the "old" select element does not show the content of the value attribute but instead shows the text:

Listing 3.2 A "datalist" with the fallback for older browsers

```
<datalist id=hompages>
<select name=homepage
  onchange="document.getElementById('url').value =
    document.forms[0].homepage[1].value" >
  <option value=www.google.com>www.google.com
  <option
  value=html5.komplett.cc/welcome>html5.komplett.cc/welcome
  <option value=slashdot.org>slashdot.org
  <option value=wired.com>wired.com
</select>
</datalist>
```

The onchange event within the select element inserts the current text of the selection menu into the text box (see Figure 3.8).

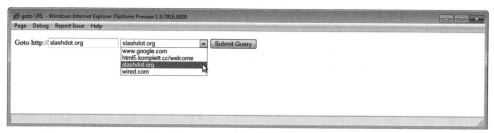

Figure 3.8 A combination of "input" and "select" elements as fallback for older browsers (here, Internet Explorer 8)

3.3.4 Cryptographic Keys with "keygen"

The keygen element has a long history in the Mozilla Firefox browser (included since version 1.0), but Microsoft still expressed great concern regarding the implementation in HTML5. keygen is used to generate cryptographic keys, which sounds complicated, and unfortunately, it is just as complicated as it sounds.

Simply put, the idea behind this element is this: The browser creates a pair of keys, one a *public key* and the other a *private key*. The public key is sent off with the other form data and is then available to the server application, whereas the private key remains saved in the browser. After this exchange of keys, the server and browser can communicate in encryption without SSL certificates. This sounds like a practical solution for those pesky self-signed certificates, which browsers keep complaining about, but sadly it is not, because the identity of the server can only be verified through a certificate that has been signed by a trustworthy authority, the *Certificate Authority (CA)*.

So if keygen cannot replace SSL, what should the new element be used for? As explained in the Mozilla documentation, the keygen element helps create a certificate that the server can sign (*signed certificate*). To make this step totally secure, it is usually necessary for the applicant to appear personally before the authority. Because the issuing of signed certificates is a task for experts, we will briefly describe this element and its attributes.

The following short HTML document creates a keygen button:

```html
<!DOCTYPE html>
  <meta charset="utf-8">
  <title>keygen Demo</title>
  <form method=post action=submit.html>
    <keygen id=kg challenge=hereismychallenge name=kg>
    <input type=submit>
  </form>
```

In addition to the familiar attributes, such as autofocus, disabled, name, and form, the keygen element has two special attributes: keytype and challenge. keytype in particular is interesting because the browser uses this entry to decide if it supports this element's function. Currently, there is only one valid keytype, which is rsa, a cryptographic system developed in 1977 at the Massachusetts Institute of Technology (MIT). If no keytype is specified (as in the preceding example), rsa is used as the default value. The specification also states that a browser does not have to support any keytype at all, which is probably because of Microsoft's veto against this element. The optional challenge attribute increases security during the key exchange. For further information, please refer to the links in the note at the end of this section.

If the browser supports the RSA key generation, it can offer a selection list to allow the user to select the length, and consequently the security, of the key (see Figure 3.9).

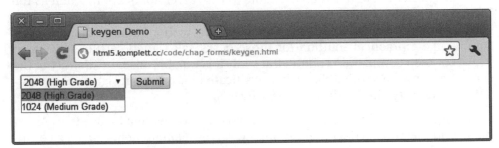

Figure 3.9   Selecting the key length in Google Chrome

Figure 3.10 shows the result after the form has been sent: The POST variable kg contains the public key required for encryption (here, rendered in the extremely useful Firefox add-on Firebug).

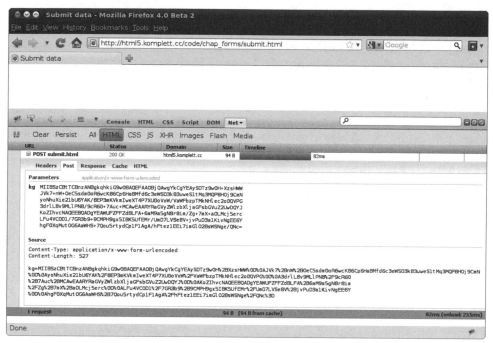

Figure 3.10 The public key of the "keygen" element, represented in Firebug

If you have not had much previous experience with cryptography but would like to find out more, Wikipedia is always a good starting point. Check out http://en.wikipedia.org/wiki/Public_key_infrastructure and http://en.wikipedia.org/wiki/Challenge-response_authentication.

3.3.5 Calculations with "output"

"The output element represents the result of a calculation." That is the very short explanation in the HTML5 specification, and you will find exactly the same text on most websites describing the new element. It all sounds very sensible, but what kind of calculations are we dealing with? Why do we need a special element for them?

As a general rule, these are calculations resulting from input fields on a website. An example familiar to most people would be an electronic shopping cart where the quantity for each product can be entered in an input field. Via the optional for attribute, you can determine which fields to include in the calculation. One or more id attributes of other fields in the document are referenced in the process.

To test the output element, we will program one of these little shopping carts for three different products. The quantity of each of these products can be changed via an input field. At the same time, the total number of items and the total price are displayed under the shopping cart. Figure 3.11 shows a shopping basket with five items.

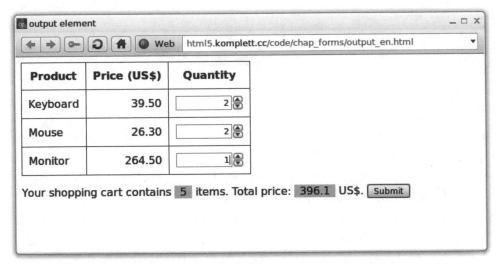

Figure 3.11   Two "output" elements show the number of products and the price in total

The code for our example can be explained quickly and simply: To update the output elements for each change in quantity, we use the form's oninput event:

```
<form oninput="updateSum();">
  <table>
    <tr><th>Product<th>Price (US$)<th>Item number
    <tr><td>Keyboard<td class=num id=i1Price>39.50<td>
    <input name=i1 id=i1 type=number min=0 value=0 max=99>
    <tr><td>Mouse<td class=num id=i2Price>26.30<td>
```

The output elements are defined after the table with the products and refer to the IDs of the input fields via the for attribute:

```
<p>Your shopping cart contains <output name=sumProd for="i1 i2 i3"
  id=sumProd></output> items. Total price:
  <output name=sum for="i1 i2 i3" id=sum></output> US$.
```

In the JavaScript code, a loop runs over all input elements, adding the quantities and calculating the total price:

```
function updateSum() {
  var ips = document.getElementsByTagName("input");
  var sum = 0;
  var prods = 0;
  for (var i=0; i<ips.length; i++) {
    var cnt=Number(ips[i].value);
    if (cnt > 0) {
      sum += cnt * Number(document.getElementById(
        ips[i].name+"Price").innerHTML);
      prods += cnt;
    }
  }
  document.getElementById("sumProd").value = prods;
  document.getElementById("sum").value = sum;
}
```

We get the product price directly from the table by using the innerHTML value of the relevant table column and converting it to a number with the JavaScript function Number(). The same applies to the value in the input field (ips[i]. value), because without this conversion, JavaScript would add up the character strings, which would not produce the desired results. The calculated values are then inserted into the value attributes of the output elements.

3.4 Client-Side Form Validation

One of the advantages of the new elements and attributes in forms is that the user can now enter data much more easily (for example, choose the date from a calendar). Another great advantage is the option of checking the form contents before the form is submitted and alerting the user of any mistakes. You might say that kind of checking is rather old hat because it has been around for years. That is true, but until now this step always had to be done via JavaScript code that you had to program. Thanks to jQuery and similar libraries, this task has become much easier and the code is more manageable, but you still must depend on an external library.

With HTML5, this situation changes fundamentally: You define the parameters of the input fields in HTML, and the browser checks whether the fields have been filled in correctly. That is a big step forward and makes many lines of JavaScript code redundant. This tiny example will convince you:

```
<form method=get action=required.html>
  <p><label>Your e-mail address:
  <input type=email name=email required></label>
  <p><input type=submit>
</form>
```

Figure 3.12 shows what will happen if you submit the form in the preceding listing without specifying an e-mail address. Opera displays the error message: *This is a required field.* If you have set the Opera user interface to another language, the error message appears in the relevant language. Of course, you can also adapt these error messages with JavaScript; more on this in section 3.4.3.

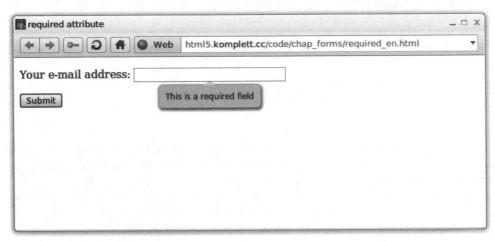

Figure 3.12 Error message for a blank input field with the "required" attribute (Opera)

But that is not all: The field is defined as the type email, so Opera also returns an error message if an invalid e-mail address is entered; for example, *Please enter a valid email address* (see Figure 3.13).

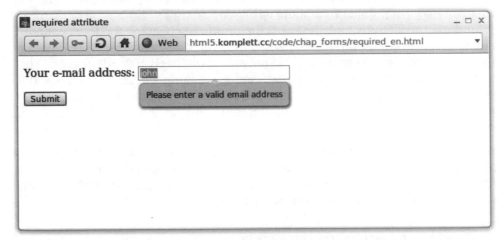

Figure 3.13 Error message in Opera after entering an invalid e-mail address

WebKit-based browsers, such as Google Chrome or Safari, currently support the validation but do not display an error message. They place a border around the invalid field and position the cursor in the field to at least provide some indication that something is not quite right.

> Despite all the euphoria about client-side validation of form input, you should not forget that this step cannot replace server-side control. A potential attacker can bypass these mechanisms with very little technical effort.

3.4.1   The "invalid" Event

During form validation, elements with an invalid content trigger the event invalid. We can use this to react individually to incorrect values:

```
window.onload = function() {
  var inputs = document.getElementsByTagName("input");
  for (var i=0; i<inputs.length; i++) {
    inputs[i].addEventListener("invalid", function() {
      alert("Field "+this.labels[0].innerHTML
        +" is invalid");
      this.style.border = 'dotted 2px red';
    }, false);
  }
}
```

After loading the page, a list of all input elements is generated (as in the example in section 3.3.5). An event listener is added to each element and deals with the error. In our example it opens an alert window, and the element is marked with a red-dotted border. The label of the input element is used as text in the alert window.

This approach is not ideal in forms with many input fields. The user must click the OK button for each incorrect input and then find the appropriate field in the form and fill in the details again. Sometimes, it would be more useful if the user could be notified immediately of invalid input while filling in the field. We will try this in the next section.

3.4.2   The "checkValidity" Function

To trigger the validation of an input element, the checkValidity function for that element is called. But you can also start "manually" what would normally happen when the form is submitted:

```
<input type=email name=email
  onchange="this.checkValidity();">
```

If you enter an invalid e-mail address and move away from the input field (either with the Tab key or by clicking elsewhere in the browser), the browser (currently, at least in Opera) returns an error message right away (refer to Figure 3.13). Error handling becomes even more elegant if we attach a function for checking input to the onchange event of all input elements:

```
window.onload = function() {
  var inputs = document.getElementsByTagName("input");
  for (var i=0; i<inputs.length; i++) {
    if (!inputs[i].willValidate) {
      continue;
    }
    inputs[i].onchange = function() {
      if (!this.checkValidity()) {
        this.style.border = 'solid 2px red';
        this.style.background = '';
      } else {
        this.style.border = '';
        this.style.background = 'lightgreen';
      }
    }
  }
}
```

The familiar loop runs over all input elements, checking first whether the element is available for validation. If willValidate does not return the value *true*, the loop continues with the next element. Otherwise, an anonymous function is assigned to the onchange event, calling the checkValidity function. this within the anonymous function refers to the input element. If the validity check fails, the element is surrounded with a red border; otherwise, the element's background is colored light green. Remember to reset the background color and border to an empty character string to make sure the browser sets the formatting back to the default value after the user has corrected an incorrect input. In Figure 3.14 you can see how the checkValidity function generates an error message as a result of incorrect time input.

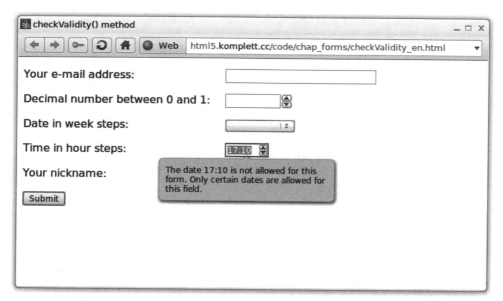

Figure 3.14   Opera displays an error message after an incorrect time input (in this case a violation of the "step" attribute)

If you would like to make error handling more interactive, you can use the new HTML5 `oninput` event instead of the `onchange` event. Unlike `onchange`, which is triggered when the field no longer has the focus, `oninput` is activated after every changed character. The `oninput` event now does what you previously had to program somewhat laboriously via the keyboard events `keyup` and `keydown`. Another advantage of `oninput` is that the event listener needs to be attached only once to the whole form, not to each input element. So in our preceding example, you could do without all the JavaScript code and change the form definition as follows:

```
<form method=get oninput="this.checkValidity();"
  action=checkValidity.html >
```

This means you forgo changing the borders and background color, but you significantly shorten the source code. An immediate reaction to each keystroke can be very helpful in some cases, but when filling in a form field, it is usually enough if the content is checked after the field has been fully completed.

3.4.3   Error Handling with "setCustomValidity()"

If you feel that all the error handling methods introduced earlier are still not quite enough, you can also program your own function for checking content. In the following example, we define an input field with the type `email`, which ensures that the browser will check for a valid e-mail address. Additionally, we want to specifically exclude three e-mail domains:

```
var invalidMailDomains = [
  'hotmail.com', 'gmx.com', 'gmail.com' ];

function checkMailDomain(item) {
  for (var i=0; i<invalidMailDomains.length; i++) {
    if (item.value.match(invalidMailDomains[i]+'$')) {
      item.setCustomValidity('E-mail addresses from '
        +invalidMailDomains[i]+' are not accepted.');
    } else {
      item.setCustomValidity('');
    }
    item.checkValidity();
  }
}
```

Each element in the array invalidMailDomains is compared to the value of the input element. The JavaScript function match() works with regular expressions, which is why we add a $symbol to the domain name, to indicate the end of the character string. If the character strings match, the setCustomValidity function is called and displays the appropriate error message. If it is not a domain name from the array, setCustomValidity() is called with an empty character string. Internally, this attaches the variable validationMessage to the input element, which Opera then displays (see Figure 3.15). The concluding call of the checkValidity function triggers the validity check and leads to the aforementioned error message.

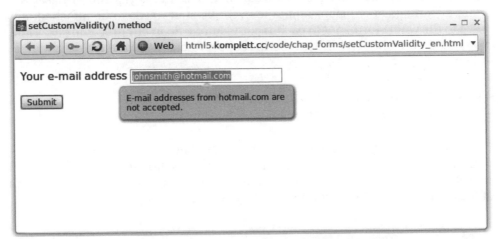

Figure 3.15   Opera displays an error message during manual error handling (checking e-mail domain)

3.4.4   Summary of Validity Checks

Table 3.3 shows a summary of all input attributes and validity functions available for validity checks, and the scenarios where they occur.

Table 3.3   Possible Errors During Validity Checks of Form Fields

Attribute/Function	Problem
required	No value was entered in the field.
type=email, url	The entered value does not match the required type.
pattern	The entered value does not match the required pattern.
maxlength	The entered value is longer than allowed.
min, max	The entered value is too small or too big.
step	The required step size of the entered value has been violated.
setCustomValidity()	The additional criteria set for this field are not fulfilled.

3.4.5   Or Perhaps Better Not to Validate? "formnovalidate"

Now that we have spent so much time discussing error handling, we will tell you how you can sneak past all the rules with the attribute formnovalidate. At first it may seem a little strange to simply disregard all the laboriously defined rules and just submit the form without validation. The specification offers a brief explanation that quickly solves the mystery. The typical application for skipping the validity check is a form that the user cannot or does not want to complete in one go. By adding the formnovalidate attribute to a submit button, the content that has been entered so far can be saved for later.

> **NOTE**
>
> If you submit a form with formnovalidate, the fields already completed are sent to the server. The server application is responsible for potentially saving the data temporarily.

Imagine, for example, that you want to fill in a support form for your faulty digital camera. After spending ages filling in all the details about the error that has occurred, the website asks you for the camera's serial number. Because you do not have the camera at hand and you do not want to lose all the information you have already entered, you click the Save button and can then calmly go looking for your camera. This button is defined as follows:

```
<p><input type=submit formnovalidate
  value="Save" name=save id=save>
```

The following example will fully illustrate the idea of the support form.

3.5   Example: A Support Form

In this example, the previously introduced new elements and attributes are used in a form. A form of this kind could, in an expanded state, be used on the website of an electronics dealer.

Initially, the client is asked to supply personal details (in this example just the name, an e-mail address, and a telephone and fax number). The second part of the form concerns the product's technical data and defect. The bottom part of the webpage shows a progress bar that is meant to encourage the user to complete the form (see Figure 3.16).

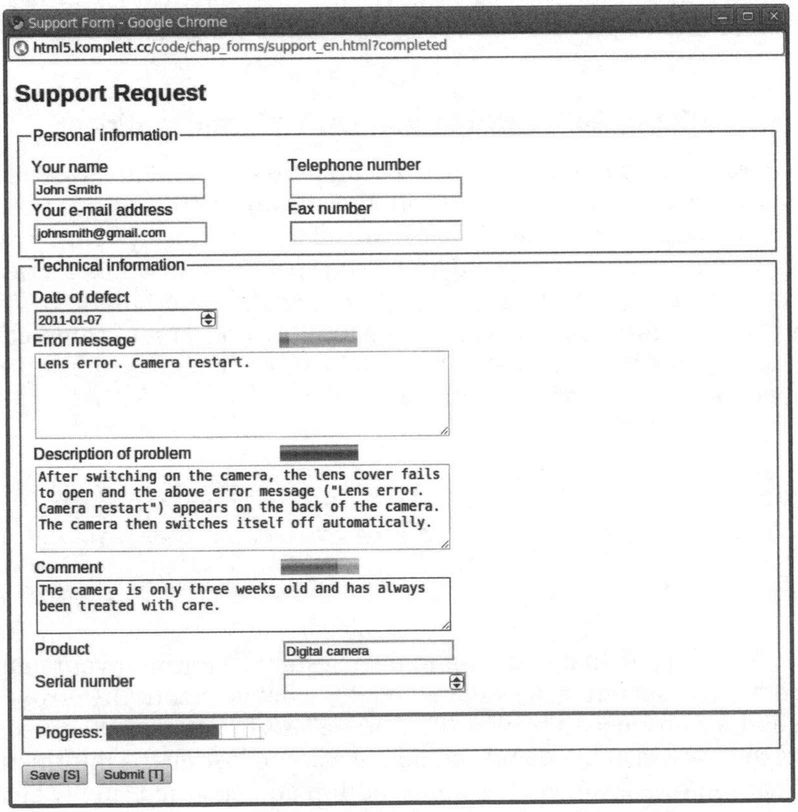

Figure 3.16   The almost completed support form

The HTML code for the form starts by loading an external JavaScript file and the already familiar call `window.onload`:

```
    <script src="support.js"></script>
    <script>
window.onload = function() {
  initEventListener();
}
    </script>
```

The `initEventListener` function runs through all `input` elements and assigns an anonymous function to the onchange event, checking the corresponding element for its validity:

```
function initEventListener() {
  var inputs = document.getElementsByTagName("input");
  for (var i=0; i<inputs.length; i++) {
    if (!inputs[i].willValidate) {
      continue;
    }
    inputs[i].onchange = function() {
      this.checkValidity();
    }
  }
}
```

The event listener is only added if the element can check validity. In our example the two buttons for submitting or saving do not have the option to check validity and therefore do not get an onchange event. As explained earlier, checking the individual form fields after they have been filled in is more convenient than checking the entire form with the oninput event.

To improve the form's user friendliness, we want to emphasize the elements marked as required to make it immediately clear to the user which are the most important fields. Fortunately, we do not have to add an extra style to each element. CSS3 gives us the new selector :required, which is intended for exactly this case. The following instruction places an orange border around all required elements:

```
:required { border-color: orange; border-style: solid; }
```

The definition of the individual input fields does not contain any great surprises. E-mail address and phone number have their own types and are required; the date when the defect occurred has the type date and can therefore be selected from a calendar window. The two-column layout in the upper part of the webpage is achieved via adjacent div elements. We still want users who jump to the next field using the Tab key to fill in the form from top to bottom and not, as

HTML logic would suggest, first fill in the left and then the right column. We can achieve this with the `tabindex` attribute, which means that pressing the Tab key in a field will move the cursor to the field with the next higher `tabindex` value:

```
<div style="float:left">
<p><label>Your name
<input tabindex=1 type=text required autofocus
   placeholder="John Smith" name=name></label>
<p><label>Your e-mail address
<input tabindex=3 type=email name=email required></label>
</div>
<div style="float:left;margin-left:10px;">
<p><label>Telephone number
<input tabindex=2 type=tel name=tel required></label>
<p><label>Fax number
<input tabindex=4 type=tel name=fax></label>
</div>
```

Now the code gets more exciting with the `textarea` fields. HTML5 does not make many changes to this type. But as you can see in Figure 3.16, each text field now has a small graphic display above it, showing how many characters you can still type into this field. You probably realized it right away: It's done with the new `meter` element, which you already know from section 3.3.1, Displaying Measurements with "meter":

```
<p><label>Error message
<textarea placeholder="Lens error. Camera restart."
   name=errmsg required rows=5 cols=50
   title="up to 200 characters">
</textarea></label><meter value=0 max=200
   tabindex=-1></meter>
```

The `meter` element is initialized with a maximum value of 200, exactly the value specified as maximum in the `title` attribute of the textarea. If a user enters more characters than the maximum allowed, the `meter` element turns red, indicating that the text entered is too long. The browser will still submit all the text, because we have not limited the textarea. So this is more a hint rather than a strict requirement. The JavaScript function for updating the `meter` elements is `updateTAMeters()` and is executed for all textareas:

```
function updateTAMeters() {
   var textfs = document.getElementsByTagName("textarea");
   for(var i=0; i<textfs.length; i++) {
      textfs[i].labels[0].nextSibling.value =
         textfs[i].textLength;
   }
}
```

The advantage of the loop is that we can now add any number of textarea elements, and as long as they have a meter element, they will be updated automatically. To achieve this, we need to resort to a DOM trick: The code printed in bold in the preceding listing accesses the DOM function nextSibling, a reference to the next element. Let's revisit the HTML code for the text field and the status bar to make things clearer. The textarea element is enclosed by a label element followed by the desired meter element. To get from the textarea element to the meter element, we use the text field's labels property. This is a *NodeList* array, and we are interested in the first element (with the index 0), because the following element (the nextSibling) is the meter element.

If you look closely, the procedure is not as complicated as it at first looks, but it has a few snags. If there is a stray whitespace or line break that sneaks in between the enclosing label element and the meter element, then our status display no longer works. The nextSibling then becomes a text element, and we can no longer reach the meter element in the for loop.

Next we want to program the progress display at the end of the form. You probably guessed that it is a progress element; More interesting is how we can elegantly express updating this element in JavaScript. First, here is the HTML code for the element:

```
<label>Progress:
  <progress id=formProgress value=0
    tabindex=-1></progress></label>
```

We assign to the progress element an id, a starting value of 0 (value), and a negative tabindex, which means that the element is never accessed with the Tab key. The JavaScript function updateProgress() updates the progress element:

```
function updateProgress() {
  var req = document.querySelectorAll(":required");
  count = 0;
  for(var i=0; i<req.length; i++) {
    if (req[i].value != '') {
      count++;
    }
  }
  var pb = document.getElementById("formProgress");
  pb.max = req.length;
  pb.value = count;
}
```

Because the progress bar is only supposed to refer to the elements that are absolutely required, we pass the character string :required to the function query-SelectorAll(). The result is a *NodeList* containing only elements that have the required attribute. A loop is then run over these elements, checking whether the value attribute matches a nonempty character string. If this condition applies (in other words, a value has already been entered), the counter variable count is increased by one value. To finish, the maximum value of the progress element is set to the number of all required fields and the value to the number of the non-empty elements.

Two buttons are available for submitting the form: Save and Submit. We have already discussed the save function in section 3.4.5, Or Perhaps Better to Not Validate? "formnovalidate"; new in this context is the attribute accesskey:

```
<p><input accesskey=T type=submit formnovalidate
   value="Save [S]"  name=save id=save>
<input accesskey=T type=submit name=submit id=submit
   value="Submit [T]">
```

Keyboard shortcuts are not new in HTML5, but they have not been used much so far. One problem with keyboard shortcuts is that they are activated by different key combinations on different platforms, so you never quite know which key you are supposed to press for a particular shortcut. The HTML5 specification has a suggestion to solve this: The value of the accessKeyLabel should return a character string that corresponds to the correct value on the platform you are using. You could then use this value in the button's label or in its title attribute. Unfortunately, at the time of this writing, not a single browser was capable of outputting this character string.

Summary

The information we supply in this chapter explains many of the new options provided in HTML5 for forms. Better times are ahead for web developers, because they will no longer need to grapple with JavaScript libraries for common input elements, such as date and time. In particular, the new form functions will be of great help when working with mobile devices where text input is usually much more difficult than on the computer. Form validation in the browser will also contribute significantly to making the code more transparent and therefore more manageable. But do not forget that client-side validation does not make the server application more secure; potential attackers can easily circumvent these checks.

If this chapter has whet your appetite and you want to try out your freshly acquired knowledge of forms on your own website, go right ahead. The syntax of the new elements and attributes is built in such a way that even older browsers will not produce errors. Users of such browsers will not be able to enjoy the full benefit of the new input elements, but text input is always possible.

4
Video and Audio

The introduction of YouTube was a quantum leap for displaying videos online. Before the video platform came along, it was practically impossible for computer novices to make a video file available to others via the Internet: The files were usually too big to send via e-mail, and if they did arrive, the likelihood was great that they could not be played on the recipient's computer.

YouTube on the other hand offers online storage, allowing you to save the video files. It also converts the different video formats, so they can be played with the Adobe Flash Player.

Adobe supports Flash on many operating systems, offering plug-ins for all common browsers. Browser plug-ins are generally a great idea, but the communication between plug-in and browser can sometimes be difficult if not impossible. Also, *closed-source* plug-ins, such as the Adobe Flash Player, are not very popular with the browser manufacturers, because they make it much harder to find the error in case of a crash.

HTML5 wanted to remedy this situation. The necessary new HTML element was easily found: video. But that was not enough to solve the problem.

4.1   A First Example

We will give you a short example to demonstrate how easy the new HTML5 video element is to use:

```
<!DOCTYPE html>
  <title>Simple Video</title>
    <video controls autoplay>
      <source src='videos/mvi_2170.webm' type='video/webm'>
      <source src='videos/mvi_2170.ogv' type='video/ogg'>
      Sorry, your browser is unable to play this video.
    </video>
```

You can play a video in the browser with remarkably little effort. In Figure 4.1 you can see the result in Mozilla Firefox. The HTML syntax is almost self-explanatory, but we will investigate it in more detail in the next section.

Figure 4.1   A video in WebM format in Mozilla Firefox

4.2   The "video" Element and Its Attributes

In the preceding example, two attributes are assigned to the video element: con-trols and autoplay. The attribute `controls` tells the browser to display control elements for the video (see Figure 4.1), and `autoplay` tells the browser to start playing the video as soon as this is possible.

Like the `canvas` element (see Chapter 5, Canvas), the `video` element belongs to the category *embedded content*; in other words it is one of the contents that is not directly connected to HTML. Within the embedded content, you can include an alternative solution (*fallback*) in case the browser does not support the video element. If this happens in our example in section 4.1, A First Example, the text *Sorry, your browser is unable to play this video* appears. Additionally, you could display a still image from the video. But let's look at the possible attributes of the video element in more detail (see Table 4.1).

Table 4.1   Attributes of the "video" element

Attribute	Value	Information
src	*url*	The URL for the video to be played. This attribute is optional and can be replaced with one or more source elements, as in our example.
poster	*url*	The URL for a picture that the browser displays while the video is loading.
preload	*none*	The browser is not supposed to try loading the video before the Play button is clicked. This saves band-width.
preload	*metadata*	Only the metadata for the video is loaded (for exam-ple, length of video, author, copyright).
preload	*auto*	In this case the entire video is loaded even before the user clicks the Play button.
autoplay	*boolean*	The browser begins playing the video as soon as enough data has been received.
controls	*boolean*	Displays simple control elements for the video. This does not determine what these elements should look like; that is mostly up to the browser manufacturers. The specification suggests several elements, such as controls for playback and pausing the video, setting the volume, an option to skip to another point in the video (provided the content supports it), switching to full screen, and possible buttons for subtitles.
loop	*boolean*	Tells the browser to repeat playback after reaching the end of the video.

Table 4.1   Attributes of the "video" element (*Contd.*)

Attribute	Value	Information
width	*in CSS pixels*	Width of video display
height	*in CSS pixels*	Height of video display
audio	*muted*	Causes the user agent to override the user's preferences, if any, and always defaults the video to muted.

If the video element does not have a src attribute, the browser processes one or more of the source elements contained within the video element. The attributes src, type, and media are intended for this purpose (see Table 4.2). In turn, if there is a source element, you must not specify a src attribute for video.

Table 4.2   Attributes of the "source" element

Attribute	Value	Information
src	*url*	The URL for the video to be played
type	*mime-type*	MIME type of the video. You can add a specification of the audio and video codec, for example, type='video/webm; codecs="vorbis,vp8"'. If there are several source elements, the browser uses this attribute (among others) to decide which video is displayed.
media	*CSS Media Query*	The output medium for which the video is intended

The browser uses two criteria to decide which of the existing source elements will be displayed: the video's MIME type and, if present, the media attribute in which you can specify additional limitations in the form of a *CSS media query*.

For CSS3, media queries were significantly expanded, so you can now have more complex instructions in addition to familiar keywords like *print, screen, handheld,* or *projection*. Here is an example:

```
media="screen and (min-width: 800px)"
```

This is where it gets interesting for video output, because depending on the browser size, the video can then be offered at different resolutions. Thanks to this trick, even mobile devices with smaller display screens and slower Internet connections can manage perfectly. A complete example for displaying a video in reduced size based on media queries looks like this:

```
<!DOCTYPE html>
  <title>Simple Video</title>
   <video controls autoplay>
    <source src='videos/mvi_2170.webm' type='video/webm'
      media="screen and (min-width: 500px)" >
    <source src='videos/mvi_2170_qvga.webm'
      type='video/webm' media="screen" >
    Sorry, your browser is unable to play this video.
   </video>
```

Browsers with less than 500 pixels in width for displaying the video will automatically display the smaller video format `mvi_2170_qvga.webm`.

> **NOTE**
>
> The specification of CSS3 Media Queries is currently in the *Editors Draft* stage. Some details are therefore likely to change. You can look up the current stage of the specification on the W3C website at http://dev.w3.org/csswg/css3-mediaqueries.

The second criterion for determining which video will be displayed is the MIME type. The optional addition of the codecs used lets the browser recognize, even before loading, whether the video can be decoded. But what are these codecs about? The following section attempts to shed light on the codec jungle.

4.3 Video Codecs

Modern video formats use a *container* file where audio and video contents can be saved separately. This flexible approach has several advantages. For example, several audio tracks can be saved in one file, allowing the user to switch between languages (as you would on a video DVD). Figure 4.2 shows the schematic representation of a video container file. The way in which audio and video are compressed within this container file is referred to as *codec*.

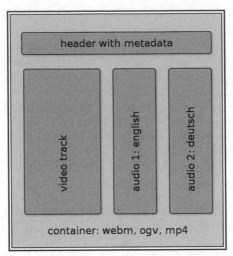

Figure 4.2   Schematic representation of a video container format

One bone of contention during the creation of the HTML5 specification was the definition of allowed audio and video codecs. These debates were caused on one hand by commercial interests of companies holding patents for certain coding processes and on the other by the desire to choose a capable and high-quality format. More precisely, the camp was divided into a group that supported the patent-protected video codec *H.264* and another group (led by the Mozilla team) calling for the open-source format *Ogg Theora*. When Ian Hickson realized that this conflict could endanger the important video element, he decided to take the definition of the format out of the specification. It is now up to the browser manufacturers to decide which formats they support and for which formats they are willing to pay license fees.

Although Mozilla fought vehemently to avoid repeating the same mistake that was made in the case of the image format GIF for which CompuServe later demanded license fees, H.264 seemed to be the favorite in the race for the new, online video format. But Google did not want to passively await the misery of potential patent infringements and decided to take care of the problem. By purchasing the video specialist *On2 Technologies*, which had already developed important video formats, Google came to own the as yet unpublished codec *VP8*. During the Google developer conference, *Google-IO 2010*, the software giant finally let the cat out of the bag: The new project *WebM,* based on the video codec VP8 and the audio format *Ogg Vorbis*, was published as an open-source project on the Internet at http://www.webmproject.org, and was soon after implemented in Firefox and Opera.

In early 2011, Google even went one step further, announcing that support for the H.264 codec would be removed from future versions of its Chrome browser. The justification for this surprising step was that Google wants to enable open innovation, believing that the core techniques of the World Wide Web need to be based on open standards, which H.264 is not.

After this brief history we will now explain a little more about the individual formats. Don't worry; we will not discuss the technical details of video compression at great length. We will just introduce the common formats for the Internet.

4.3.1   Ogg: Theora and Vorbis

When the Fraunhofer society began to demand license fees for the popular MP3 format at the end of the last millennium, the *Xiph.Org Foundation* developed the free audio codec *Vorbis*. Based on the video codec *VP3.2*, which was released in 2002 (developed by the aforementioned company *On2*), Xiph also created the video format *Theora*. Video and audio are combined in a container format, *Ogg*, and the container can contain one or more audio and video tracks. The MIME type for Ogg video files is *video/ogg,* and the corresponding filename extension is .ogv. (The file extension .ogg also works, but according to Xiph.org, we should avoid it and instead use the more explicit file extension .ogv for Ogg video and .oga for Ogg audio.)

Do not confuse the *Ogg Media* container format (file extension .ogm) with the Ogg container discussed here. The Ogg Media (OGM) container is an extension that supports a large number of additional video codecs. Initially, this sounds very useful, but it does lead to some problems: Xiph insists that Ogg should be mentioned only in the context of free formats, but this is not the case with Ogg Media, which can also use patented formats.

4.3.2   MPEG-4: H.264 and AAC

The MPEG-4 (MP4) container is a derivation of the multimedia format *Quick-Time* commonly used in Apple operating systems. Like the Ogg container, MP4 can have audio and video tracks; it even goes one step further and can embed images and text. The most common codecs in MP4 are the patented video codec H.264 and the audio codec *Advanced Audio Coding (AAC)*. The file extension is .mp4, and common media types are *video/mp4, audio/mp4,* and *application/mp4.*

NOTE

Apple created some confusion when files with the extension .m4a started to appear on iPods and other Apple devices. These are MP4 files, but Apple wanted the file extension to indicate that it is a pure audio file. Other file extensions used are .m4b for audio books and .m4r for iPhone ringtones.

It was mostly the huge success of Apple's mobile devices (iPod, iPhone, iPad) that contributed to the rapid spreading of the MP4 file format. To achieve an acceptable performance when playing back videos on devices with weak processors (such as cell phones), the computer-intensive process is transferred to a separate chip. This hardware acceleration saves energy and prolongs battery life.

The patent problem regarding the H.264 codec should not be underestimated. The type of encoding is patent protected until at least 2028—a veritable sword of Damocles hanging over the software manufacturers who could be required at any time to pay fees for the encoding process.

4.3.3   WebM: VP8 and Vorbis

As mentioned at the beginning of this section, Google caused some excitement and euphoria by founding the WebM project. The video codec VP8 received very good feedback in general, and the audio codec Vorbis had already proven successful. Google decided to use the open-source format *Matroska* as a container, which was already tried and tested as well. But although the Matroska format supports a number of different codecs, the WebM container only allows for the video codec VP8 and the audio codec Vorbis.

The standard file extension for WebM videos is `.webm`, and the corresponding MIME type is *video/webm*.

Immediately after Google's announcement, the browser manufacturers of Mozilla Firefox, Opera, and even Microsoft for Internet Explorer announced that they would support the WebM format. It goes without saying that Google's browser Chrome offers support for WebM, so there is only one browser without support for the new codec (at least at the time of this writing): Apple's Safari.

4.4   Tools for Video Conversion

Because most peoples' digital cameras usually do not produce videos in WebM or Ogg format, the next section introduces different tools for converting videos. They are all open-source products that run on Windows, Mac OS, and Linux, except for the *Miro Video Converter*.

4.4.1   FFmpeg

FFmpeg is sometimes referred to as the *Swiss army knife* of video conversion. And rightly so, because the list of audio and video formats that FFmpeg can read and write is remarkably long. It can also split multimedia files into their components; for example, it can strip out only the audio track of a film and then convert it. If you are thinking of adding converted YouTube videos to your MP3 collection, be warned: The quality of the audio track on YouTube is usually rather disappointing.

Because the developers of FFmpeg did not bother with such trivialities as the programming of a graphic user interface, the user is expected to be none too shy about using the command line. If you do not change the FFmpeg default settings, you only need the following function call to convert an existing Flash Video (FLV) to the WebM format:

```
$> ffmpeg -i myflashvideo.flv myflashvideo.webm
```

FFmpeg is also excellent for finding out the format of a video:

```
$> ffmpeg -i myflashvideo.flv
...
Input #0, flv, from '/tmp/myflashvideo.flv':
 Duration: 00:05:12.19, start: 24.8450, bitrate: 716 kb/s
    Stream #0.0: Video: h264, yuv420p, 480x360 [PAR 1:1
      DAR 4:3], 601 kb/s, 25 tbr, 1k tbn, 49.99 tbc
    Stream #0.1: Audio: aac, 44100 Hz, stereo, s16,
      115 kb/s
```

In this example, we are dealing with an approximately five-minute long video in a Flash container in which the video track is saved using the H.264 codec, and the audio track is in AAC.

Since version 0.6, FFmpeg has supported WebM videos. But the developers were not satisfied with using the *libvpx* library available through Google: They reimplemented VP8 based on the existing FFmpeg code, hoping to achieve considerably better performance in converting videos.

A significant part of the FFmpeg project is the *libavcodec* library where supported audio and video formats are saved. Players like *vlc*, *mplayer*, or *xine* use this library to play or re-encode videos.

The list of parameters for FFmpeg is practically endless and cannot be reproduced in detail within the scope of this book. If you are interested in finding out more, please refer to the excellent FFmpeg Documentation available online at http://www.ffmpeg.org/ffmpeg-doc.html.

Table 4.3 shows some important parameters for encoding with FFmpeg.

Table 4.3   Some important FFmpeg parameters

Parameter	Effect
-h	Help for all parameters (very long list)
-formats	List of all supported file formats
-codecs	List of all supported audio and video codecs
-i *file*	Sets *file* as input file / stream
-f *fmt*	Sets *fmt* as output format (for example, webm, ogg, or mp4)
-ss *start*	Searches the input medium up to the point *start* (in seconds)
-t *duration*	Records for *duration* seconds
-b *bitrate*	Video quality (bitrate, default: 200 kilobits/s)
-r *fps*	Frames per second (default: 25)
-s *widthxheight*	Video size (in pixels, specified in width times height, or specifications such as *vga*)
-ab *bitrate*	Audio quality (bitrate, default: 64 kilobits/s)

Thanks to the option of letting FFmpeg work without user interaction, it is particularly suitable for automatic video conversion.

4.4.2   VLC

For many years, the *VideoLan* project has been developing the popular media player *VLC*, available for various operating systems (Windows, Mac OS, Linux, and other UNIX variations) with a simple graphic interface. The media player uses, among others, the *libavcodec* library of the FFmpeg project and therefore also supports the WebM format.

VLC does not just play videos of different formats and sources; you also have the option to convert multimedia content via the menu item Convert / Save. As you can see in Figure 4.3, you can use predefined profiles for converting to common formats—a very useful feature.

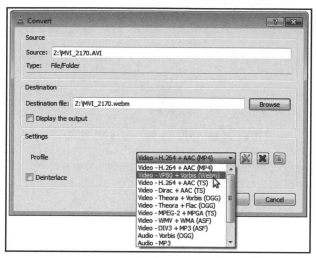

Figure 4.3   Dialog for converting videos in VLC

If you want to set quality and size of the video more precisely, you can open another dialog via Tools.

If you examine VLC more closely, you will discover further interesting functions. For example, you have the option of capturing the screen as a video (screencast) so you can record your current work or the option of streaming videos to the Net via different protocols. Of course, FFmpeg can do that, too, but VLC even has a GUI on top of that. You can download VLC at http://www.videolan.org for all common platforms.

4.4.3 Firefogg

If you are not completely comfortable using the command line and you do not want to install VLC, you can use the Firefox extension *Firefogg*. After installation, you can go to http://firefogg.org/make to easily select a video on your computer and convert it to the Ogg or WebM video format. Firefogg.org only offers the GUI buttons in this case; the conversion takes place on the local computer. An adapted version of FFmpeg, downloaded during the Firefogg installation, is working in the background.

In the menu item Preset you will find defaults for Ogg and WebM video in high and low quality (see Figure 4.4). You can also conveniently set metadata, such as title, author, recording date, and copyright, via the user interface.

Figure 4.4 Settings for video conversion in Firefogg

But Firefogg is more than just a graphic interface for FFmpeg. The extension comes with a JavaScript library, which makes it very easy for web developers to implement video uploads for users. The advantage is obvious: Instead of uploading a video format in low compression and then converting it on the server, the conversion takes place on the client side before the upload. This saves bandwidth and computing power on the web server's side. Wikipedia is also betting on this concept, so we can hope that the development of Firefogg will continue.

NOTE

The website http://firefogg.org/dev/chunk_post_example.html shows in a few lines of source code how the Firefogg JavaScript library works. Firefogg divides the upload into 1MB chunks, which means that if the Internet connection fails, you do not need to upload the entire video again.

4.4.4 Miro Video Converter

The *Miro Video Converter* was developed as an offshoot of the *Miro Media Player* (http://www.getmiro.com), an innovative open-source audio and video player available for all common operating systems. The Miro Video Converter is only available for Windows and Mac OS. Figure 4.5 shows the simple user interface, which offers selection not only by video codec but also by device (iPad, iPhone, PlayStation, and Android phones).

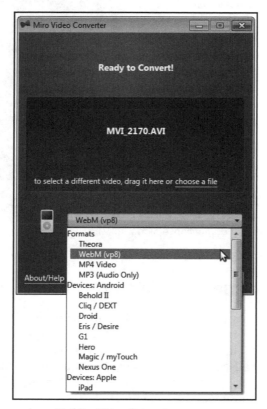

Figure 4.5 Video conversion with Miro Video Converter

Load the video file via drag and drop, and FFmpeg starts the conversion. If FFmpeg should fail for any reason (which can occasionally happen), the FFmpeg Output button can help: Apart from the exact commands, it also shows all conversion status messages (see Figure 4.6). A quick Google search for the relevant error message will usually help you.

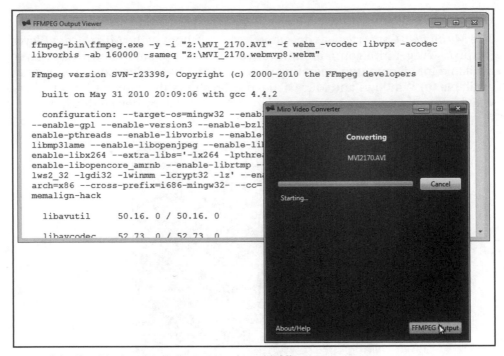

Figure 4.6   Troubleshooting during conversion with Miro

4.5   Which Format for Which Browser?

If you want to make videos available online for as many different browsers as possible, you will currently have to resort to a fallback solution for the video element. As shown in Table 4.4, there is no single video format at the moment that can be displayed by all common browsers. For the correlation of browser versions and release dates, please refer to the end of the Introduction chapter or look at the timeline shown on the website at

http://html5.komplett.cc/code/chap_intro/timeline.html?lang=en

Table 4.4 Codec support in current browsers

Codec	Firefox	Opera	Chrome	Safari	IE	iOS*	Android
OGG	3.5	10.50	3.0				
MP4			3.0			3.0	2.0
WebM	4.0	10.60	6.0		9**		
Flash	Plug-In	Plug-In	Plug-In	Plug-In	Plug-In		2.2

* Apple's operating system for mobile devices, such as iPhone, iPad, iPod (since June 2010 *iOS*, previously *iPhone OS*).
** According to Microsoft, the WebM codec must be installed in the operating system, unlike with other browsers.

4.6 Interim Solutions for Older Browsers

Fortunately, not every web developer who wants to cater to different platforms or browsers has to completely reinvent the wheel. There are several free libraries online focusing on this problem. Currently, Kaltura's JavaScript library *mwEmbed* has reached a very good stage of development. Wikipedia uses it to make video and audio elements available for most platforms. The main focus of this library is on the Ogg format. If you want to offer WebM and MP4 as well, use of the *html5media* library is a good solution.

4.6.1 mwEmbed

The mwEmbed library gained wider recognition mainly through the integration in Wikipedia. Kaltura, the company behind mwEmbed, offers integration not only for *MediaWiki*, the free encyclopedia's wiki software, but also for ready-made plug-ins for common CMS and blog software like *Drupal* or *WordPress*.

To ensure that even older browsers do not choke on the new HTML5 syntax, this example adds the elements head and body:

```
<!DOCTYPE html>
<html>
 <head>
  <title>mwEmbed fallback</title>
  <script type="text/javascript"
    src="http://html5.kaltura.org/js" > </script>
 </head>
 <body>
  <h1>mwEmbed fallback</h1>
   <video controls autoplay>
```

```
      <source src='videos/mvi_2170.mp4' type='video/mp4'>
      <source src='videos/mvi_2170.webm' type='video/webm'>
      <source src='videos/mvi_2170.ogv' type='video/ogg'>
      Sorry, your browser is unable to play this video.
    </video>
  </body>
</html>
```

The JavaScript library mwEmbed is downloaded directly from the project website (http://html5.kaltura.org/js) and then sorts out how the video can be played. In any case, a small control bar appears at the bottom edge of the video. Figure 4.7 shows the reaction of Internet Explorer 8, which does not yet know the HTML5 video element: To play the Ogg video, it loads the Java applet *Cortado*.

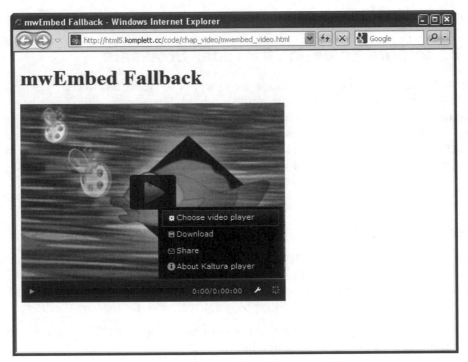

Figure 4.7   Internet Explorer 8 with Kaltura's fallback library mwEmbed

If you are not happy with Java applets as replacements for native video in the browser, you can use the *html5media* library instead.

4.6.2 html5media

The JavaScript library *html5media* works even more reservedly than mwEmbed and only takes action if the browser cannot play any of the specified video formats. In that case, it loads the open-source Flash Video Player *Flowplayer* and expects an MP4 (H.264) video as input. Unfortunately, the library contains a bug in the current version, which means that older browsers return a JavaScript error and output nothing if several source elements are specified:

```
<!DOCTYPE html>
<html>
 <head>
  <title>html5media fallback</title>
  <script type="text/javascript"
    src="libs/html5media.min.js" > </script>
 </head>
 <body>
  <h1>html5media fallback</h1>
  <video src="videos/mvi_2170.mp4" width=640 height=480
    controls>
  </video>
 </body>
</html>
```

In this case it is important to specify the width and height; otherwise, the Flowplayer will be displayed with a height of only a few pixels. Figure 4.8 provides an example.

Figure 4.8   A video in Internet Explorer 8 playing on the free Flowplayer (Flash fallback)

4.7   Video and Scripting—A Simple Video Player

Not only can you display videos in the browser, you can also control them directly with JavaScript via the HTMLMediaElement interface. This section shows you how this works. We will implement a simple JavaScript HTML5 video player with the following features:

- Start and stop the video

- Display and set the playback position on a control bar

- Fast forward and backward

- Select specific scenes in the movie

- Switch volume between high, low, and mute

A suitable video for our video player is easily found: *Big Buck Bunny*—a roughly ten-minute long computer-animated cartoon, which is the result of a free film project, as its URL http://bigbuckbunny.org indicates. The project was initiated by the *Blender Foundation*. From October 2007 to April 2008, seven 3D animation specialists used free software, like *Blender, Gimp, Inkscape,* or *Python,* all running on *Ubuntu,* to create this film and made it available online under an open license. A summary of the action, based on the motto *funny and furry,* can be found on Wikipedia at http://en.wikipedia.org/wiki/Big_Buck_Bunny. But our main concern is the video player. Figure 4.9 shows what it will look like.

Figure 4.9   Screen shot of the JavaScript HTML5 video player

The video player's HTML page with JavaScript library and CSS styles can be found on this book's companion website at the following links:

- http://html5.komplett.cc/code/chap_video/js_videoPlayer_en.html
- http://html5.komplett.cc/code/chap_video/js_videoPlayer.js
- http://html5.komplett.cc/code/chap_video/js_videoPlayer.css

4.7.1 Integrating the Video

Most likely, you are already familiar with the HTML code for integrating video. Apart from the two event handler attributes oncanplay and ontimeupdate, which will play an important role later on, there is not much new here:

```
<video preload=metadata
       poster=videos/bbb_poster.jpg
       width=854 height=480
       oncanplay="initControls()"
       ontimeupdate="updateProgress()">
  <source src='videos/bbb_480p_stereo.ogv'
          type='video/ogg;codecs="theora, vorbis"'>
  <!-- further source elements as alternatives -->
  Sorry, your browser is unable to play this video.
</video>
```

With preload=metadata, we first load only so much of the film that the film duration and at least the first frame are available. During loading, we display the picture specified in the poster attribute and then the first frame, which, unfortunately, is completely black in our case.

The width and height is specified for demo purposes to reenlarge the original video—reduced from 854 x 480 to 428 x 240 after downloading—back to 854 x 480 pixels. Why? Well, the reduced version is 39MB and is easier to test than the original video at 160MB. Also, explicitly specifying the attributes width and height can help explain 80% of the short HTMLVideoElement interface. This interface consists of only four attributes for the video dimensions; an attribute for the poster frame's URL, if there is one; and the audio attribute that reflects whether the audio track is muted or not.

Provided that the variable video contains a reference to our video element, we have the following attribute values:

- video.width = 854 (specified width)
- video.height = 480 (specified height)

- `video.videoWidth = 428 (original width)`
- `video.videoHeight = 240 (original height)`
- `video.poster = URL for bbb_poster.jpg (poster frame)`

These few attributes are of course not enough to implement our video player. And indeed they are only additional elements of the HTMLVideoElement, which also represents an HTMLMediaElement—the object that contains all the necessary methods and attributes. If you are curious, you can look it up in the specification at http://www.w3.org/TR/html5/video.html#htmlmediaelement.

The real work starts with oncanplay, because it refers to the JavaScript function to be executed as soon as the browser can play the video. In our example this function is initControls() where a reference to the video is created and saved in the global variable video. In the course of implementing our video player, we will have to add entries to initControls() a few more times, but for now we only need the following code:

```
var video;
var initControls = function() {
  video = document.querySelector("VIDEO");
};
```

The method document.querySelector() is part of the *CSS Selectors API*. In the video variable it provides a reference to the first video element in the document. This gives us access to the HTMLMediaElement interface, and we can now start implementing our first feature—starting and stopping playback.

4.7.2 Starting and Stopping the Video

To start and stop playback, we first need a button in the HTML document that can react to a user clicking it:

```
<input type=button
       value="&#x25B6;"
       onclick="playPause(this);">
       id="playButton"
```

▶ is a character reference to the Unicode symbol *BLACK RIGHT-POINTING TRIANGLE*, which we can conveniently use as Play button. The function of starting and stopping playback is contained in playPause(), a callback function called with every click, which gets passed the button object in the argument this:

```
var playPause = function(ctrl) {
  if (video.paused) {
    video.play();
    ctrl.value = String.fromCharCode('0x25AE','0x25AE');
  }
  else {
    video.pause();
    ctrl.value = String.fromCharCode('0x25B6');
  }
};
```

The attribute `video.paused` tells us if the film is playing or not. It returns `true` if the film is paused and `false` if it is playing. This makes starting and stopping playback easy. `video.start()` and `video.pause()` are the suitable methods that in turn set `video.paused` to `false` or `true` accordingly.

The `button` object passed in the argument `ctrl` is used to change the button to a Pause or Play button via `ctrl.value`, depending on the current state. If we were to assign ▶ directly, this would not have the desired result; instead, the character string ▶ would be displayed literally as text written on the button. The correct method of creating Unicode symbols in JavaScript is via `String.fromCharCode()`. To this, we pass the desired UTF 16 hexadecimal codes as strings, separated by commas. Incidentally, the label text on the Pause button is made up of two *BLACK VERTICAL RECTANGLE* symbols (▮).

We will need the `playButton` ID again later on.

4.7.3 Displaying and Setting the Playback Position

To display the current playback position, we use the new input type `range`, previously mentioned in Chapter 3, Intelligent Forms:

```
<input type="range"
       min=0 max=1 step=1 value=0
       onchange="updateProgress(this)"
       id="currentPosition">
```

The attributes `min` and `max` set the permitted value range, and `step` determines the interval by which the `value` will be changed when the user drags the slider. Applied to our video, `min` specifies the start and `max` the end of our film, which means that we have to set the value `max` to the total length of the video in seconds. The right place to do this is `initControls()`, the right attribute to do it with is `video.duration`. So we add the following lines to our `initControls()` function:

```
curPos = document.getElementById("currentPosition");
curPos.max = video.duration;
```

This now gives max the value 596.468017578125, which means the video is about ten-minutes long. Setting the playback position directly is done in the onchange event handler callback updateProgress()when the slider is dragged or clicked:

```
var updateProgress = function(ctrl) {
  video.currentTime = ctrl.value;
};
```

A single instruction is sufficient here; the attribute video.currentTime not only reflects the current playback position, but can also be set directly. We get the suitable value from the slider's value attribute. To implement the display of the current playback position in the format MM:SS, we still need the following steps:

1. Add a span element in connection with the slider:
    ```
    <span id="timePlayed"> </span>
    ```

2. Save a reference to the span in the initControls() function and initialize this variable curTime with the value 0:00:
    ```
    curTime = document.getElementById("timePlayed");
    curTime.innerHTML = '0:00';
    ```

3. Update the timestamp curTime at each call of updateProgress():
    ```
    mm = Math.floor(video.currentTime / 60.0);
    ss = parseInt(video.currentTime) % 60;
    ss = (ss < 10) ? '0'+ss : ss;
    curTime.innerHTML = mm+':'+ss;
    ```

We are nearly finished. Only one essential slider feature is still missing: While the video is playing, it has to stay synchronized with the running time. The solution lies in the HTML code for integrating the video: ontimeupdate. The specification states that a timeupdate event should be triggered at intervals of at least 15 and up to 250 milliseconds during media stream playback. The event handler attribute ontimeupdate determines which callback function is called. If we set it to updateProgress(), we have found the perfect timer for synchronizing our slider.

Compared to setting the position manually by clicking or dragging the slider, we now must not change the playback position but instead set the slider and the time display to the value of video.currentTime. The slightly adapted and thus final version of our updateProgress() function is shown in Listing 4.1:

Listing 4.1   Change and update playback position

```
var updateProgress = function(ctrl) {
  if (ctrl) {
    video.currentTime = ctrl.value;
  }
  else {
    curPos.value = video.currentTime;
  }
  // Setting the time in format MM:SS
  mm = Math.floor(video.currentTime / 60.0);
  ss = parseInt(video.currentTime) % 60;
  ss = (ss < 10) ? '0'+ss : ss;
  curTime.innerHTML = mm+':'+ss;
};
```

The purpose of the if/else block is to find out if updateProgress() was called with the slider or with ontimeupdate. In the former case, the passed slider object is assigned to ctrl, and we need to set the playback position to the slider value. In the latter case, a timeupdate event is present, and we need to set the slider to the current playback time in the variable curPos.

Now that the playback and controlling the playback position are sorted out, you have some time to sit back and relax. Take ten minutes off and go explore Big Buck Bunny with your very own, homemade, and almost finished video player!

4.7.4   Fast Forward and Backward

For these two features, we first need buttons in the HTML document. Their labels will again be Unicode symbols, this time *guillemets*—angle quotation marks. The Unicode name describes what they look like: *LEFT-POINTING DOUBLE ANGLE QUOTATION MARK* («) and *RIGHT-POINTING DOUBLE ANGLE QUOTATION MARK* (»). Two event listener attributes start and stop the quick search, which starts onmousedown and ends onmouseup:

```
<input type="button"
       value="&#x00AB;"
       onmousedown="fastFwdBwd(-1)"
       onmouseup="fastFwdBwd()">
 <input type="button"
        value="&#x00BB;"
        onmousedown="fastFwdBwd(1)"
        onmouseup="fastFwdBwd()">
```

The JavaScript callback fastFwdBwb() is rather short and looks like this:

```
var fastFwdBwd = function(direct) {
  _pause();
  _play();
  if (direct) {
    video.playbackRate = 5.0 * direct;
  }
};
```

Two attributes play an important role in speeding up a video. One of them we can see in our callback function with video.playbackRate. It represents the current playback rate. The second one is video.defaultPlaybackRate, a default value that determines the film's normal speed as 1.0. For faster playback, we need to change the playback rate; for example, 2.0 would mean *twice as fast*, 4.0 would be *four times as fast*, and so on. The number and where applicable the minus sign determines the direction of playback—positive values fast forward, negative ones rewind.

According to the definition in the specification, the attribute video.playbackRate must be set to the value of video.defaultPlaybackRate each time video.play() is called. So as long as we do not crank up the defaultPlaybackRate, we can be sure that the original speed applies at each restart. To increase the speed, we therefore only need to change the video.playbackRate.

This makes the implementation of fastFwdBwd() very easy: The video is first stopped briefly. Then it is played again, and if 1 or -1 is assigned to the variable direct, the video.playbackRate is set accordingly and the speed is increased.

The functions _pause() and _play() contain code blocks for starting and stopping the video, previously found in the callback playPause(). With these functions, we can now not only control playback and pausing by clicking the Play button, but also directly via the script. To detach the functionality from the Play button, we need to define a reference to the button in initControl() via getElementById() and make it available as variable pButton. The split version of playPause() is shown in Listing 4.2:

Listing 4.2   Starting and stopping the video

```
var _play = function() {
  video.play();
  pButton.value = String.fromCharCode('0x25AE','0x25AE');
};
var _pause = function() {
  video.pause();
  pButton.value = String.fromCharCode('0x25B6');
};
```

```
var playPause = function() {
  if (video.paused) {
    _play();
  }
  else {
    _pause();
  }
};
```

4.7.5   Selecting Specific Scenes in the Film

To select individual scenes, we first need a list with timestamps and titles. A pull-down menu provides the basis:

```
<select name="scenes" onchange="selectScene(this)" size=19>
  <option value="0:00" selected>0:00 Opening scene</option>
  <option value="0:23">0:23 Title sequence</option>
  <!-- 17 other entries -->
</select>
```

The rest is simple and taken care of by the callback selectScene(). We pass it the selected entry as the argument. Then we convert its timestamp to seconds and set video.currentTime to the resulting value. The method _play() serves us well once again and starts playing the video at the desired point:

```
var selectScene = function(ctrl) {
  arr = ctrl.value.split(":");
  video.currentTime = parseFloat((arr[0]*60)+(arr[1]*1));
  updateProgress();
  _play();
};
```

4.7.6   Set Volume to High, Low, or Mute

All that's left is the volume control. Let's start with a simple exercise—*on/off*. Once more, we need a button in the HTML code with a label formed from a Unicode symbol, this time *BEAMED EIGHTH NOTES* (♫):

```
<input type="button"
       value="&#x266B;"
       onclick="mute(this)">
```

The mute() function uses the *read/write* attribute video.muted to switch to mute or loud, depending on the initial setting. To give the user optical feedback, the button label is displayed in the CSS color silver when the tone is muted and in black when the volume is switched on:

```
var mute = function(ctrl) {
  if (video.muted) {
    video.muted = false;
    ctrl.style.color = 'black';
  }
  else {
    video.muted = true;
    ctrl.style.color = 'silver';
  }
};
```

Setting the volume is not complicated, either. In addition to the slider as input type range, we also need to control the label in a span. The basic HTML structure then looks like this:

```
<input type="range"
       min=0.0 max=1.0 step=0.1 value=1.0
       onchange="adjustVolume(this)"/>
<span id="currentVolume"> </span>
```

We define a reference to the span element in initControls(), as before, and use video.volume to initialize the volume with 100 %:

```
curVol = document.getElementById("currentVolume");
curVol.innerHTML = "100 %";
video.volume = 1;
```

The callback function adjustVolume() reacts if the slider is changed. The slider reflects with min=0 and max=1 the exact value range of video.volume and changes the volume via step=0.1 in 10% steps if the slider is dragged:

```
var adjustVolume = function(ctrl) {
  video.volume = ctrl.value;
  curVol.innerHTML = (Math.round(ctrl.value*100))+'%';
};
```

Our video player is now complete. This practical example has given you the chance to explore about half of the attributes and methods of the HTMLMediaElement interface. A few interesting attributes and methods are still missing; we will look at those next.

4.7.8 Other Attributes and Methods of the "HTMLMediaElement" Interface

All media elements (including not only video, but also audio) have five attributes in common, which are shown in the HTMLMediaElement interface. Apart from src as source of the *media stream*, there are the *boolean* attributes autoplay, loop, and controls, plus preload with its three values none, metadata, and auto. The code for dynamically creating a video could then look like this:

```
var video = document.createElement("VIDEO");
video.src = 'videos/bbb_240p_stereo.ogv';
video.autoplay = false;
video.loop = true;
video.controls = true;
video.preload = 'metadata';
```

But this video is not loaded yet. The loading process only starts with the next method of the HTMLMediaElement interface, video.load(). To be able to see the video in the browser, we need to append it to the DOM tree. So we add two lines to our listing:

```
video.load();
document.documentElement.appendChild(video);
```

The dynamic counterpart of the oncanplay attribute of our video player's video element is an event listener with event type, callback function, and a flag that determines if the event should become active in the *capture* phase or not. Confused? Just use false for the third argument, which activates the event listener in the *bubbling* phase instead. If you want to know the details of how the event order works, look online at http://www.quirksmode.org/js/events_order.html. Our event listener listens for the event canplay and then immediately starts playing the film:

```
video.addEventListener("canplay", function() {
  video.play();
}, false);
```

NOTE

The HTML version of our brief code example can of course be found online at http://html5.komplett.cc/code/chap_video/js_dynamicVideo_en.html.

As simple as this example may seem, the processes during loading a media stream are actually rather complicated. The specification distinguishes between *network state* and *ready state*, devoting two `readonly` attributes to these two states in the `HTMLMediaElement` interface, with several constants for describing the relevant state.

The attribute `networkState` is for monitoring the network state. It can be queried at any time and returns the possible values listed in Table 4.5.

Table 4.5   Constants of the "networkState" attribute

Value	Constant	Description
0	NETWORK_EMPTY	The video/audio has not yet been initialized.
1	NETWORK_IDLE	The video/audio source is selected but is not currently being loaded.
2	NETWORK_LOADING	The browser is actively loading the video/audio.
3	NETWORK_NO_SOURCE	No suitable source for the video/audio can be found.

When selecting a suitable source, you need to remember that there are two options for doing this: either via the `src` attribute of the relevant element or via several `source` elements from which the browser can choose the most suitable one. If we are working with several `source` elements for a video, the question arises as to how we know which of the offered elements was in fact chosen by the browser. The answer is in the *readonly* attribute `video.currentSrc`. In the screen shot of the video player, you can see it at the bottom left before the copyright.

Actively asking if media types are supported by the relevant browser or not can be done not only by the browser when selecting the suitable `source` element, but also by the programmer with a script. The method we use for this is `canPlayType(type)` and requires a corresponding media type as an argument. The answer is `probably` if the browser is fairly sure that it can play the format, `maybe` if the browser is rather skeptical, or `' '` as an empty character chain if it can definitely not deal with it.

NOTE

See for yourself what selection of common types `canPlayType(type)` returns for your browser at http://html5.komplett.cc/code/chap_video/js_canPlayType.html.

The attribute readyState describes which state a media element is currently in. It has the possible values listed in Table 4.6.

Table 4.6   Constants of the "readyState" attribute

Value	Constant	Description
0	HAVE_NOTHING	No data is available on the current playback position.
1	HAVE_METADATA	Metadata, such as length and dimension, are present, but no data can be played yet.
2	HAVE_CURRENT_DATA	Data for the current position is available but is not really enough to begin playback.
3	HAVE_FUTURE_DATA	Sufficient data for current and future playback positions is available to start playback.
4	HAVE_ENOUGH_DATA	The browser is sure that it can keep playing the media stream without interruption if the network state remains the same.

If anything should really go wrong during loading or playback, an error event is fired, narrowing down the relevant error in its code attribute:

```
video.addEventListener("error", function(e) {
  alert(e.code);
}, false);
```

This callback function therefore returns one of the possible values shown in Table 4.7 in e.code.

Table 4.7   Constants in the "code" attribute of the "MediaError" interface

Value	Constant	Description
1	MEDIA_ERR_ABORTED	Loading was aborted by the user.
2	MEDIA_ERR_NETWORK	A network error has occurred.
3	MEDIA_ERR_DECODE	An error occurred while decoding the media stream.
4	MEDIA_ERR_SRC_NOT_SUPPORTED	The media format is not supported.

We have nearly reached the end of our journey through the HTMLMediaElement interface. The remaining attributes are:

- Two *boolean* attributes for displaying if the browser is currently searching for other data (seeking) or if the end of the stream has been reached (ended)

- An attribute for giving information on the start time of the stream (initialTime)

- An attribute that represents the current timeline offset as a Date object (startOffsetTime)

- Three attributes for implementing the TimeRanges interface—buffered, played, and seekable.

The basic idea of TimeRanges is, as its name indicates, recording periods of time:

```
interface TimeRanges {
  readonly attribute unsigned long length;
  float start(in unsigned long index);
  float end(in unsigned long index);
};
```

Using the example of played helps you understand how this works: If we are playing the intro of the *Big Buck Bunny* video and then click Pause, we get a first time range consisting of a start and an end time. The corresponding attributes are played.start(0) and played.end(0), and the number of existing time ranges in played.length is 1. If we then switch to the eighth chapter and continue playback there for a bit, we create the next time range with played.start(1) and played. end(1), and the played.length becomes 2. If two time ranges should overlap, they are combined into one. All ranges are sorted in the TimeRanges object.

This way we can track which areas of a media stream are buffered, played, or marked as seekable. A little online example helps visualize the individual TimeRanges while playing the *Big Buck Bunny* video—take a look at http://html5.komplett.cc/code/chap_video/js_timeRanges.html.

4.7.9 The Long List of Media Events

The list of events fired on loading or playing of a media stream at certain times is long and basically reflects the three main status conditions of the HTMLMediaElement interface.

In the *network state*, we encounter loadstart, progress, suspend, abort, error, emptied, and stalled, and their names indicate in which network scenarios they appear. In the *ready state* are loadedmetadata, loadeddata, waiting, playing, canplay, or canplaythrough, all relating directly to the availability of data for the current or future playback position. In the *playback state* are play, pause, timeupdate, ended, ratechange, and durationchange, and again their names are as self-explanatory as is the last element we need to mention, volumechange.

When and how each event is used depends entirely on the purpose of your script. For our video player, we needed only two, oncanplay and ontimeupdate. But if we wanted to refine the details, we would almost certainly need many others as well.

If you want to read details on the various events, you should refer to the very helpful *Event summary* in the specification. There you will find not only a description of each event, but also indications as to when it is actually fired. Browse to http://www.w3.org/TR/html5/video.html#mediaevents.

If you want to see media events *live in action*, go to Philippe Le Hégaret's *HTML5 Video, Media Events, and Media Properties* test page at W3C: http://www.w3.org/2010/05/video/mediaevents.html.

4.8   And What About Audio?

There is not much new to announce about audio in HTML5. Conveniently, video and audio share the HTMLMediaElement interface, which means that everything we have told you about scripting and video is also applicable to audio elements. Understandably, the additional video attributes for width, height, audio, and poster frame of the HTMLVideoElement interface are omitted. audio elements can be easily created via a constructor and have a src attribute assigned to them at the same time:

```
var audio = new Audio(src);
```

Following the pattern of our video player, let's program an audio player for the Big Buck Bunny soundtrack. Slider, time display, and starting or stopping work in the same way as in the video example. A new feature is the menu for selecting the track: Different audio files are involved plus two buttons for jumping ahead or backward on the track list. Additionally, we implement *looping* at the end of all tracks plus random selection of the next track. You can see the result in Figure 4.10.

Figure 4.10 Screen shot of the JavaScript HTML5 audio player

NOTE
The individual tracks were extracted from the video's soundtrack using the free, cross-platform, sound editor Audacity (http://audacity.sourceforge.net). For private use, you can also download the soundtrack without background noises for free from the homepage of the score's composer, Jan Morgenstern, at http://www.wavemage.com/category/music.

The screen shot of the audio player will look familiar, because the new buttons once more use certain Unicode symbols for their labels. To be specific, you can see the symbols listed in Table 4.8.

Table 4.8 Unicode symbols for audio player buttons

Button	Entity	Unicode Name
Skip back	&#x25C3;	*WHITE LEFT-POINTING SMALL TRIANGLE*
Skip forward	&#x25B9;	*WHITE RIGHT-POINTING SMALL TRIANGLE*
Loop	&#x21BA;	*ANTICLOCKWISE OPEN CIRCLE ARROW*
Shuffle	&#x219D;	*RIGHTWARDS WAVE ARROW*

The pull-down menu also looks familiar, but this time we do not jump to certain points in the playback time as in the video player; instead, we switch between whole tracks. The menu and the Skip backward, forward, Loop, and Shuffle buttons have this effect of changing from one track to the next, so the script logic becomes a bit more complicated.

Let's start with the audio element:

```
<audio src="music/bbb_01_intro.ogg"
       oncanplay="canPlay()"
       ontimeupdate="updateProgress()"
       onended="continueOrStop()">
</audio>
```

On loading the page, we set the src attribute to the first track and define three callbacks. You have already encountered the updateProgress()function, which moves the slider along and updates the time display (see Listing 4.1). The two new callbacks are canPlay(), which is called when a track is ready to play, and continueOrStop(), which decides what to do next at the end of a track. The on-canplay callback canPlay() is rather short and looks like this:

```
canPlay = function() {
  curPos.max = audio.duration;
  if (pbStatus.keepPlaying == true) {
    _play();
  }
};
```

Obviously, curPos.max adapts the slider's max attribute, just as in the video player, but what is the subsequent if block all about? The answer is simple: We try to take the current playback status into account and only keep playing if the player was already in play mode.

So the status of the Play button determines if the audio player starts playing after switching to another track. If it is playing, it should keep playing after every track change, but if it is paused, it should only switch tracks and stay paused. This may sound complicated, but the implementation in the play button's callback is easy; we just add the following code:

```
pbStatus.keepPlaying =
  (pbStatus.keepPlaying == true) ? false : true;
```

This alternates the status variable pbStatus.keepPlaying between true and false with every click, and the correct decision is reached in canPlay().

Back to our example. With canPlay()and pbStatus.keepPlaying, we now have control of the situation if the track is ready to play. But how do we manage switching from one track to the next? As mentioned earlier, there are several options for this: We can choose via the menu, click the Skip back and Skip forward buttons, or let the audio player do it automatically at the end of a track as a result of the settings for the Loop and Shuffle buttons. All of these options have one thing in common: They need to load a new track, and that is done via the method loadTrack():

```
var loadTrack = function(idx) {
  audio.src = 'music/'+tracks.options[idx].value;
  audio.load();
};
```

Two details need explaining:

1. What is hiding behind the argument idx? Hiding behind idx is the index of the track to be loaded from the pull-down menu in the variable tracks, from which we can extract file names.
2. What does the call audio.load() do? As you may have guessed, it starts loading the new track, which can be played as soon as it has reached the status canplay.

loadTrack() is called in various ways. First, when changing tracks directly in the menu via the onchange event handler changeTrack(this):

```
changeTrack = function(ctrl) {
  loadTrack(ctrl.options.selectedIndex);
};
```

Of course it is also called by the Skip forward and Skip backward buttons; their respective onclick event handler calls the callback function advanceTrack(n) and passes it the step value in the argument n as well as the desired direction via the positive or negative sign. The step value is the same in both cases, which means -1 is *skip backward* and 1 is *skip forward*:

```
advanceTrack = function(n) {
  var idx = tracks.options.selectedIndex + n;
  if (idx < 0) {
    idx = idx + tracks.options.length;
  }
  if (idx > tracks.options.length-1) {
    idx = idx - tracks.options.length;
  }
  tracks.options.selectedIndex = idx;
  loadTrack(idx);
};
```

The algorithm for determining the new track is simple and consists of two phases. We first add n to the index of the selected track, and then we deal with two special cases that may arise from this: If we are currently in the first track and click Skip backward, the index becomes negative and we therefore have to keep playing the last track. If we are in the last track and click Skip forward, this also does not work, so we have to make sure the player selects the first track as next track.

The advantage of the method advanceTrack() is that we can use it even for the last two features—looping at the end of the track and random track selection. First, we quickly need to discuss exactly how the two buttons signal *inactive* and *active*. Switching between the two modes is done via onclick event handlers, which trigger the callback toggleOnOff(node) and assign the appropriate button in the argument node:

```
toggleOnOff = function(node) {
  var cls = node.getAttribute("class");
  node.setAttribute("class",
    (cls == 'off') ? 'on' : 'off'
  );
  pbStatus[node.id] = node.getAttribute("class");
};
```

As the first line of the function indicates, the status is determined by the button element's class attribute, defining the appearance via CSS. The formats for *on* and *off* can be found in the stylesheet js_audioPlayer.css:

```
.off {
  opacity: 0.2;
}
.on {
  opacity: 1.0;
}
```

Additionally, the current status of the relevant button is specified in the status variable pbStatus[node.id] where the node.id indicates *loop* or *shuffle* and therefore pbStatus.loop or pbStatus.shuffle is assigned *on* or *off*. The correct moment for reacting to this status is always at the end of a track. Now the callback function continueOrStop() takes effect:

```
continueOrStop = function() {
  if (pbStatus.shuffle == 'on') {
    advanceTrack(
      Math.round(Math.random()*tracks.options.length)
    );
  }
  else if (tracks.options.selectedIndex ==
          tracks.options.length-1) {
    if (pbStatus.loop == 'on') {
      advanceTrack(1);
    }
    else {
      pbStatus.keepPlaying = false;
    }
  }
  else {
    advanceTrack(1);
  }
};
```

If we are in shuffle mode, rounding the result of Math.random(), multiplied by the number of all tracks, generates a random number between 0 and the total number of tracks. We then advance by this value in advanceTrack(), and it does not matter by how much we overshoot the target: If we are, for example, in the second-last track and want to skip forward five positions, the algorithm in advanceTrack() ensures that the fourth item on the menu is played.

The question *"To loop or not to loop?"* only ever arises in the last track. If the corresponding button is set to *on* mode, we start again from the beginning with advanceTrack(1); if it is in *off* mode, we stop here and set pbStatus.keepPlaying to false. In all other cases we simply go to the next track and start playing it.

At this point we have not only completed our audio player, but also reached the end of the chapter on video and audio. Many of the features we programmed manually in the video and audio player are of course also implemented by the browser and can be activated more easily via the `controls` attribute. But it still makes sense to look behind the scenes to discover the options available when scripting video and audio.

Summary

With video and audio, two important functions that previously required plug-ins become part of the HTML specification. It is difficult to predict which video co-dec will eventually prevail, although in light of Google's commitment in favor of WebM, we can hope for a patent-free open format.

As the second part of the chapter shows, the HTMLMediaElement Interface makes video and audio accessible for scripting. Using JavaScript allows for an interaction that was not possible previously with the available plug-in solutions.

As for every HTML5 topic, there are many more impressive examples to be found online. Take some time to search and discover them for yourself! By reading this chapter you have laid the foundation for understanding these new and fascinating HTML5 features.

5
Canvas

One of the most interesting and at the same time one of the oldest new HTML5 elements is *Canvas*. In July 2004, just one month after the WHATWG was formed, Apple's David Hyatt presented a proprietary HTML extension named Canvas, an announcement that caused an uproar among the still young HTML5 movement. *"The real solution is to bring these proposals to the table,"* was Ian Hickson's first reaction, and after a brief debate, Apple submitted its idea to the WHATWG. This paved the way for including Canvas in the HTML5 specification, and a first draft was published in August 2004.

NOTE

You can find Apple's Canvas announcement and Ian Hickson's reaction at:

● http://weblogs.mozillazine.org/hyatt/archives/2004_07.html#005913

● http://ln.hixie.ch/?start=1089635050&count=1

5.1   A First Example

Canvas is, simply put, a programmable picture on which you can draw via a JavaScript API. In addition to the canvas via the canvas element, we also need a script element for the drawing commands. Let's start with the canvas element:

```
<canvas width="1200" height="800">
  alternative content for browsers without canvas support
</canvas>
```

The attributes width and height determine the dimension of the canvas element in pixels and reserve the corresponding amount of space on the HTML page. If one or both attributes are missing, default values come into effect: 300 pixels for width and 150 pixels for height. The area between the start and end tag is reserved for alternative content, which will be displayed if a browser does not support Canvas. Similar to the alt tag for pictures, this alternative content should describe the content of the Canvas application or show a suitable screen shot. Phrases like *Your browser does not support Canvas* without any further information are not very helpful and should be avoided.

Our canvas is now finished. In the next step, we can add the drawing commands in a script element. A few lines of code are enough to turn our first, and admittedly quite trivial, Canvas example into reality:

```
<script>
  var canvas = document.querySelector("canvas");
  var context = canvas.getContext('2d');
  context.fillStyle = 'red';
  context.fillRect(0,0,800,600);
  context.fillStyle = 'rgba(255,255,0,0.5)';
  context.fillRect(400,200,800,600);
</script>
```

Even if we do not yet know anything about the syntax of the Canvas drawing commands, the result in Figure 5.1 will not come as a surprise if you look closely at the code. We now have a red and a light yellow rectangle with 50% opacity, resulting in an orange tone where the two rectangles overlap.

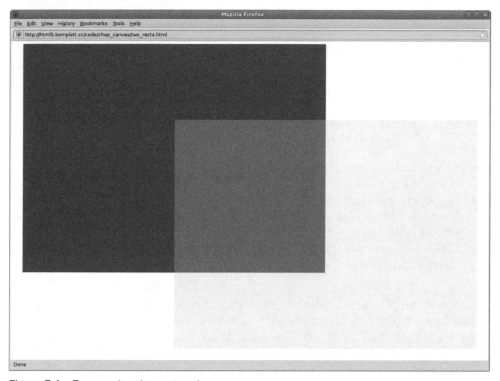

Figure 5.1   Two overlapping rectangles

> All figures in this chapter were created as HTML pages using Canvas and can be found online either at the URL visible in the screen shot or via the Index page of the companion website at http://html5.komplett.cc/code/chap_canvas/index_en.html. Take a look at the source code!

Before we can draw on the canvas, we need to create a reference to it. The first line in the script does exactly that. In the variable canvas and using the *W3C CSS Selectors API* method document.querySelector(), it saves a reference to the first canvas element found in the document:

```
var canvas = document.querySelector("canvas");
```

Apart from the attributes canvas.width and canvas.height, this object, also called HTMLCanvasElement, has the method getContext(). It allows us to get to the heart of Canvas, the CanvasRenderingContext2D, by passing *2d* as context parameter:

```
var context = canvas.getContext('2d');
```

Now we have defined the *drawing context* and can start drawing the two rectangles. Without going into details of the attribute fillStyle or the method fill-Rect(), the basic procedure for both is the same: Define the fill color and then add the rectangle:

```
context.fillStyle = 'red';
context.fillRect(0,0,800,600);
context.fillStyle = 'rgba(255,255,0,0.5)';
context.fillRect(400,200,800,600);
```

The current Canvas specification only defines a 2D context (see *HTML Canvas 2D Context* specification at http://www.w3.org/TR/2dcontext) but does not rule out that others, for example *3D*, could follow at a later stage. First initiatives in this direction have already been launched by the Khronos group: In cooperation with Mozilla, Google, and Opera, they are working on a JavaScript interface called WebGL based on OpenGL ES 2.0 (http://www.khronos.org/webgl). First implementations of this emerging standard are present in Firefox, WebKit, and Chrome.

But back to the 2D context: The possibilities of the CanvasRenderingContext2D interface are manifold and certainly well-suited for creating sophisticated applications. Figure 5.2 shows a simple bar chart, which will accompany us through an explanation of the first three features of the drawing context: rectangles, colors, and shadows.

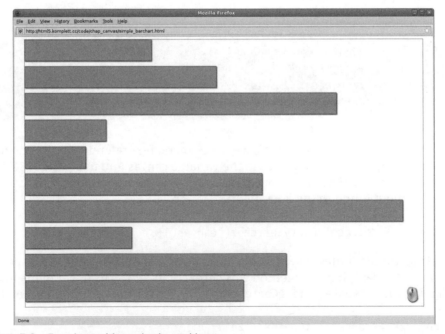

Figure 5.2   Bar chart with ten horizontal bars

5.2 Rectangles

Canvas has four methods for creating rectangles. Three of these we will discuss now, the fourth we will encounter later in connection to paths:

```
context.fillRect(x, y, w, h)
context.strokeRect(x, y, w, h)
context.clearRect(x, y, w, h)
```

The names of these methods are self-explanatory: `fillRect()`creates a filled rectangle, `strokeRect()` a rectangle with border and no filling, and `clearRect()` a rectangle that clears existing content like an eraser. The rectangle's dimensions are determined by four numerical parameters: origin x/y, width w, and height h.

In Canvas, the coordinate origin is at the top left, which means the x coordinates increase toward the right and the y coordinates toward the bottom (see Figure 5.3).

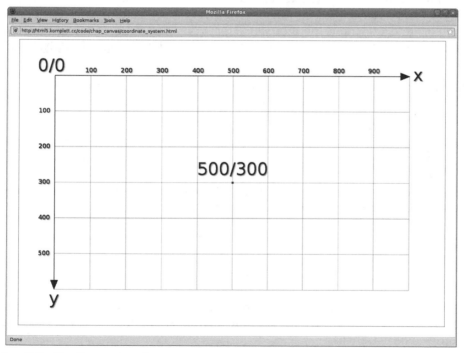

Figure 5.3   The Canvas coordinate system

In parallel to the first example, we first define a reference to the `canvas` element in our bar chart and then the drawing context. The function `drawBars()`is responsible for doing the main job, drawing the horizontal bars. We pass the desired number of bars we want to draw to this function:

```
<script>
var canvas = document.querySelector("canvas");
var context = canvas.getContext('2d');
var drawBars = function(bars) {
  context.clearRect(0,0,canvas.width,canvas.height);
  for (var i=0; i<bars; i++) {
    var yOff = i*(canvas.height/bars);
    var w = Math.random()*canvas.width;
    var h = canvas.height/bars*0.8;
    context.fillRect(0,yOff,w,h);
    context.strokeRect(0,yOff,w,h);
  }
};
drawBars(10);
</script>
```

Calling this function with drawBars(10) deletes any existing content with clear-Rect() and then draws the ten filled rectangle outlines in the for loop with fill-Rect() and strokeRect(). The width w of the bars varies between 0 pixels and the full width of the canvas element, and is determined randomly via the JavaScript function Math.random(). The function Math.random() generates a number between 0.0 and 1.0, and is therefore ideal for producing random values for width, height, and the position, depending on the canvas dimension. Multiplying with the corresponding attribute value does the job.

The equally spaced, horizontal arrangement of the bars follows the canvas height. The spaces between the bars result from multiplying the calculated maximal bar height h by the factor 0.8.

The canvas width and height can be easily seen in the attributes canvas.width and canvas.height as mentioned in the first example. Just as easily, we can access the HTMLCanvasElement from the drawing context via its attribute context. canvas and use it to generate new bars with each click on the canvas. Three lines of code added after the drawBars(10) call are enough:

```
context.canvas.onclick = function() {
  drawBars(10);
};
```

We have clarified how the ten bars are drawn, but how do we make them light gray with black outlines? We will find the answer by looking at the options of assigning color in Canvas.

5.3 Colors and Shadows

The attributes fillStyle and strokeStyle serve to specify colors for fills and lines. The color specification follows the rules for CSS color values and can have a number of different formats. Table 5.1 shows the available options, using the color red as an example.

Table 5.1 Valid CSS color values for the color red

Method	Color Value
Hexadecimal	#FF0000
Hexadecimal (short)	#F00
RGB	rgb(255,0,0)
RGB (percent)	rgb(100%,0%,0%)
RGBA	rgba(255,0,0,1.0)
RGBA (percent)	rgba(100%,0%,0%,1.0)
HSL	hsl(0,100%,50%)
HSLA	hsla(0,100%,50%,1.0)
SVG (named color)	red

To specify the current fill and stroke color in Canvas, you just need to enter the appropriate color values as a character string for fillStyle and strokeStyle. In the bar chart example, we will choose the SVG named color silver as fill and a semitransparent black outline in RGBA notation. We want all bars to look the same, so we define the styles before the drawBars() function:

```
context.fillStyle = 'silver';
context.strokeStyle = 'rgba(0,0,0,0.5)';
var drawBars = function(bars) {
  // code for drawing bars
};
```

Valid opacity values range from 0.0 (transparent) to 1.0 (opaque) and can be used as a fourth component in RGB and HSL color space. The latter defines colors not via their red, green, and blue components, but via a combination of hue, saturation, and lightness.

NOTE

You can find more information on the topic CSS colors with HSL color palettes and a list of all valid SVG color names in the *CSS Color Module Level 3* specification at http://www.w3.org/TR/css3-color.

If you look closely, you can see shadows behind the bars. These are created by four additional drawing context attributes:

```
context.shadowOffsetX = 2.0;
context.shadowOffsetY = 2.0;
context.shadowColor = "rgba(50%,50%,50%,0.75)";
context.shadowBlur = 2.0;
```

The first two lines determine the shadow offset with shadowOffsetX and shadowOffsetY, shadowColor assigns its color and opacity, and shadowBlur causes the shadow to be blurred. As a general rule, the higher the value of shadowBlur, the stronger the blur effect.

Before moving on to color gradients in the next section, we need to clarify how the dotted border in the bar chart and the subsequent graphics is achieved. The answer is very simple: with CSS. Every canvas element can of course also be formatted with CSS. You can specify spacing, position, and z-index just as easily as background color and border. In our example, the following style attribute creates the dotted border:

```
<canvas style="border: 1px dotted black;">
```

5.4 Gradients

In addition to solid colors for fills and lines, Canvas offers two kinds of gradients: linear and radial gradients. The basic principle of creating gradients in Canvas is easily demonstrated using the example of a simple gradient from red to yellow and orange and then to purple (see Figure 5.4).

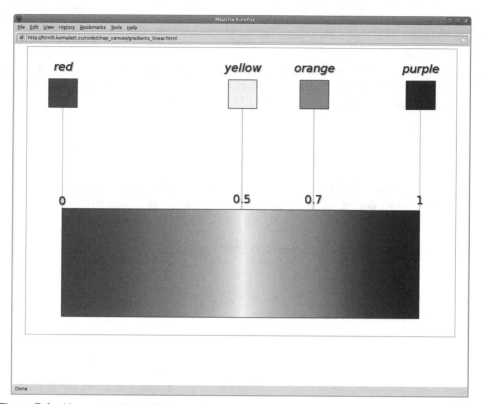

Figure 5.4 Linear gradient with four colors

First, context.createLinearGradient(x0, y0, x1, y1) creates a CanvasGradient object and determines the direction of the gradient via the parameters x0, y0, x1, y1. We still need to specify the color offsets in another step, so we save this object in the variable linGrad:

```
var linGrad = context.createLinearGradient(
  0,450,1000,450
);
```

The method addColorStop(offset, color)of the CanvasGradient object is the next step and selects the desired colors and offsets on our imaginary gradient line. Offset 0.0 represents the color at the point x0/y0 and offset 1.0 the color at the end point x1/y1. All colors in between are divided up according to their offset, and transitions between the individual stops are interpolated by the browser in RGBA color space:

```
linGrad.addColorStop(0.0, 'red');
linGrad.addColorStop(0.5, 'yellow');
```

```
linGrad.addColorStop(0.7, 'orange');
linGrad.addColorStop(1.0, 'purple');
```

Colors are specified following the rules for CSS color values and are identified as SVG named colors in our examples to make it more readable. Our linear gradient is now finished and can be assigned via fillStyle or strokeStyle:

```
context.fillStyle = linGrad;
context.fillRect(0,450,1000,450);
```

Unlike linear gradients, the start and end points of radial gradients are not points, but circles. So to define a radial gradient, we now need to use the method context.createRadialGradient(x0, y0, r0, x1, y1, r1) (see Figure 5.5).

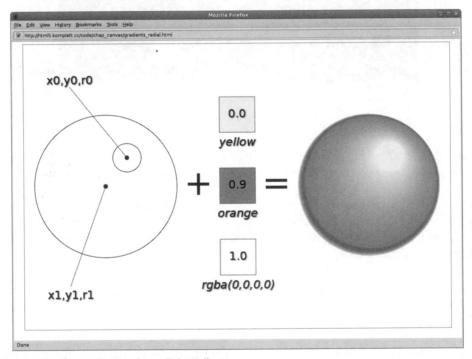

Figure 5.5   Components of a radial gradient

On the left side of the graphic, you can see the start and end circle, in the middle the three color stops with offset values, and on the right the final result: a sphere that appears to glow. A very appealing result is generated by a bit of clear and simple source code:

```
var radGrad = context.createRadialGradient(
  260,320,40,200,400,200
);
radGrad.addColorStop(0.0,'yellow');
radGrad.addColorStop(0.9,'orange');
radGrad.addColorStop(1.0,'rgba(0,0,0,0)');
context.fillStyle = radGrad;
context.fillRect(0,200,400,400);
```

The shadow effect around the sphere is incidentally created by the last two color stops, interpolating from orange to transparent black, which means the visible part of the gradient ends directly at the outer circle.

After this quick trip through the world of colors and gradients, we now move on to other geometric forms: paths.

5.5 Paths

The process of creating paths in Canvas is comparable to drawing on a piece of paper: You put the pencil on the paper at one point, draw, lift the pencil off again, and continue drawing at another point on the paper. The content you draw can range from simple lines to complex curves or even polygons formed from these. An initial example illustrates the concept, translating each step of writing the letter A into Canvas path commands:

```
context.beginPath();
context.moveTo(300,700);
context.lineTo(600,100);
context.lineTo(900,700);
context.moveTo(350,400);
context.lineTo(850,400);
context.stroke();
```

The results are shown in Figure 5.6.

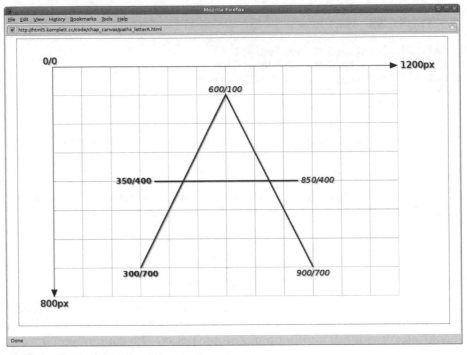

Figure 5.6   The letter A as a path

Let's look closer at the source code for this example. We can see the three phases of creating the path:

1. Initialize a new path with beginPath()
2. Define the path geometry with moveTo() and lineTo() calls
3. Draw the lines with stroke()

Each path must be initialized with beginPath() and can then contain any number of segments. In our example, we have two segments that reproduce the hand movements when writing through combinations of moveTo() and line-To(). This creates first the roof shape and then the horizontal line of the letter A. With stroke(), we then draw the defined path onto the canvas.

The decision whether and when segments of a path will be separated into several individual paths is entirely dependent on the layout. Each path can only be formatted in its entirety. So, if we wanted the horizontal line of the letter A to have a different color, we would need to define two separate paths.

Let's look at the main path drawing methods in more detail.

5.5.1 Lines

To create lines as in our example of the letter A, Canvas offers the method lineTo():

```
context.lineTo(x, y)
```

The effect of the method is shown in Figure 5.7.

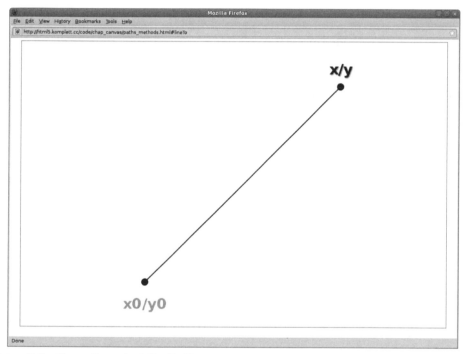

Figure 5.7   The path method "lineTo()"

Expressed in words, this means *line to point x/y*, which means we have to already have defined a starting point with moveTo() or still have an end point from the previous drawing step. After drawing the line, the coordinate x/y becomes the new current point.

In all graphics used to demonstrate the path drawing methods, we have marked the starting point x0/y0 in light gray and the new current point in bold type.

5.5.2 Bézier Curves

Canvas knows two kinds of Bézier curves: quadratic and cubic, the latter incorrectly referred to only as bezierCurveTo(). Figure 5.8 illustrates the former, and Figure 5.9 illustrates the latter.

```
context.quadraticCurveTo(cpx, cpy, x, y)
context.bezierCurveTo(cp1x, cp1y, cp2x, cp2y, x, y)
```

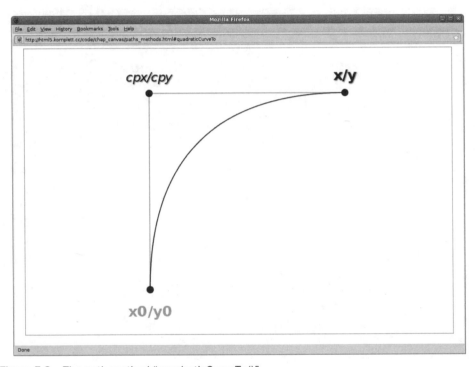

Figure 5.8   The path method "quadraticCurveTo()"

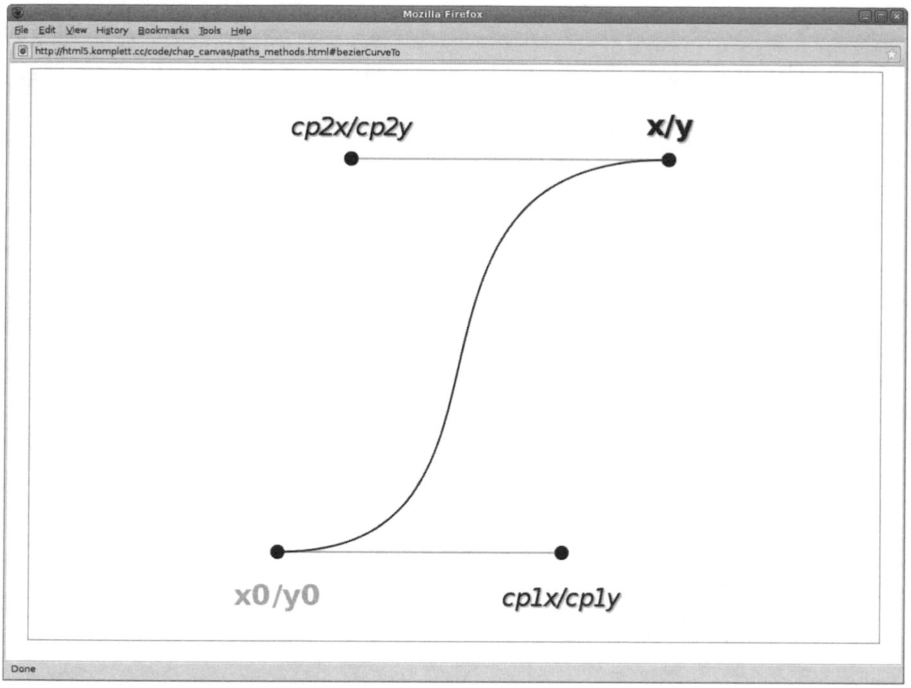

Figure 5.9   The path method "bezierCurveTo()"

To create Bézier curves, we need the current point as a starting coordinate plus a target coordinate and, depending on the type of curve, one or two control points. In both cases, the coordinate x/y becomes the new current point after drawing the curve.

5.5.3   Arcs

Methods for creating arcs are not quite as straightforward. The first method is defined by two coordinates and a radius:

```
context.arcTo(x1, y1, x2, y2, radius)
```

As shown in Figure 5.10, arcTo() creates the new path as follows: A circle with a given radius is added to the line from x0/y0 to x1/y1 and then to x2/y2, so that the circle touches the line in exactly two points, the start tangent t1 and the end tangent t2. The arc between these two points becomes part of the path, and the end tangent t2 becomes the new current point.

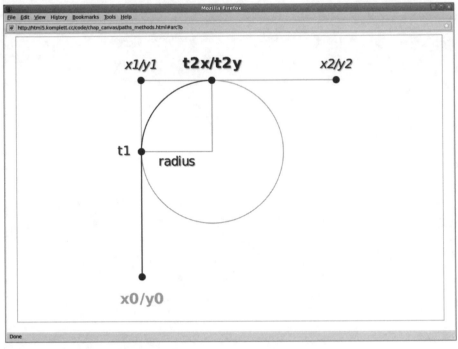

Figure 5.10   The path method "arcTo()"

In practice, this method is very useful for rectangles with rounded corners. A reusable function will come in handy to do the job shown in Figure 5.11.

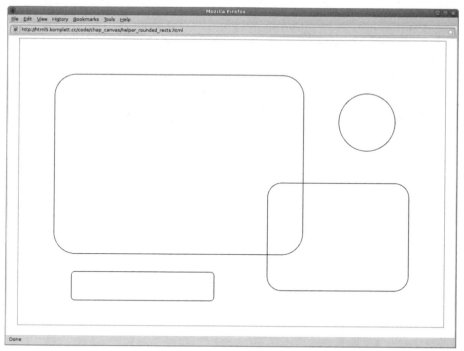

Figure 5.11 Four different rectangles with rounded corners; the circle is an extreme example of a rounded rectangle

```
var roundedRect = function(x,y,w,h,r) {
  context.beginPath();
  context.moveTo(x,y+r);
  context.arcTo(x,y,x+w,y,r);
  context.arcTo(x+w,y,x+w,y+h,r);
  context.arcTo(x+w,y+h,x,y+h,r);
  context.arcTo(x,y+h,x,y,r);
  context.closePath();
  context.stroke();
};
roundedRect(100,100,700,500,60);
roundedRect(900,150,160,160,80);
roundedRect(700,400,400,300,40);
roundedRect(150,650,400,80,10);
```

The function roundedRect() requires the basic values for the rectangle plus the radius for rounding. It then draws the desired rectangle with a moveTo() method, four arcTo() methods, and a closePath() method. You have not yet encountered the method closePath(): It closes the rectangle by joining the last point back up to the start point.

The second option for creating arcs—the method arc()—seems even more complicated at first glance. In addition to center and radius, we now have to specify two angles and the direction of rotation:

```
context.arc(x, y, radius, startAngle, endAngle, anticlockwise)
```

The center point of the arc in Figure 5.12 is the center of a circle with a given radius. Originating from this point, the angles startAngle and endAngle create two handles, intersecting the circle in two points. The direction of the arc between these two coordinates is determined by the parameter anticlockwise, where 0 means *clockwise* and 1 *counterclockwise*.

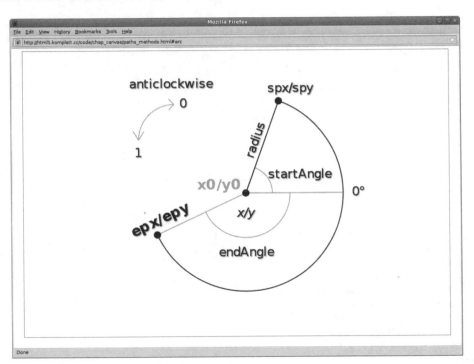

Figure 5.12   The path method "arc()"

The resulting arc begins in the center of the circle at the point x0/y0, joins this point in a straight line to the first intersection point spx/spy, and from there draws an arc to the end point epx/epy, which now becomes the new current point.

The biggest drawback in creating arcs is that all angles must be specified in radians instead of degrees. So here's a quick helper to refresh your memory on how to convert:

```
var deg2rad = function(deg) {
  return deg*(Math.PI/180.0);
};
```

Talking of helper functions, let's use two more to facilitate drawing circles and sectors. For circles, we really only need center and radius, the rest will be taken care of by the function circle():

```
var circle = function(cx,cy,r) {
  context.moveTo(cx+r,cy);
  context.arc(cx,cy,r,0,Math.PI*2.0,0);
};
```

Especially for circle diagrams, also called pie charts, specifying the angles in radians seems hardly intuitive. Our function sector() does the tedious conversion chore for us and allows us to specify start and end angles in degrees:

```
var sector = function(cx,cy,r,
    startAngle,endAngle, anticlockwise
  ) {
  context.moveTo(cx,cy);
  context.arc(
    cx,cy,r,
    startAngle*(Math.PI/180.0),
    endAngle*(Math.PI/180.0),
    anticlockwise
  );
  context.closePath();
};
```

Now, just a few lines of code are enough to draw circles and pie charts without losing track:

```
context.beginPath();
circle(300,400,250);
circle(300,400,160);
circle(300,400,60);
sector(905,400,250,-90,30,0);
sector(900,410,280,30,150,0);
sector(895,400,230,150,270,0);
context.stroke();
```

Figure 5.13 shows the result.

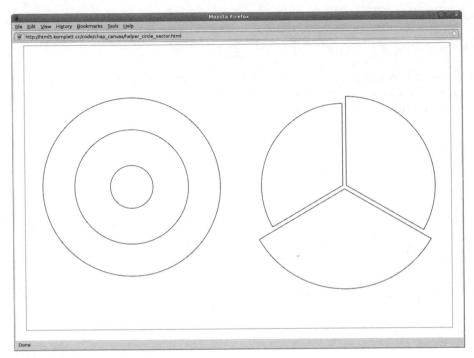

Figure 5.13   Circles and sectors

5.5.4   Rectangles

The method rect() handles a bit like our helpers, unlike the other methods:

```
context.rect(x, y, w, h)
```

In contrast to the previous path drawing methods, the current point x0/y0 is ignored altogether when drawing with rect(); instead, the rectangle is defined via the parameters x, y, width w, and height h. The origin point x/y then becomes the new current point after drawing (see Figure 5.14).

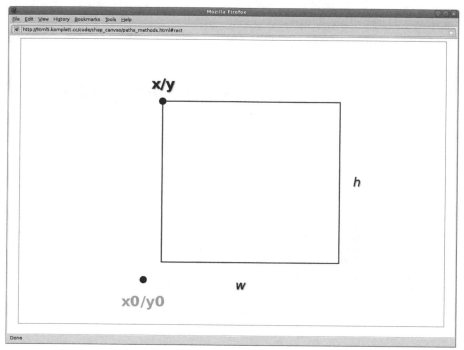

Figure 5.14   The path method "rect()"

5.5.5   Outlines, Fills, and Clipping Masks

If we think back to the three stages of creating a path with initialization—determining path, geometry, and drawing—we have now reached the third and last stage: the drawing. Here we decide what the path should look like. In all previous examples, we chose a simple outline at this point, created via the following method:

```
context.stroke()
```

The line color is determined by the attribute strokeStyle. You can also define the width of the line (lineWidth), what the ends of the line should look like (lineCap), and the join between lines (lineJoin) using three other Canvas attributes (the asterisk indicates default values; we will encounter it repeatedly from now on):

```
context.lineWidth = [ Pixel ]
context.lineCap = [ *butt, round, square ]
context.lineJoin = [ bevel, round, *miter ]
```

Figure 5.15 provides examples of the width, end, and join attributes.

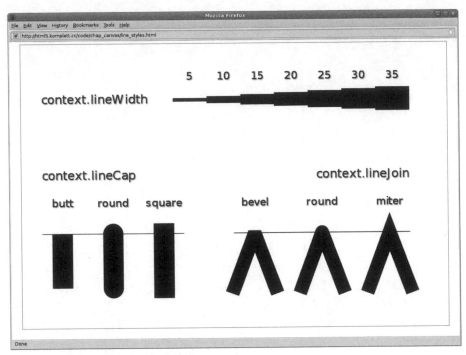

Figure 5.15   Attributes for determining line styles

The lineWidth is specified in pixels; the default setting is 1.0. As with the two other line attributes, the line width applies not only to lines and polygons, but also to rectangles created with strokeRect().

If we want to add a cap to a line with lineCap, we can choose butt, round, or square; butt is the default value. If we use round, the line gets a round cap by adding a semicircle at the end of the line with half the lineWidth as a radius. For square, the semicircle is replaced by a rectangle with a height of half the line width.

To create beveled line joins, we use the attribute lineJoin with bevel; we can also round the corners and create mitered joins with miter, which is the default value. To stop the angle of miter lines from becoming too acute, the specification provides the attribute miterLimit with a default value of 10.0. This is the ratio of the length of the tapered point (the distance between the intersection of lines and point) to half the line width. If the miterLimit is exceeded, the point will be trimmed, creating the same effect as in bevel.

To fill paths with a color or gradient, we first need to set the appropriate style attribute with fillStyle and then call the following path method:

```
context.fill()
```

This may sound simple but can get very complicated if paths self-intersect or are nested. In such cases, the so-called *non-zero* winding number rule takes effect: It decides whether to fill or not depending on the winding direction of the subpaths involved.

Figure 5.16 shows the *non-zero* rule in action. On the left, both circles were drawn in clockwise direction; on the right, the inner circle was drawn counterclockwise, leading to the hole in the center.

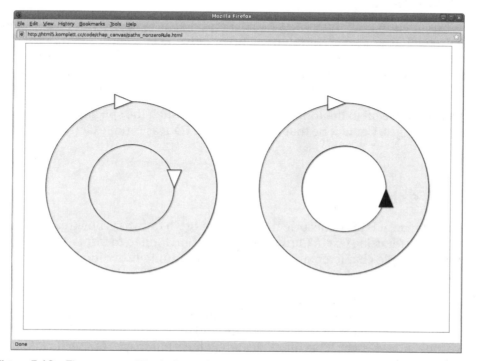

Figure 5.16   The non-zero fill rule for paths

To help us draw the directional circles, we used the helper from the arc() section, this time slightly modified: The desired direction is now passed as an argument. Valid settings for anticlockwise are 0 and 1:

```
var circle = function(cx,cy,r,anticlockwise) {
  context.moveTo(cx+r,cy);
  context.arc(cx,cy,r,0,Math.PI*2.0,anticlockwise);
};
```

The code for the circle on the right with the hole in it looks like this:

```
context.beginPath();
context.fillStyle = 'yellow';
```

```
circle(900,400,240,0);
circle(900,400,120,1);
context.fill();
context.stroke();
```

After `stroke()` and `fill()`, we need only one other method for drawing paths—the method

```
context.clip().
```

The explanation is as short as its name: `clip()` ensures that the defined path is not drawn but used as a cutout for all other drawing elements. Anything within the mask remains visible; the rest is hidden. You can reset the mask by creating another clipping mask using the entire canvas area as geometry. We will encounter a more elegant method later on, in section 5.13, with `save()` and `restore()`.

Let's now move on to the topic of text, a topic to which the specification devotes only four pages. Could it be that text support in Canvas is not exactly great?

5.6 Text

At first glance, it is probably true that text support in Canvas is not great, because the options for using text in Canvas are meager and limited to formatting and positioning simple character strings. There is no running text with automatic line breaks, nor paragraph formats or the option to select already existing texts.

We are left with three attributes for determining text attributes, two methods for drawing text, and one method for determining text length of a character string while taking into account the current format. This does not seem like much, but if we look more closely, it becomes clear that those four pages of specification are based on well-thought-out details.

5.6.1 Fonts

The definition of the `font` attribute simply refers to the CSS specification and states that `context.font` is subject to the same syntax as the CCS font shorthand notation:

```
context.font = [ CSS font property ]
```

In this manner, all font properties can be easily specified in a single string. Table 5.2 lists the individual components and their possible values.

Table 5.2 The components of the CSS "font" property

Property	Values
font-style	*normal, italic, oblique
font-variant	*normal, small-caps
font-weight	*normal, bold, bolder, lighter 100, 200, 300, 400, 500, 600, 700, 800, 900
font-size	xx-small, x-small, small, *medium, large, x-large, xx-large, larger, smaller em, ex, px, in, cm, mm, pt, pc, %
line-height	*normal, \<number>, em, ex, px, in, cm, mm, pt, pc, %
font-family	Font family or generic font family, such as serif, sans- serif, cursive, fantasy, monospace

When assembling the font attribute, only the properties font-size and font-family are required. All others are optional, and if omitted, default to the values marked with an asterisk as shown in Table 5.2. Because Canvas text does not recognize line breaks, the attribute line-height has no effect and is always ignored. The cleaned-up pattern for assembling the components is therefore:

```
context.font = [
  font-style font-variant font-weight font-size font-family
]
```

Regarding the font-family, the same rules apply as for defining fonts in stylesheets: You can specify any combination of font families and/or generic font families. The browser then picks the first known font from that priority list.

You can achieve complete independence from the browser or the relevant platform and its fonts by using webfonts. Once they are integrated into a stylesheet via @font-face, they are available as font-family in Canvas, too, via the font name assigned:

```
@font-face {
  font-family: Scriptina;
  src: url('fonts/scriptina.ttf');
}
```

Figure 5.17 shows brief examples of valid CSS font attributes and their rendering in Canvas. The source of the webfont *Scriptina* in the preceding example is http://www.fontex.org—a well-organized collection of free fonts that are available for download.

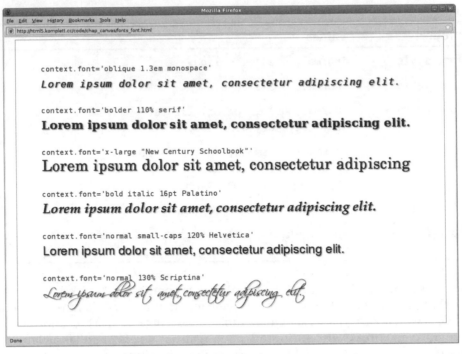

Figure 5.17   Font formatting with the "font" attribute

At the time of this writing, no browser supported @font-face without problems. In Firefox, for example, the webfont *Scriptina* in the last line only appears in Canvas if it is used at least once in the HTML document. The correct implementation of small-caps is also missing in Firefox, which is why the second to last example is not displayed correctly either.

5.6.2 Horizontal Anchor Point

The attribute textAlign determines the horizontal anchor point of Canvas texts:

```
context.textAlign = [
  left | right | center | *start | end
]
```

The keywords left, right, and center are familiar from the CSS attribute text-align, whereas start and end are already CSS3 extensions that allow for text direction, depending on the appropriate language. Some languages are written not from left to right but sometimes from right to left, as for example, Arabic and Hebrew.

Figure 5.18 presents the horizontal anchor points for writing with textflow ltr (left to right) and rtl (right to left), demonstrating the effect of directionality on the attributes start and end.

In the browser, the directionality of a document can be changed via the global attribute document.dir:

```
document.dir = [ *ltr | rtl ]
```

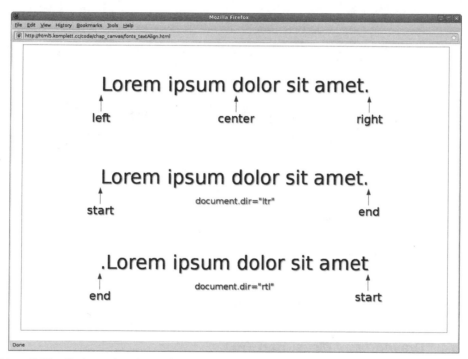

Figure 5.18 Horizontal anchor points with "textAlign"

5.6.3 Vertical Anchor Point

The vertical anchor point and therefore the baseline on which all glyphs are aligned is determined by the third and last text attribute, textBaseline:

```
context.textBaseline = [
  top | middle | *alphabetic | bottom | hanging | ideographic
]
```

The first four `textBaseline` keywords, *top*, *middle*, *alphabetic* and *bottom* are self-explanatory. A *hanging* baseline is required by Devanagari, Gurmukhi, and Bengali, three Indian alphabets used for writing the languages Sanskrit, Hindi, Marathi, Nepali or Panjabi, and Bengali. The group of *ideographic* writing systems includes Chinese, Japanese, Korean, and Vietnamese. Figure 5.19 illustrates the `textBaseline` vertical anchor points.

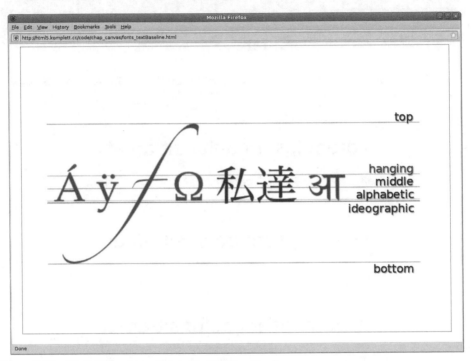

Figure 5.19   Vertical anchor points with "textBaseline"

5.6.4 Drawing and Measuring Text

Once font and anchor point have been determined, you only need to draw the text. Similar to rectangles, you can decide on a fill and/or outline, and you can even specify the maximum text width with an optional parameter, `maxwidth`:

```
context.fillText(text, x, y, maxwidth)
context.strokeText(text, x, y, maxwidth)
```

Finally, you can measure the text dimension with the method `measureText()`, which can at least determine the width while taking into account the current format. In our example in Figure 5.20, the bottom right value (759) was calculated using this method:

```
TextWidth = context.measureText(text).width
```

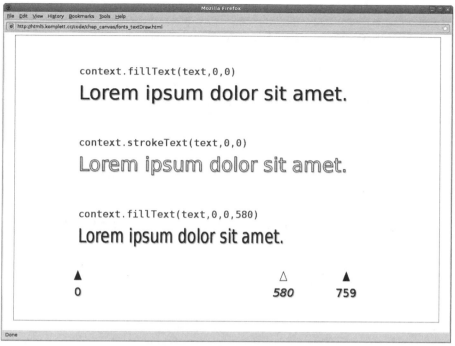

Figure 5.20   "fillText()", "strokeText()", and "measureText()"

It is not currently possible to determine the height and origin point of the *bounding box*, but this may be implemented in a future version of the specification, together with multiline text layout. The final note in the text chapter of the Canvas specification sounds promising: It indicates that in the future, fragments of documents (e.g., formatted paragraphs) might also find their way into Canvas via CSS.

The Canvas API offers a multitude of options for working in Canvas with raster-based formats not only in the future, but right now. In addition to embedding images and videos, you also have optional reading and writing access to every pixel on the canvas area. You can read up on how to do this in section 5.8, Pixel Manipulation.

5.7   Embedding Images

For embedding images, Canvas offers the method `drawImage()`,which we can invoke with three different parameter sets (the method can take three, five, or nine arguments):

```
context.drawImage(image, dx, dy)
context.drawImage(image, dx, dy, dw, dh)
context.drawImage(image, sx, sy, sw, sh, dx, dy, dw, dh)
```

In all three cases we need an image, canvas, or video element in the first parameter, which can be dynamically integrated via JavaScript or statically in the HTML code. Animated pictures or videos are not rendered in animation but displayed statically as the first frame or a poster frame if present.

All other arguments of the method drawImage() affect position, size, or cropping the source image to render in the target canvas. Figure 5.21 shows the graphic interpretation of the possible position parameters; the prefix s stands for source and d for destination.

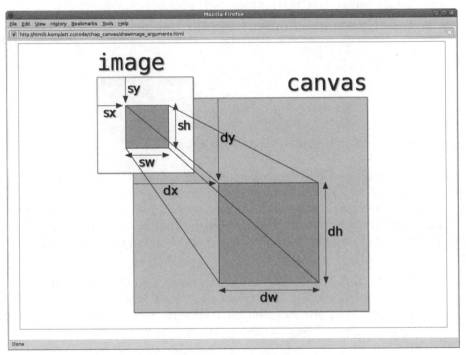

Figure 5.21   Position parameters of the "drawImage()" method

Let's now compare the individual drawImage() methods using three simple examples. The common setup is a picture measuring 1200 × 800 pixels, created dynamically as a JavaScript object (see Figure 5.22):

```
var image = new Image();
image.src = 'images/yosemite.jpg';
```

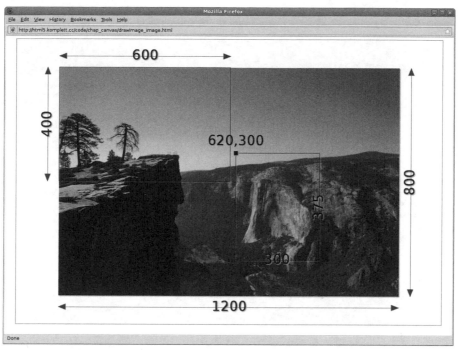

Figure 5.22   The source image of all "drawImage()" examples

In addition to pixel sizes, which we will encounter in the examples, Figure 5.22 shows the impressive 1000-meter-high rock face of El Capitan in Yosemite National Park: The photo was taken from Taft Point. This picture is now drawn onload onto the 600 × 400 pixel target canvas, using one of the three possible sets of arguments. The first and simplest option determines the top-left corner of the image in the target canvas with dx/dy. In our case, this is the position 0/0:

```
image.onload = function() {
  context.drawImage(image,0,0);
};
```

Width and height are copied directly from the original image, and because our image is bigger than the target canvas, it will come as no surprise that we only see the top-left quarter of Taft Point on our canvas (see Figure 5.23).

Figure 5.23   Taft Point in Yosemite National Park

If we want to represent the whole image in the canvas, we also have to specify the desired width and height in the arguments dw/dh. The browser then takes care of scaling the image to 600 × 400 pixels. The result is shown in Figure 5.24:

```
image.onload = function() {
  context.drawImage(image,0,0,600,400);
};
```

Figure 5.24 Taft Point with El Capitan in Yosemite National Park

In contrast to the two previous variations of drawImage(), which could have been realized with CSS as well, the third variation offers completely new possibilities of working with images. We can now copy any section of the source image (sx, sy, sw, sh) into the defined area of the target canvas (dx, dy, dw, dh). So nothing stands in the way of image montage:

```
image.onload = function() {
  context.drawImage(image,0,0);
  context.drawImage(
    image, 620,300,300,375,390,10,200,250
  );
};
```

The result is shown in Figure 5.25.

Figure 5.25   Yosemite National Park postcard

The first `drawImage()` call returns again the top-left quarter of Taft Point; the second extracts the area of El Capitan and draws it as icon into the top-right corner. Text with shadows completes the rudimentary layout of our postcard.

If you would rather have El Capitan in the foreground and Taft Point as a stamp at the top right, you just need to slightly modify the `drawImage()` calls. In our example you can do this by clicking on the canvas:

```
canvas.onclick = function() {
  context.drawImage(
    image,600,250,600,400,0,0,600,400
  );
  context.drawImage(
    image,0,0,500,625,390,10,200,250
  );
};
```

This yields the image shown in Figure 5.26.

Figure 5.26   Yosemite National Park postcard (alternative layout)

This was a brief introduction to the topic drawImage(), using an image as a source. You will find a detailed example of using the video element as the first parameter of drawImage() in section 5.14.2, Playing a Video with "drawImage()", but first we will discuss how you can get both read and write access to pixel values on the canvas area.

5.8 Pixel Manipulation

As methods for reading and manipulating pixel values, we have three choices: getImageData(), putImageData(), and createImageData(). Because all three contain the term ImageData, we first need to define what this refers to.

5.8.1 Working with the "ImageData" Object

Let's approach the ImageData object with a 2 × 2 pixel-sized canvas, onto which we draw four rectangles 1 × 1 pixels big and filled with the named colors navy, teal, lime, and yellow:

```
context.fillStyle = 'navy';
context.fillRect(0,0,1,1);
context.fillStyle = 'teal';
context.fillRect(1,0,1,1);
context.fillStyle = 'lime';
context.fillRect(0,1,1,1);
context.fillStyle = 'yellow';
context.fillRect(1,1,1,1);
```

In the next step, we use the method getImageData(sx, sy, sw, sh) to get the ImageData object. The four arguments determine the desired canvas section as a rectangle, as shown in Figure 5.27:

```
ImageData = context.getImageData(
  0,0,canvas.width,canvas.height
);
```

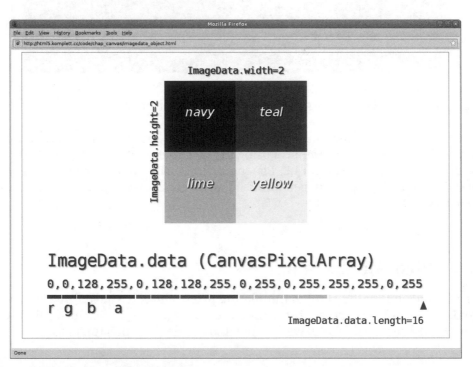

Figure 5.27   The "ImageData" object

The ImageData object has the attributes ImageData.width, ImageData.height, and ImageData.data. The latter hides the actual pixel values in the so-called CanvasPixelArray. This is a flat array with red, green, blue, and alpha values for each pixel in the selected section, starting at the top left, from left to right and top to bottom. The number of all values is saved in the attribute ImageData. data.length.

Using a simple for loop, we can now read the individual values of the CanvasPixelArray and make them visible with alert(). Starting at 0, we work from pixel to pixel by increasing the counter by 4 after each loop. The RGBA values are the result of offsets from the current position. Red can be found at counter i, green at i+1, blue at i+2, and the alpha component at i+3:

```
for (var i=0; i<ImageData.data.length; i+=4) {
  var r = ImageData.data[i];
  var g = ImageData.data[i+1];
  var b = ImageData.data[i+2];
  var a = ImageData.data[i+3];
  alert(r+" "+g+" "+b+" "+a);
}
```

Modifying pixel values works exactly the same: We change the Canvas-PixelArray *in-place* by assigning new values. In our example, the RGB values are set to random numbers between 0 and 255 via Math.random(); the alpha component remains unchanged:

```
for (var i=0; i<ImageData.data.length; i+=4) {
  ImageData.data[i]   = parseInt(Math.random()*255);
  ImageData.data[i+1] = parseInt(Math.random()*255);
  ImageData.data[i+2] = parseInt(Math.random()*255);
}
```

After this step, the canvas still looks the same. The new colors only become visible after we write the modified CanvasPixelArray back to the canvas via the method putImageData(). When calling putImageData(), we can have a maximum of seven parameters:

```
context.putImageData(
  ImageData, dx, dy, [ dirtyX, dirtY, dirtyWidth, dirtyHeight ]
)
```

The first three attributes are required; in addition to the ImageData object, they contain the coordinate of the origin point dx/dy, from which the CanvasPixelArray is applied via its width and height attributes. The optional dirty parameters cut out only a specified section of the CanvasPixelArray and write back only that section with reduced width and height. Figure 5.28 shows our 4-pixel canvas before and after modification, with a list of the relevant values of the CanvasPixelArray.

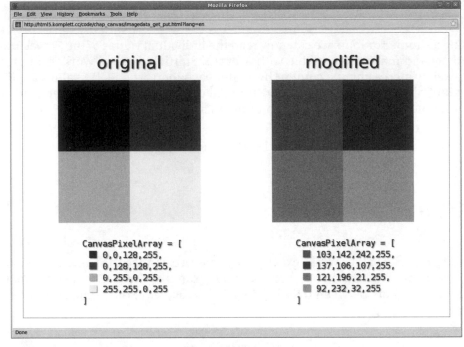

Figure 5.28   Modifying colors in the "CanvasPixelArray"

You can initialize an empty ImageData object directly via the method createImageData(). Width and height correspond to the arguments sw/sh or the dimensions of an ImageData object passed in the call. In both cases, all pixels of the CanvasPixelArray are set to transparent/black, which is rgba(0,0,0,0):

```
context.createImageData(sw, sh)
context.createImageData(imagedata)
```

So we could also create the 2 × 2 pixel modified canvas of Figure 5.28 directly via createImageData() and draw it via putImageData():

```
var imagedata = context.createImageData(2,2);
for (var i=0; i<ImageData.data.length; i+=4) {
  imagedata.data[i] = parseInt(Math.random()*255);
  imagedata.data[i+1] = parseInt(Math.random()*255);
  imagedata.data[i+2] = parseInt(Math.random()*255);
}
context.putImageData(imagedata,0,0);
```

That's it for now on dry CanvasPixelArray theory. In practice, things get much more exciting: With getImageData(), putImageData(), createImageData(), and a little bit of math, we can even write our own color filters for manipulating images. We will show you how in the next section.

5.8.2 Color Manipulation with "getImageData()", "createImageData()", and "putImageData()"

The starting picture for all examples is once again the photo of Yosemite National Park, drawn onto the canvas onload via drawImage(). In a second step, we define the original CanvasPixelArray via getImageData() and then modify it in the third step. In a for loop, each pixel's RGBA values are calculated following a mathematical formula and inserted into a CanvasPixelArray created previously via createImageData(). At the end we write it back to the canvas with putImageData().

Listing 5.1 provides the basic JavaScript frame of all filters used in Figure 5.29. The function grayLuminosity() is not part of the code example but will be addressed later, together with the other filters:

Listing 5.1 Basic JavaScript frame for color manipulation

```
var image = new Image();
image.src = 'images/yosemite.jpg';
image.onload = function() {
  context.drawImage(image,0,0,360,240);
  var modified = context.createImageData(360,240);
  var imagedata = context.getImageData(0,0,360,240);
  for (var i=0; i<imagedata.data.length; i+=4) {
    var rgba = grayLuminosity(
      imagedata.data[i+0],
      imagedata.data[i+1],
      imagedata.data[i+2],
      imagedata.data[i+3]
    );
    modified.data[i+0] = rgba[0];
    modified.data[i+1] = rgba[1];
    modified.data[i+2] = rgba[2];
    modified.data[i+3] = rgba[3];
  }
  context.putImageData(modified,0,0);
};
```

The server icon in the bottom-right corner of Figure 5.29 indicates that if you are using Firefox as your browser, this example can only be accessed via a server with http:// protocol. We will explain the reasons in section 5.15.3, Security Aspects.

Figure 5.29　Color manipulation with "getImageData()" and "putImageData()"

For converting the color to shades of gray, the documentation of the free, image-editing program GIMP offers three formulae in the chapter Desaturate (see the web link http://docs.gimp.org/en/gimp-tool-desaturate.html) with which you can calculate the shade of gray via *Lightness, Luminosity,* or average lightness (*Average*). If we implement these calculations with JavaScript, we get our first three color filters:

```
var grayLightness = function(r,g,b,a) {
  var val = parseInt(
    (Math.max(r,g,b)+Math.min(r,g,b))*0.5
  );
  return [val,val,val,a];
};

var grayLuminosity = function(r,g,b,a) {
  var val = parseInt(
    (r*0.21)+(g*0.71)+(b*0.07)
  );
  return [val,val,val,a];
};

var grayAverage = function(r,g,b,a) {
  var val = parseInt(
```

```
      (r+g+b)/3.0
   );
   return [val,val,val,a];
};
```

With grayLuminosity(), we are using the second formula in Figure 5.29, replacing the RGB component of each pixel with the new calculated value. In this and all following calculations, we must not forget that RGBA values can only be integers; the JavaScript method parseInt() makes sure of it.

The algorithm for sepiaTone() was taken from an article by Zach Smith, titled *How do I ... convert images to grayscale and sepia tone using C#?* (see the shortened web link http://bit.ly/a2nxI6):

```
var sepiaTone = function(r,g,b,a) {
   var rS = (r*0.393)+(g*0.769)+(b*0.189);
   var gS = (r*0.349)+(g*0.686)+(b*0.168);
   var bS = (r*0.272)+(g*0.534)+(b*0.131);
   return [
      (rS>255) ? 255 : parseInt(rS),
      (gS>255) ? 255 : parseInt(gS),
      (bS>255) ? 255 : parseInt(bS),
      a
   ];
};
```

Adding up the multiplied components can lead to values larger than 255 in each of the three calculations; in this case, 255 is inserted as a new value.

Inverting colors is very easy with the filter invertColor(): You simple deduct each RGB component from 255:

```
var invertColor = function(r,g,b,a) {
   return [
      (255-r),
      (255-g),
      (255-b),
      a
   ];
};
```

The filter swapChannels() modifies the sequence of the color channels. We first need to define the desired order as the fourth parameter in an array, where 0 is red, 1 is green, 2 is blue, and 3 is the alpha channel. To swap channels, we use the array rgba with the corresponding starting values and then return it in the new order. So changing from RGBA to BRGA, as in our example, can be achieved via order=[2, 0, 1, 3]:

```
var swapChannels = function(r,g,b,a,order) {
  var rgba = [r,g,b,a];
  return [
    rgba[order[0]],
    rgba[order[1]],
    rgba[order[2]],
    rgba[order[3]]
  ];
};
```

The last method, monoColor(), sets each pixel's RGB component to a particular color, using the starting pixel's gray value as an alpha component. When the function is called, the fourth parameter defines the desired color as an array of RGB values—in our case, blue with color= [0, 0, 255]:

```
var monoColor = function(r,g,b,a,color) {
  return [
    color[0],
    color[1],
    color[2],
    255-(parseInt((r+g+b)/3.0))
  ];
};
```

The filters we have introduced here are still rather simple, changing the color values of individual pixels without taking into account the neighboring pixels. If you factor these into the calculation, you can achieve more complex methods, such as sharpen, unsharp mask, or edge detection.

NOTE

Discussing such filters in detail would go beyond the scope of this book. If you want to explore more, check out Jacob Seidelin's *Pixastic Image Processing Library* (http://www.pixastic.com/lib). More than 30 JavaScript filters, available free under the Mozilla Public License, are just waiting to be discovered.

In the meantime, let's turn to Thomas Porter and Tom Duff, two Pixar Studios gurus who created a sensation back in 1984 with their article on alpha blending techniques. The digital compositing techniques they described not only earned them a prize at the *Academy of Motion Picture Arts and Sciences,* but also found their way into the Canvas specification.

5.9   Compositing

The possibilities of compositing in Canvas are many and varied, but you will only find a few good examples of their use on the Internet. Most are limited to presenting the methods per se, and to start with, that's what we will do, too. Figure 5.30 shows valid keywords of the globalCompositeOperation attribute, their Porter-Duff equivalent (in italics, with *A*,*B*), and the result after drawing.

First, we draw the blue rectangle as background, then we set the desired composite method, and finally we add the red circle. So for the first method, source-over, which is also the default value of the globalCompositeOperation attribute, the code looks like this:

```
context.beginPath();
context.fillStyle = 'cornflowerblue';
context.fillRect(0,0,50,50);
context.globalCompositeOperation = 'source-over';
context.arc(50,50,30,0,2*Math.PI,0);
context.fillStyle = 'crimson';
context.fill();
```

The image looks like that shown in Figure 5.30.

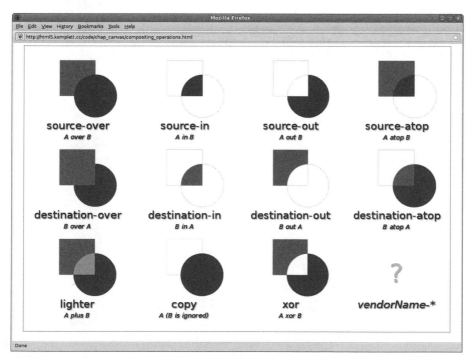

Figure 5.30   Values of the "globalCompositeOperation" attribute

The circle is the *source* (*A*); the rectangle is the *destination* (*B*). Let's use the Porter-Duff terms to explain the different methods, because they are much more intuitive and describe more precisely what is going on.

With source-over, we draw *A* over *B*; with source-in, only that part of *A* that is in *B*; with source-out, only that part of *A* that is outside of *B*; and with source-atop, we draw both *A* and *B* but only the part of *A* that overlaps *B*. The second line reverses the whole thing, so we do not need to explain it again.

The method lighter adds colors in the overlapping area, which makes it lighter. copy eliminates *B* and only draws *A*, and xor removes the intersection of *A* and *B*. The question mark indicates that vendor-specific compositing operations are also allowed, similar to the getContext() method.

Unfortunately, compositing is not yet fully implemented in any browser, which makes it difficult to sensibly present all methods. We will pick two and take a look at some examples for using the operations destination-in and lighter.

If we use destination-in to combine image and text, we can achieve a cutout effect, as shown in Figure 5.31. First, we draw the image with drawImage(), set the compositing method, and then insert the text with a maximum width of 1080 pixels. The text formatting corresponds to a font-size of 600 px with a text anchor point at the center top and a 60 pixel border with round line caps and joins:

```
context.drawImage(image,0,0,1200,600);
context.globalCompositeOperation = 'destination-in';
context.strokeText('HTML5',600,50,1080);
```

Figure 5.31 Compositing operation "destination-in" with image and text

The light gray text is again written with the default compositing method source-over and therefore not affected by the effect. Currently, it is not possible to define several texts as cutout at the same time because of the already mentioned shortfall in browser implementation.

Our second example uses the method `lighter`, expanding the previously mentioned options for color manipulation in images. With `lighter`, Figure 5.32 combines the Yosemite picture with 16 rectangles in the named standard colors, offering a CPU-friendly alternative to the color filter `monoColor()` mentioned in section 5.8.2, Color Manipulation with "getImageData()", "createImageData()", and "putImageData()". So we could implement the example used in that section differently and achieve a similar result:

```
context.drawImage(img,0,0,210,140);
context.globalCompositeOperation = 'lighter';
context.fillStyle = 'blue';
context.fillRect(0,0,210,140);
```

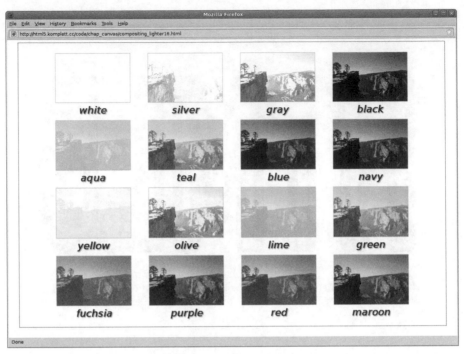

Figure 5.32   Compositing operation "lighter" with 16 base colors

We will encounter the compositing operator destination-out once more in the mirror effect in Figure 5.37 in section 5.11, Transformations. Let's first turn to user-defined patterns in Canvas.

5.10   Patterns

To create user-defined patterns for fills and lines, the specification offers the method createPattern(). Similar to drawImage(), it accepts both image elements and canvas or video elements as input, defining the type of pattern repetition in the parameter repetition:

```
context.createPattern(image, repetition)
```

Permitted values of the repetition argument are, as with the CSS specification's background-color attribute, repeat, repeat-x, repeat-y, and no-repeat. If we again use the 16 named basic colors, we can use a few lines of code to create checkered patterns, each with two pairs of colors (see Figure 5.33).

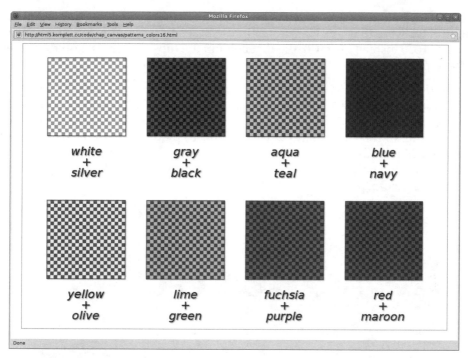

Figure 5.33 Checkered pattern in eight color combinations

The pattern is created as an in-memory canvas with a 20 × 20 pixel width and four 10 × 10 pixel squares. Illustrated using the example of the green pattern, this step looks as follows:

```
var cvs = document.createElement("CANVAS");
cvs.width = 20;
cvs.height = 20;
var ctx = cvs.getContext('2d');
ctx.fillStyle = 'lime';
ctx.fillRect(0,0,10,10);
ctx.fillRect(10,10,10,10);
ctx.fillStyle = 'green';
ctx.fillRect(10,0,10,10);
ctx.fillRect(0,10,10,10);
```

We then define the canvas cvs as a repeating pattern using createPattern(), assign it to the attribute fillStyle, and use it to fill the square:

```
context.fillStyle = context.createPattern(cvs,'repeat');
context.fillRect(0,0,220,220);
```

Patterns are anchored to the coordinate origin and applied starting from that point. If we were to begin `fillRect()` in the preceding example ten pixels to the right, at 10/0 instead of at 0/0, the first color in the top-left corner would be green instead of `lime`.

In addition to user-defined canvas elements, we can also use images as sources of patterns. Figure 5.34 shows an example using `createPattern()` to fill the background, to create a pattern for the title text, and to cut out individual sections of the familiar Yosemite picture. The two other pictures, *pattern_107.png* and *pattern_125.png*, are part of the *Squidfingers* pattern library, where you have the choice of nearly 160 other appealing patterns to download: http://www.squidfingers.com/patterns.

Figure 5.34   Pattern using images as a source

Let's first look at how the background is created:

```
var bg = new Image();
bg.src = 'icons/pattern_125.png';
bg.onload = function() {
  context.globalAlpha = 0.5;
  context.fillStyle = context.createPattern(bg,'repeat');
  context.fillRect(0,0,canvas.width,canvas.height);
};
```

The first two lines create a new Image object, setting its src attribute to the image pattern_125.png in the folder icons. Just as with drawImage(), we need to make sure that the image is really loaded before defining the pattern. The function bg.onload() contains the real code for generating the repeating pattern, which we apply at 50% opacity to the whole canvas area. With the same procedure, we fill the title text *Yosemite!* with the image *pattern_107.png*.

For the overlapping image sections, we simply enter the whole Yosemite photo *yosemite.jpg* as the pattern and then work in a for loop through the input array extents, which contains the x-, y-, width-, and height-values of the sections we want. By calling fillRect(), the relevant image area is shown as fill pattern and receives an additional border with strokeRect():

```
var extents = [
  { x:20,y:50,width:120,height:550 } // and 7 others ...
];
var image = new Image();
image.src = 'images/yosemite.jpg';
image.onload = function() {
  context.fillStyle = context.createPattern(
    image,'no-repeat'
  );
  for (var i=0; i<extents.length; i++) {
    var d = extents[i]; // short-cut
    context.fillRect(d.x,d.y,d.width,d.height);
    context.strokeRect(d.x,d.y,d.width,d.height);
  }
};
```

Three different images are used in Figure 5.34, and all three must be fully loaded before they can be used, so we need to nest the three onload functions. This ensures that we can control the correct order during drawing. The pseudo-code for a possible nesting looks like this:

```
// create all images
bg.onload = function() {
  // draw background
  image.onload = function() {
    // add image cutouts
    pat.onload = function() {
      // fill title with pattern
    };
  };
};
```

The only option to avoid this kind of nesting would be to link all involved images in the page's HTML code as hidden img elements via visibility:hidden and to reference them with getElementById() or getElementsByTagName() after loading the page in window.onload().

Before moving on to another section of the Canvas specification, *Transformations*, we should mention that when using a video element as the source of `createPattern()`, the first frame of the video or the poster frame, if present, is used as a pattern, similar to the `drawImage()` method.

5.11 Transformations

Canvas transformations manipulate the coordinate system directly. When moving a rectangle, you are not only moving the actual element, but also shifting the whole coordinate system and only then redrawing the rectangle. The three basic transformations are `scale()`, `rotate()`, and `translate()`, as shown in Figure 5.35.

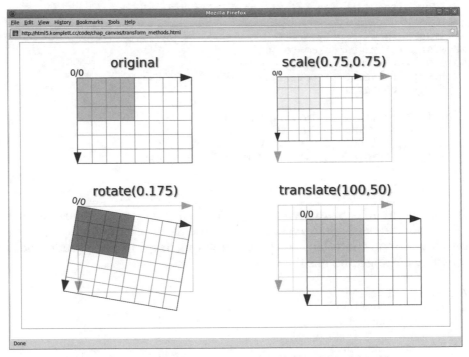

Figure 5.35   The basic transformations "scale()", "rotate()", and "translate()"

```
context.scale(x, y)
context.rotate(angle)
context.translate(x, y)
```

For scaling via `scale()`, we need two multiplicands as arguments for the size change of the x and y dimension, rotations using `rotate()` require the angle of clockwise rotation in radiant, and moving via `translate()` defines offsets in x- und y-directions in pixels. If combining these methods, the individual transformations must be carried out in reverse order: In terms of JavaScript code, they basically must be read from back to front.

To first scale and then rotate, we write:

```
context.rotate(0.175);
context.scale(0.75,0.75);
context.fillRect(0,0,200,150);
```

If we want to rotate first and then translate, the JavaScript code would have to be:

```
context.translate(100,50);
context.rotate(0.175);
context.fillRect(0,0,200,150);
```

You need to be careful in any case where rotations are involved, because they are always carried out with the origin 0/0 as the center of rotation. The rule of thumb is that rotate() is usually the last action. Figure 5.36 shows an example using all three basic methods, depicting our Yosemite image from a different perspective as a kind of ski jump.

Figure 5.36   Rotate, scale and move

Listing 5.2 shows the very short source code in Figure 5.36.

Listing 5.2 Source code of the transformations shown in Figure 5.36

```
image.onload = function() {
  var rotate = 15;
  var scaleStart = 0.0;
  var scaleEnd = 4.0;
  var scaleInc = (scaleEnd-scaleStart)/(360/rotate);
  var s = scaleStart;
  for (var i=0; i<=360; i+=rotate) {
    s += scaleInc;
    context.translate(540,260);
    context.scale(s,s);
    context.rotate(i*-1*Math.PI/180);
    context.drawImage(image,0,0,120,80);
    context.setTransform(1,0,0,1,0,0);
  }
};
```

As soon as the image is loaded, we define the angle of rotation rotate as 15°, the start and end scaling scaleStart as 0.0 and scaleEnd as 4.0, and derived from this the increment for scaling scaleInc with the aim of achieving the end scale 4.0 within a full rotation. In the for loop we then rotate the image counterclockwise by 15° each time, scale it from 0.0 to 4.0, and set its top-left corner to the coordinate 540/260.

So why do we have the method setTransform() at the end of the for loop?

Apart from the basic transformations scale(), rotate(), and translate(), Canvas offers two other methods for changing the coordinate system and therefore the *transformation matrix*: transform() and setTransform(), which were already mentioned in Listing 5.2:

```
context.transform(m11, m12, m21, m22, dx, dy);
context.setTransform(m11, m12, m21, m22, dx, dy);
```

Both have the arguments m11, m12, m21, m22, dx, and dy in common, representing the transformation properties listed in Table 5.3.

Table 5.3 Components of a Canvas matrix transformation

Component	Content
m11	Scale in x-axis
m12	Horizontal shear
m21	Vertical shear
m22	Scale in y-axis
dx	Translate along x-axis
dy	Translate along y-axis

The main difference between them is that `transform()` changes the current transformation matrix via multiplication, whereas `setTransform()` overwrites the existing matrix with the new one.

The three basic methods could also be formulated as attributes of `transform()` or `setTransform()` and are basically nothing else than convenient shortcuts for corresponding matrix transformations. Table 5.4 lists these attributes and other useful matrices for flipping (`flipX/Y`) and skewing (`skewX/Y`). The angles for skewing are again specified in radiant.

Table 5.4 Matrices of basic transformations and other useful transformation methods

Method	Transformation Matrix (m11, m12, m21, m22, dx, dy)
`scale(x, y)`	x,0,0,y,0,0
`rotate(angle)`	cos(angle),sin(angle), -sin(angle), cos(angle),0,0
`translate(x, y)`	1,0,0,1,x,y
`flipX()`	-1,0,0,1,0,0
`flipY()`	1, 0, 0, -1, 0, 0
`skewX(angle)`	1,0,tan(angle),1,0,0
`skewY(angle)`	1,tan(angle),0,1,0,0

Before further exploring Canvas transformations using a detailed example, we should mention that both `getImageData()` and `putImageData()` are not affected by transformations, according to the specification. The call `getImageData(0,0,100,100)` always gets the 100 × 100 pixel square in the top-left corner of the canvas regardless of whether the coordinate system was translated, scaled, or rotated. The same goes for `putImageData(imagedata,0,0)`, where the top-left corner serves as an anchor point for applying the content of `imagedata`.

Let's move on to the example where we will apply all mentioned transformation methods. Figure 5.37 shows the appealing result—a collage of three image sections of our Yosemite picture with mirror effect in pseudo-3D.

Figure 5.37 Photo collage with mirror effect in pseudo-3D

Let's start by punching out the three square sections for Taft Point, Merced River, and El Capitan. The result will be saved in the array `icons`:

```
var icons = [
  clipIcon(image,0,100,600,600),
  clipIcon(image,620,615,180,180),
  clipIcon(image,550,310,400,4];
```

The function `clipIcon()` takes care of clipping and adapting the size of the differently sized image portions. In this function, we first create a new *in-memory* canvas with a size of 320 × 320 pixels, onto which we then copy the appropriately reduced (or enlarged) icon with `drawImage()` before adding a 15-pixel white border:

```
var clipIcon = function(img,x,y,width,height) {
  var cvs = document.createElement("CANVAS");
  var ctx = cvs.getContext('2d');
  cvs.width = 320;
  cvs.height = 320;
  ctx.drawImage(img,x,y,width,height,0,0,320,320);
  ctx.strokeStyle = '#FFF';
  ctx.lineWidth = 15;
  ctx.strokeRect(0,0,320,320);
  return cvs;
};
```

In a second step, we create the reflection effect for each of these three image sections and save it in the array effects:

```
var effects = [];
  for (var i=0; i<icons.length; i++) {
  effects[i] = createReflection(icons[i]);
}
```

The main work is done in the function createReflection(), the slightly modified code of which has been taken from a blog post in Charles Ying's *blog about art, music, and the art of technology* about the iPhone's *CoverFlow* effect (see the shortened web link http://bit.ly/b5AFW6):

```
var createReflection = function(icon) {
  var cvs = document.createElement("CANVAS");
  var ctx = cvs.getContext('2d');
  cvs.width = icon.width;
  cvs.height = icon.height/2.0;

  // flip
  ctx.translate(0,icon.height);
  ctx.scale(1,-1);
  ctx.drawImage(icon,0,0);

  // fade
  ctx.setTransform(1,0,0,1,0,0);
  ctx.globalCompositeOperation = "destination-out";
  var grad = ctx.createLinearGradient(
    0,0,0,icon.height/2.0
  );
  grad.addColorStop(0,'rgba(255,255,255,0.5)');
  grad.addColorStop(1,'rgba(255,255,255,1.0)');
  ctx.fillStyle = grad;
  ctx.fillRect(0,0,icon.width,icon.height/2.0);
  return cvs;
};
```

In createReflection() we first use another *in-memory* canvas to flip the lower half of the image section passed in icon. Thinking back to the shortcuts for transformation matrices, we could achieve flipping via the matrix for flipY(). But in this case we use another option of creating reflection, using the method scale(), where scale(1,-1) corresponds to the method flipY() and scale(-1,1) corresponds to the method flipX(). The fade-out effect is achieved via a gradient from semitransparent white to opaque white, placed over the icon using the compositing method destination-out.

Now we have defined the individual image sections and can start drawing. A black/white gradient with almost complete black in the center of the gradient creates the impression of 3D space, in which we then place the three images:

```
var grad = context.createLinearGradient(
  0,0,0,canvas.height
);
grad.addColorStop(0.0,'#000');
grad.addColorStop(0.5,'#111');
grad.addColorStop(1.0,'#EEE');
context.fillStyle = grad;
context.fillRect(0,0,canvas.width,canvas.height);
```

The center picture of Merced River is the easiest to position via setTransform(); we can then draw it with a reflection effect:

```
context.setTransform(1,0,0,1,440,160);
context.drawImage(icons[1],0,0,320,320);
context.drawImage(effects[1],0,320,320,160);
```

The width of the El Capitan image on the right is scaled by 0.9 to achieve a better 3D effect. The result is skewed by 10° downward via the matrix for skewY() and positioned to the right of the center:

```
context.setTransform(1,0,0,1,820,160);
context.transform(1,Math.tan(0.175),0,1,0,0);
context.scale(0.9,1);
context.drawImage(icons[2],0,0,320,320);
context.drawImage(effects[2],0,320,320,160);
```

Drawing the Taft Point image on the left is a bit more complicated. After skewing, the top-left corner of our section forms the anchor point; we then have to skew upward by 10° and then move the result downward again. Pythagoras' theorem will help us determine the required dy value: It results as tangent of the rotation angle in radians multiplied by the length of the cathetus corresponding to the width of the icon, so Math.tan(0.175)*320. We also have to compensate for scaling the image width by 0.9 by shifting it to the right by 320*0.1:

```
context.setTransform(1,0,0,1,60,160);
context.transform(1,Math.tan(-0.175),0,1,0,0);
context.translate(320*0.1,Math.tan(0.175)*320);
context.scale(0.9,1);
context.drawImage(icons[0],0,0,320,320);
context.drawImage(effects[0],0,320,320,160);
```

We have now completed our most difficult Canvas example so far. The result is quite impressive, so we should probably save it as JPEG or PNG file. Unlike the other browsers, Firefox makes it easy for you—just right-click on the canvas to save your creation. If you click on View Image, a bizarre and very, very, very long URL address appears, starting with data:image/png;base64..., which takes us straight to the next section—canvas.toDataURL().

5.12   Base64 Encoding with "canvas.toDataURL( )"

Base64 describes a method of encoding binary data as ASCII strings. In Canvas it is used to turn the canvas content, which only really exists as raster in memory, into a processable data: URL. The method to achieve this is

canvas.toDataURL(type, args)

We pass the MIME type of the desired output format as type using either image/png or image/jpeg. The former is the default encoding format and is also used if we omit type or specify a format with which the browser cannot cope. Any additional parameters can be accommodated by the optional argument args—for example, the image quality if selecting image/jpeg with valid numbers between 0.0 and 1.0.

The result of toDataURL() is a base64-encoded string. In the case of the 2 × 2 pixel canvas in the named colors navy, teal, lime, and yellow of Figure 5.27, it looks as follows:

data:image/png;base64,iVBORwOKGgoAAAANSUhEUg
AAAAIAAAACCAYAAABytgOkAAAAFOlEQVQImQXBAQEAAA
CCIKb33ADLFqlOPuYIemXXHEQAAAAASUVORK5CYII=

These encoded strings can get rather long. The base64 version of our photo collage with the reflection effect, for example, has no less than 1,298,974 characters and would fill 325 pages of this book (with each page containing 50 lines of 80 characters each)!

So what is toDataURL()used for? Why convert binary image data to character strings? The answer is simple: With toDataURL(), we can make the fleeting *in-memory* canvas permanently available in HTML, enabling the user or an application to save it.

The first use of toDataURL() is copying a Canvas graphic into an HTMLImageElement. This becomes possible because the src attribute can also be a data: URI. The necessary code is short and requires an empty image in addition to a dynamically created canvas:

```
<!DOCTYPE html>
<title>Copy canvas onto image</title>
<img src="" alt="copied canvas content, 200x200 pixels">
<script>
  var canvas = document.createElement("CANVAS");
  canvas.width = 200;
  canvas.height = 200;
  var context = canvas.getContext('2d');
  context.fillStyle = 'navy';
  context.fillRect(0,0,canvas.width,canvas.height);
  document.images[0].src = canvas.toDataURL();
</script>
```

The crucial line in the listing is printed in bold and shows how easy it is to copy—define the reference to the first image in the document and specify its src attribute as canvas.toDataURL(). As a result, we get a regular img element, which we treat just like any other image in the browser and can save as PNG.

With a simple onclick handler on the canvas element, we demonstrate the next use of toDataURL()—directly assigning the resulting data: URI as URL, but this time the output is not as PNG, but as JPEG:

```
document.images[0].onclick = function() {
  window.location = canvas.toDataURL('image/jpeg');
};
```

The disadvantages of this method are that the URL can get painfully long sometimes (remember the 1.3 million characters?), and the fact that images in this format do not end up in the cache and therefore must be created anew with every call. Other potential applications of toDataURL() are with localstorage or XMLHttpRequest, allowing saving and accessing existing Canvas graphics both on the client side and server side. toDataURL() also serves us well for creating CSS styles with background-image or list-style-image where we can insert it as url() value.

5.13 "save( )" and "restore( )"

Our journey through CanvasContext2D is nearly at an end. Only two methods are left to explain: context.save() and context.restore(). Without them, we could probably not manage any complex Canvas graphics; if you had a quick glance at the figures' source code, you would probably agree. To help you better understand the methods context.save() and context.restore(), we need to recapitulate first.

By defining the drawing context with canvas.getContext('2d'), all attributes are assigned default values, which then have a direct effect when drawing:

```
context.globalAlpha = 1.0;
context.globalCompositeOperation = 'source-over';
context.strokeStyle = 'black';
context.fillStyle = 'black';
context.lineWidth = 1;
context.lineCap = 'butt';
context.lineJoin = 'miter';
context.miterLimit = 10;
context.shadowOffsetX = 0;
context.shadowOffsetY = 0;
context.shadowBlur = 0;
context.shadowColor = 'rgba(0,0,0,0)';
context.font = '10px sans-serif';
context.textAlign = 'start';
context.textBaseline = 'alphabetic';
```

At the same time, the coordinate system is initialized with the identity matrix, and a clipping mask is created, which comprises the entire canvas area:

```
context.setTransform(1, 0,0,1,0,0);
context.beginPath();
context.rect(0,0,canvas.width,canvas.height);
context.clip();
```

If we change attributes, transformations, or clipping masks, they remain valid until we change them again. In more complicated graphics, it is easy to lose track of all these changes. This is where context.save() and context.restore() become useful.

With context.save(), we can create a snapshot at any time, which saves the currently set attributes and transformations while taking into account the current clipping mask. Later, we can easily access this snapshot with context.restore(). The specification mentions the *stack of drawing states* in this context, because snapshots can also be nested.

This technique is excellent where transformations or clipping masks are concerned. And for shadow effects, it is much easier to reset the four shadow components back to their default values with `context.save()` and `context.restore()` than setting each component individually. For the animations we will discuss next, `context.save()` and `context.restore()` are practically indispensable.

5.14 Animations

Unlike SVG or SMIL animations, Canvas animations are done purely manually. The ingredients are a function for drawing plus a timer calling it in regular intervals. JavaScript offers `window.setInterval()` for this purpose; the rest is up to the imagination of the Canvas programmer.

5.14.1 Animation with Multicolored Spheres

This is our animation premiere: Spheres of different colors appear in random places on the canvas, fade slowly, and are covered by other spheres. The animation speed should correspond to an adult's resting pulse of about 60 beats per minute. As an additional feature, we want to be able to stop or restart the animation by clicking on the canvas.

About 50 lines of JavaScript code are sufficient. But before turning to the analysis of Listing 5.3, let's look at a static screen shot of the result in Figure 5.38.

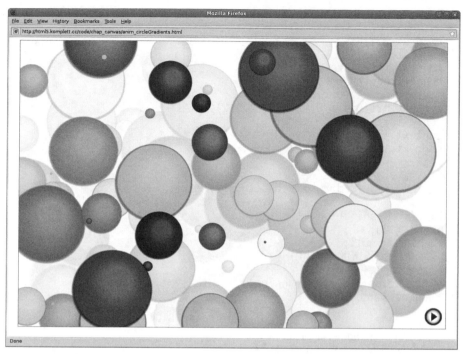

Figure 5.38 Animation with multicolored spheres

Listing 5.3 JavaScript code for animation with multicolored spheres

```
var canvas = document.querySelector("canvas");
var context = canvas.getContext('2d');
var r,cx,cy,radgrad;

var drawCircles = function() {
  // fade existing content
  context.fillStyle = 'rgba(255,255,255,0.5)';
  context.fillRect(0, 0,canvas.width,canvas.height);

  // draw new spheres
  for (var i=0; i<360; i+=15) {
    // random position and size
    cx = Math.random()*canvas.width;
    cy = Math.random()*canvas.height;
    r = Math.random()*canvas.width/10.0;

    // define radial gradient
    radgrad = context.createRadialGradient(
      0+(r* 0.15),0-(r* 0.25),r/3.0,
      0,0,r
    );
    radgrad.addColorStop(0.0,'hsl('+i+',100%,75%)');
    radgrad.addColorStop(0.9,'hsl('+i+',100%,50%)');
```

```
        radgrad.addColorStop(1.0,'rgba(0,0,0,0)');

        // draw circle
        context.save();
        context.translate(cx,cy);
        context.beginPath();
        context.moveTo(0+r,0);
        context.arc(0,0,r,0,Math.PI*2.0,0);
        context.fillStyle = radgrad;
        context.fill();
        context.restore();
    }
};
drawCircles();   // draw first set of spheres

// start/stop animation at pulse speed
var pulse = 60;
var running = null;
canvas.onclick = function() {
    if (running) {
        window.clearInterval(running);
        running = null;
    }
    else {
        running = window.setInterval(
            "drawCircles()",60000/pulse
        );
    }
};
```

After defining canvas, context, and some other variables, the proper work starts with the function drawCircles(). A semitransparent white rectangle fades existing content from previous drawCircles() calls, and then the for loop draws new spheres. The position of each sphere and its radius are randomized once again with Math.random(), placing the center in each case into the canvas area and limiting the radius to a tenth of the canvas width.

To make sure the circles look like spheres, we create a radial gradient. Its geometry consists in a light spot at the top right and the total circle. The choice of increment of the for loop reflects the desire to have colors in HSL color space as colorStops of the gradient. With each loop, the color angle increases by 15°, causing the color change from red to green to blue and back to red.

We can then in each case derive pairs of matching colors from the lightness: The first one represents the light spot and the second one the darker color near the sphere's edge. The third call of addColorStop() causes the very edges of the sphere to fade to transparent black. We create a total of 24 spheres in this way; to make things clearer, the spheres' color pairs are shown in Figure 5.39.

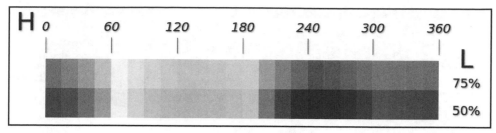

Figure 5.39   HSL colors for multicolored spheres animation

Then the sphere is drawn as a circle with the defined gradient. Embedding in `context.save()` and `context.restore()` ensures that the temporary displacement with `translate()` is not applied to the subsequent circles. Now the function `drawCircles()` is complete, and we can draw a first set of spheres and then move on to the timer.

About 15 lines are sufficient to implement starting and stopping the animation via an `onclick` event listener. With the first click on the canvas, we start the animation with `window.setInterval()` and save the unique interval ID in the variable `running`. Times are specified in milliseconds for `window.setInterval()`, so we need to convert the beats per minute accordingly in the variable `pulse`.

Once the animation is running, the unique interval ID is assigned to the variable `running`, and with the next click, we can interrupt it using `window.clearInterval(running)`. If we then set `running` back to `null`, the next click on the canvas signals: *no animation is running*. In this case, we restart and the fun starts over.

5.14.2   Playing a Video with "drawImage()"

As you already know from section 5.7, Embedding Images, an `HTMLVideoElement` can also be used as a source for `drawImage()`. But if you are hoping that videos embedded in this way will play automatically, you will be disappointed, because the logic for this must be implemented fully in JavaScript. This is not difficult, as you can see from the final Canvas animation example—an extension of our Yosemite National Park postcard in Figure 5.25. Instead of the static image section with El Capitan, we now place a dynamic video into the top-right corner, offering a 360° panoramic view from Taft Point. While the video is playing, ten small snapshots of the running video appear as a gallery along the bottom of the canvas. After the end of the video, you can see the picture shown in Figure 5.40.

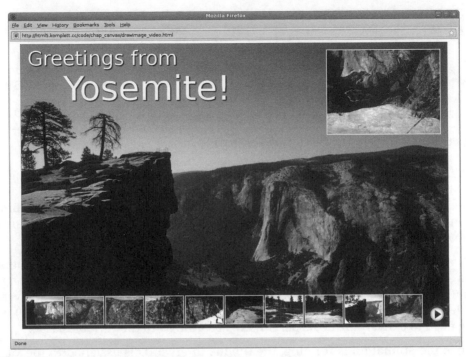

Figure 5.40   Yosemite National Park video postcard

> **NOTE**
>
> The video was kindly provided by YouTube user *pos315*, converted to *WebM* via *ffmpeg*, and reduced to 320 × 240 pixels. You can see the original online at http://www.youtube.com/watch?v=NmdHx_7b0h0.

Unlike images, which up to now have always found their way into the canvas via the JavaScript method new Image(), we integrate the panoramic view directly into the HTML page as a video element. As additional attributes, we need pre-load, oncanplay as an event listener to give us the point in time when we can lay out the postcard and prepare for starting and stopping, and a style instruction for hiding the embedded original video. We only use the original video to copy the current video frame onto the canvas in brief intervals during playing. The alternative text for browsers without video support gives a quick reference to the content of the video:

```
<video src="videos/yosemite_320x240.webm"
  preload="auto"
  oncanplay="init(event)"
  style="display:none;"
>
```

```
Panoramic view of Yosemite Valley from Taft Point
</video>
```

To ensure that the function init(event) as a reference in the oncanplay attribute really exists, we set the script element before our video element. The schematic structure of this central function, which implements both the layout and the function of the video postcard, looks like this:

```
var init = function(evt) {
  // save reference to video element
  // create background image
  image.onload = function() {
    // draw background image
    // add title
    // draw first frame
    canvas.onclick = function() {
      // implement starting and stopping
      // copy video frames while playing
      // create icons at regular intervals while playing
    };
  }
};
```

The reference to the video object of the video element can be found in evt.target, and we save it in the variable video. As before, we create a new background image via new Image(), and as soon as the image is fully loaded, we continue drawing the background and title. The steps up to this point probably do not require further explanation, but perhaps we should explain drawing the first frame:

```
context.setTransform(1,0,0,1,860,20);
context.drawImage(video,0,0,320,240);
context.strokeRect(0,0,320,240);
```

We first position the coordinate system at the top-right corner with setTransform(), and then draw the first frame with a border using draw-Image(). This procedure will later be repeated over and over while playing, and it is crucial that the HTMLVideoElement video of the drawImage() method always offers the image of the current frame.

Stopping, starting, and then copying the current frames of the original video running in the background, as well as creating scaled-down image sections, is implemented via the function canvas.onclick() by clicking on the canvas. Listing 5.4 shows the JavaScript code needed to do all that:

Listing 5.4 Code for animating the video postcard

```
var running = null;
canvas.onclick = function() {
  if (running) {
    video.pause();
    window.clearInterval(running);
    running = null;
  }
  else {
    var gap = video.duration/10;
    video.play();
    running = window.setInterval(function () {
      if (video.currentTime < video.duration) {
        // update video
        context.setTransform(1,0,0,1,860,20);
        context.drawImage(video,0,0,320,240);
        context.strokeRect(0,0,320,240);
        // update icons
        var x1 = Math.floor(video.currentTime/gap)*107;
        var tx = Math.floor(video.currentTime/gap)*5;
        context.setTransform(1,0,0,1,10+tx,710);
        context.drawImage(video,x1,0,107,80);
        context.strokeRect(x1,0,107,80);
      }
      else {
        window.clearInterval(running);
        running = null;
      }
    },35);
  }
};
```

As in the first animation example, the variable running contains the unique interval ID of window.setInterval() and allows for controlling the animation. If a value is assigned to running, we pause the hidden video with video.pause(), stop copying frames by removing the interval, and set running back to null. Otherwise, we start the video with video.play() at the first or next click and copy the current video frame onto the canvas in the callback function of the interval every 35 milliseconds. We continue the whole process until the video has finished playing or the canvas is clicked again. The two attributes video.currentTime and video.duration of the video object in the variable video can help check whether the current playback position is still less than the total time of the video.

Drawing the copied video at the top right happens in parallel to drawing the first frame. For the strip of mini snapshots, we use the total length of the video and the desired number of snapshots to calculate the interval gap after which we need to shift the anchor point x1 further right with a small gap tx. As long as x1 has the same value, the animation in the reduced-size image keeps running. If x1 is shifted to the right, the last frame remains static and the animation continues running from the new position. After about 40 seconds of playing time, the video is over, ten new mini snapshots have been drawn, and we can restart the sequence all over again by clicking on the canvas.

That's it for now for our video postcard. But before we can finish this chapter, we need to mention a few more topics.

5.15 Anything Still Missing?

The next section describes the method isPointInPath() and considers aspects of accessibility and security in Canvas. The chapter concludes with a quick update on the improved level of browser support and a selection of links for all those who want to find out more about Canvas.

5.15.1 "isPointInPath(x, y)"

As you can guess from the method's name, isPointInPath() returns either *true* or *false*, depending on whether the point specified by the coordinates x/y is inside or outside of the current path. A brief example demonstrates the application of this method; in this case, it returns true in alert():

```
context.beginPath();
context.rect(50,50,100,100);
alert(
   context.isPointInPath(75,75)
);
```

One practical use of isPointInPath() is for determining if the user has clicked on a particular area of the canvas. All we need for this is an onclick event handler, which uses the mouse position in clientX/clientY and the position of the canvas element in offsetLeft/offsetTop to calculate the current x/y position in relation to the canvas area:

```
canvas.onclick = function(evt) {
  context.beginPath();
  context.rect(50,50,100,100);
  alert(
    context.isPointInPath(
      evt.clientX - canvas.offsetLeft,
      evt.clientY - canvas.offsetTop
    )
  );
};
```

Unfortunately, `isPointInPath()` does not allow for path transformations: Even if we had moved the coordinate system 200 pixels to the right before issuing the `beginPath()` instruction, clicking on the coordinate 75/75 would still return true. It does, however, take the *non-zero* fill rule into account when determining inside/outside; as already indicated for the two code examples, the path to be tested does not necessarily have to be drawn with `fill()` or `stroke()`.

5.15.2   Accessibility in Canvas?

The question mark in this section heading is deliberate: Canvas is definitely still lacking with regard to accessibility. This is partly due to the fact that during the conception of Canvas, accessibility was given hardly any attention, and partly due to the nature of the issue—raster-based formats without DOM are innately anything but accessible.

In the context of the HTML5 specification, SVG with its DOM would probably be better suited for realizing accessible content. But practice proves that even big projects, such as the web-based code editor *Skywriter* (https://mozillalabs.com/skywriter), use Canvas instead of SVG for the sake of performance, which really breaks the basic rule stated at the beginning of the HTML5 specification's Canvas section: *Authors should not use the canvas element in a document when a more suitable element is available.*

The second requirement, demanding that when *authors use the canvas element, they must also provide content that, when presented to the user, conveys essentially the same function or purpose as the bitmap canvas*, also does not hold true in reality. The area between the canvas start tag and end tag would be intended for such alternatives but is usually only used to specify fallback content for browsers without Canvas support.

For interactive Canvas applications, the HTML Canvas 2D Context specification also suggests including focusable HTML elements in the fallback content, for example, an `input` element for each focusable area of the canvas. Authors should use the method `drawFocusRing()` to mark with a ring those areas of the canvas that currently have the focus in fallback. The example listed in the specification in this context, with a couple of checkboxes that are meant to be kept synchronous in the fallback and canvas area via `drawFocusring()`, demonstrates how complicated the whole thing is and leads us to suspect that this is not the best solution.

Since July 2009, the *Canvas Accessibility Task Force* has been trying to remedy the unsatisfactory situation. They are investigating potential improvements of focus and cursor management. The first lot of suggestions are on the table, being discussed intensely, and may well find their way into the specification in one form or another.

But until that happens, we will just have to deal with it: *Accessibility—please hold!*

5.15.3 Security Aspects

From a security point of view, accessing images and their content (pixels) via scripts in other domains is especially problematic in Canvas. The specification refers to this as *information leakage* and tries to counter this leakage with the *origin-clean flag*.

The concept of *origin-clean* is two-stage and mainly based on certain method calls and attribute assignments setting the *origin-clean flag* from true to false during a running script. If getImageData() or todataURL() are called in such a case, the script aborts with a SECURITY_ERR exception.

The main protagonists are drawImage(), fillStyle, and strokeStyle. They contribute to a redefinition of the *origin-clean flag* whenever images or videos from another domain, or canvas elements that are not *origin-clean* themselves, come into play.

Assuming that the variable image contains a reference to the WHATWG logo at http://www.whatwg.org/images/logo and the script is not running on the WHATWG server, the following drawImage() call sets the *origin-clean flag* to false:

```
context.drawImage(image,0,0);
```

If we use the logo as a pattern, the properties fillStyle and strokeStyle have the same result—*origin-clean* becomes false:

```
var pat = context.createPattern(image);
context.fillStyle = pat;
context.strokeStyle = pat;
```

Each call of getImageData() or toDataURL() from that point on will invariably result in the script being terminated.

In the Firefox browser, this mechanism is handled even more restrictively: Any images loaded via the file:// protocol are classified as not *origin-clean*. So what is the consequence for our chapter? All graphics with a server icon in the bottom-right corner do not work in Firefox if they are opened locally via file://; instead, they can only be displayed by a web server.

TIP

If you do not want to install an Apache server and you have access to Python, you can use just one line to start a rudimentary web server in the current directory at port 8000 and then address the content of this directory in the browser via the url http://localhost:8000:

```
python -m SimpleHTTPServer
```

5.15.4 Browser Support

The current versions of Firefox as well as Safari, Chrome, and Opera support a large part of the Canvas specification. If you want to see Canvas in IE, you will have to use IE9, which offers hardware-accelerated support for Canvas. This makes workarounds for IE8 such as Google's Chrome Frame Plugin (http://code.google.com/chrome/chromeframe) or the JavaScript shim *explorercanvas* (http://code.google.com/p/explorercanvas) obsolete.

As you would expect, there are slight differences in the degree to which those browsers that already support Canvas have implemented it. A useful source for determining the degree of implementation is the *Canvas Testsuite* by Philip Taylor with approximately 800 tests and a table of test results for the main browsers at http://philip.html5.org/tests/canvas/suite/tests.

All examples in this Canvas chapter were created with Firefox, as you can see in the screen shots. At the time of this writing, all examples worked fine in Firefox except for the representation of fonts in small-caps. Safari, Opera, IE9, and Chrome also score quite well with our examples—Safari and Opera more so than IE9 and Chrome.

Because every new release of the common browsers can result in improvements regarding Canvas implementation, regularly updated details of how the examples in our book run in different browsers are provided in the Canvas index on the companion website at http://html5.komplett.cc/code/chap_canvas/index_en.html.

5.15.5 Further Links

A good starting point for exploring Canvas is a portal describing itself as *Home to applications, games, tools and tutorials that use the HTML 5 <canvas> element* at http://www.canvasdemos.com; it offers a series of interesting links. Worth a look is also the extensive Canvas tutorial in Mozilla's *developer center* at https://developer.mozilla.org/en/canvas_tutorial and http://hacks.mozilla.org/category/canvas, a blog of the Mozilla community focusing on advanced application examples.

If you want to get into the details of Canvas, your best bet is the Canvas specification. The current version of the two documents can be found at:

- http://www.w3.org/TR/html5/the-canvas-element.html
- http://www.w3.org/TR/2dcontext

If you prefer an interactive version with stages of implementation and the option of leaving comments directly or reporting errors on the individual sections, go to the WHATWG at http://www.whatwg.org/specs/web-apps/current-work/multipage/the-canvas-element.html.

Summary

Our journey through the world of Canvas has come to an end. It was a long way from drawing two overlapping rectangles in red and yellow to programming a video postcard. You learned how to work with colors, create shadow effects, and draw lines, Bézier curves, arcs, rectangles, and clipping masks. We spent quite some time exploring the key features of Canvas—manipulating images and creating appealing effects by combining pixel manipulation methods with patterns, transformations, and compositing. We even dared to hand-code animations. But although this chapter is the longest in the book, it can only provide a small glimpse into the myriad possibilities offered through Canvas. Many other impressive examples are waiting to be discovered on the Internet—go explore!

6

SVG and MathML

Just two paragraphs are devoted to the vector standard *SVG* and the Mathematical Markup Language *MathML* in the HTML5 specification. Yet the integration of these two XML dialects is another milestone on the way toward web applications of the future. Whereas MathML delights primarily the science sector, everyone profits from SVG: Incorporating a standardized vector format into the browser is long overdue. The topic SVG alone fills entire books and would be far beyond the scope of this book, just as a detailed guide to MathML would not be appropriate here either. So in this chapter, we will only discuss the integration of SVG and MathML in an HTML5 document.

Prerequisite for using SVG and MathML in HTML5 is of course the implementation of both components in the browser. In addition, the *parser* also has to recognize svg and math elements and be able to pass their values to the *layout engine* to be represented as a graphic. At the time of this writing, only Firefox 4 fulfilled all the requirements. Figure 6.1 shows the result using the example of three MathML formulae with corresponding SVG graphics.

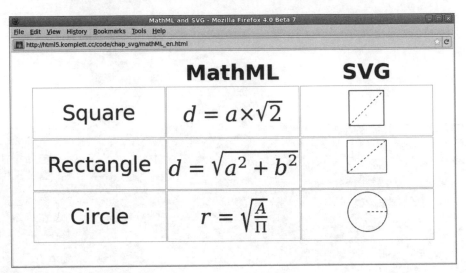

Figure 6.1 MathML and SVG in action

6.1 MathML

To explain the necessary markup, let's use the example with the circle: In Listing 6.1 you can see the source code for the formula to calculate the radius r of a circle with a given area A.

Listing 6.1 MathML markup and formula for circle radius with given area

```
<math>
  <mrow>
    <mi>r</mi>
    <mo>=</mo>
    <msqrt>
      <mfrac>
        <mrow>
          <mi>A</mi>
        </mrow>
        <mrow>
          <mn>&Pi;</mn>
        </mrow>
      </mfrac>
    </msqrt>
  </mrow>
</math>
```

Each MathML block within an HTML5 document begins with `<math>` and ends with `</math>`. In between, you have optional tags for defining the formula—in our case, six different ones, introduced in the order in which they appear in Table 6.1.

Table 6.1   The MathML tags of Listing 6.1 and their meaning

Element	Name	Purpose
mrow	*row*	Element for grouping expressions
mi	*i* for *identifier*	Variable, function name, or constant
mo	*o* for *operator*	Operators such as equal, plus, minus, or multiplication sign
msqrt	*sqrt* for *square root*	Square root expression
mfrac	*frac* for *fraction*	Fractions, division
mn	*n* for *number*	Number

The element `mrow` for grouping expressions appears three times: once for the whole expression and then twice more for distinguishing between numerator and denominator in the division `mfrac`. Radius `r` and area `A` are represented as `mi` elements, the equals sign is represented as a `mo` element, and the root expression is formed with a `msqrt` element. For *pi* we use the `mn` element in combination with the MathML entity `&Pi;`—one of more than 2,000 MathML entities, which we could also have written as Unicode symbol `&#x03A0;` (*GREEK CAPITAL LETTER PI*).

> **NOTE**
>
> The table for converting the named MathML entities to Unicode characters can be found in the MathML specification at http://www.w3.org/TR/REC-MathML/chap6/byalpha.html.

The formula for calculating the diagonal of the square in Figure 6.1 contains another entity as a multiplication sign, `&times;` (as Unicode symbol `&#x00D7;` MULTIPLICATION SIGN), and for squaring the rectangle sides a, b in the center example, we use the `msup` element (*sup* for *superscript*).

Of course, these three MathML examples only show the tip of the iceberg. Starting points for exploring the world of MathML can be found on the following websites. Do not miss the *MathML Basics* examples on the Mozilla project demo page. You will be surprised to see that writing complicated formulas is made possible by MathML! Check out these websites to learn more about MathML:

- **MathML specification:** http://www.w3.org/TR/MathML
- **W3C Math working group:** http://www.w3.org/Math
- **Planet MathML:** http://www.w3.org/Math/planet
- **MathML Demos:** http://www.mozilla.org/projects/mathml/demo

6.2 SVG

To the right of the relevant MathML formula, you can see the corresponding SVG graphic that illustrates the formula's components. Let's again stick with the example of the circle and look at the SVG code in Listing 6.2 for the circle graphic in Figure 6.1.

Listing 6.2   The SVG source code for the circle graphic

```
<svg width="100" height="100">
  <circle cx="50" cy="50" r="45"
          fill="none" stroke="black" />
  <path d="M 50 50 h 45"
        stroke="black" stroke-dasharray="5,5"/>
</svg>
```

At the beginning of the SVG block, we now have <svg> and at the end </svg>. In contrast to MathML, the start tag also specifies the width and height of the graphic, reserving the corresponding amount of space on the HTML page. The circle is a circle element with the center cx/cy and the radius r. The attributes fill and stroke determine what the circle looks like.

The dashed line to indicate the radius is created via a path element whose geometry data is determined in its d attribute. Similar to the canvas element, SVG allows not only lines, but also complex curves in open or closed form as polygons. The syntax for geometry instructions in the d attribute uses numbers for coordinates plus letters for identifying the path type, which follows the relevant abbreviation: So, d="M 50 50 h 45" means *Move to point 50/50 and then draw a horizontal line to the right with a length of 45.*

The square and rectangle demonstrate that other notations are also possible. Capital letters indicate absolute movements; lowercase letters indicate relative movements. The square's diagonal is created with d="M 10 90 L 90 10". That would be the equivalent of *Move to point 10/90 and then draw a line to point 90/10*. The rectangle's diagonal is done with d="M 5 80 l 90 -75", which means *Move to point 5/80 and then draw a line from there to the point located 90 pixels to the right and 75 pixels up.*

The dashed lines for the circle radius and the diagonals for the square and rectangle are created by the attribute `stroke-dasharray`, a feature that is unfortunately missing in the Canvas specification. Its attribute value determines the switch between *draw line* and *insert space*, and the switching process is repeated until the line is finished. For more complicated patterns, any number of values separated by commas can be entered.

Last but not least, the geometric forms square and rectangle are two `rect` elements with `x`, `y`, `width`, and `height` attributes, which means we have covered all elements and attributes appearing in the SVG code of the graphics. Of course, the same applies here as with MathML: This is just the tip of the iceberg, and this time really just the tiniest top bit of it. Beneath, geometric shapes of all kinds are lurking, as are mighty path drawing methods, text layouts, transformations, freely definable coordinate systems, filters, gradients, symbols, masks, patterns, compositing, clipping, scripting, styling, and even animations.

If you want to dive more deeply into the topic SVG, you should definitely invest in a book on SVG. The following links offer further opportunities to start exploring the topic online:

- **The SVG specification:** http://www.w3.org/TR/SVG11

- **An SVG Primer for Today's Browsers:** http://www.w3.org/Graphics/SVG/IG/resources/svgprimer.html

- **W3C SVG Working Group:** http://www.w3.org/Graphics/SVG

- **Learn SVG: The Web Graphics Standard:** http://www.learnsvg.com

Summary

With the arrival of IE9, all browsers finally offer native SVG support, after ten years of vector standard. We hope the same will apply to MathML; its integration in the HTML5 specification will play its part, just as it did with SVG. As essential components of the new web platform, MathML, and especially SVG, will certainly play an even more important role in the future.

7

Geolocation

The Geolocation API was removed from the core of the HTML5 specification and is, according to the W3C nomenclature, just in its early stages. But it is already largely implemented, particularly in mobile browsers. One reason for the rapid implementation is most likely because the interface is short and abstract: Only three JavaScript calls cover the whole range of functions. The specification does not state how the browser has to determine locations, only the format in which the result should be returned.

After a brief introduction regarding the nature of geographical data, we will demonstrate the new functions using several brief examples. If you try our examples on a smartphone, you will quickly experience that *Aha! Effect.*

7.1   Introduction to Geolocation

This section introduces you to the basics of geolocation. It covers geographical data and online map services.

7.1.1   About Geographical Data

You may already have come across a coordinate in the format N47 16 06.6 E11 23 35.9. The position is specified in degrees-minutes-seconds. In this example, the desired location is at a latitude of 47 degrees, 16 minutes, and 6.6 seconds north, and a longitude of 11 degrees, 23 minutes, and 35.9 seconds east. These kinds of coordinates are referred to as geographical coordinates. Unfortunately, the great drawback with these values is that they are very difficult to calculate with, not just because we are used to thinking in decimal numbers. Because the coordinates specify a position on the spheroid Earth, the curvature of the planet's surface has to be taken into account when calculating distances.

To simplify the situation, projected coordinates are used in practice. The spheroid Earth is divided into strips where the linear distance between points can be measured. Many countries use their own coordinate system, adapted to local requirements. In Austria, for example, data is referenced in the *Bundesmelde-netz*, a Cartesian coordinate system. All common coordinate systems have a numeric identifier, the *EPSG* code (administrated by the *European Petroleum Survey Group*).

Obviously, the Geolocation API cannot take into account every existing coordinate system. The x and y coordinates are therefore not projected but are specified in geographical coordinates in decimal degrees. The standard specifies the widely used *World Geodetic System 1984* (*WGS84*) as a geodetic reference system. It basically describes the underlying reference ellipsoid. The y value is specified in meters above this ellipsoid. Any point on or near Earth can be described with sufficient accuracy using this system.

7.1.2   Online Map Services

To represent geographical data in a browser, you have several options: SVG is very well suited due to its flexible coordinate system, and data can be drawn as a raster image using canvas. The easiest solution is to use an existing JavaScript library. Of the free libraries available online, we will look closer at Google Maps and OpenStreetMap. Microsoft's map service *Bing Maps* can only be used after registering, so we will not discuss it here.

The two libraries introduced in this chapter use a mixture of raster and vector data for display. To enable faster loading times, the raster images are subdivided into tiles and calculated in advance for all zoom levels, allowing for step-by-step image construction. Vector information is displayed, depending on the browser, in SVG or in the Microsoft specific VML format for Internet Explorer.

7.1.2.1 Google Maps

Google Maps is undoubtedly the most widely used map service on the Internet. Many companies use the free service to cartographically represent their location. But Google Maps can do much more than place position markers on a map. As you can see from the website http://maps.google.com/help/maps/casestudies, more than 150,000 websites use Google Maps, including large companies, such as the *New York Times*.

The library's current version, V3, is very different from earlier versions: To use it, you no longer need an API key (so registration with Google is not required), and the library was optimized for use on mobile devices. As is so often the case with Google products, programming is very straightforward. For a simple road map of Central Europe, you need only a few lines of HTML and JavaScript, as shown in Listing 7.1:

Listing 7.1 Road map of Central Europe with Google Maps

```html
<html>
 <head>
 <script type="text/javascript"
  src="http://maps.google.com/maps/api/js?sensor=true">
 </script>
 <script type="text/javascript">
  window.onload = function() {
    var map =
      new google.maps.Map(document.getElementById("map"),
        { center: new google.maps.LatLng(47,11),
          zoom: 7,
          mapTypeId: google.maps.MapTypeId.ROADMAP
        }
    );
  }
 </script>
 <body>
  <div id="map" style="width:100%; height:100%"></div>
```

When loading the library, you must specify the `sensors` parameter. If it is set to true, the device can determine its position and inform the application. This is particularly useful for mobile devices (such as smartphones with GPS). Once the entire page is loaded (`window.onload`), a new object with the type `google.maps.Map` is created, whose constructor receives as its first parameter the HTML element provided for displaying the map. The second parameter determines a list of options of what is displayed on the map and how. In this case, the center of the map is set to 47 degrees north and 11 degrees east with a zoom level of 7 (zoom level 0 is equivalent to a view of the whole Earth), and the map type is specified as road map via the constant `google.maps.MapTypeId.ROADMAP`.

NOTE

Because the map object's constructor contains a reference to the content of the HTML page, it can only be called once the website is loaded; that is, at `window.onload`.

7.1.2.2   OpenStreetMap/OpenLayers

OpenStreetMap was introduced in 2004 with the ambitious aim of becoming a comprehensive and free platform for geodata worldwide. Following the successful method adopted by Wikipedia, it was supposed to be easy for users to record geographical elements in their surrounding area and save them online. Considering the difficulty of editing geodata, the current state of the project is impressive. Thousands of users have uploaded their GPS data to the platform openstreetmap.org or corrected and commented on data on the website. Also, existing geodata with a suitable license was integrated into the database (for example, the US *TIGER* data and the *Landsat 7* satellite images).

Several tools were created in association with the project, with which you can download data from the OpenStreetMap servers and – provided you have permission – upload and save that data to the server. The open interface makes it easy for software developers to integrate their products into the system.

A significant factor in the success of OpenStreetMap is the simple option for web developers to integrate maps into their websites through the OpenLayers project. This JavaScript library is not limited to OpenStreetMap but can definitely show its strength through this interaction. With OpenLayers, you can also access maps by Google, Microsoft, Yahoo, and countless other geographic services (based on the standards *WMS* and *WFS*).

A mini example of a road map in Central Europe with OpenLayers and OpenStreetMap is provided in Listing 7.2:

Listing 7.2   Road map of Central Europe with OpenStreetMap and OpenLayers

```
<!DOCTYPE html>
<html>
<head>
<title>Geolocation - OpenLayers / OpenStreetMap</title>
<script src=
"http://www.openlayers.org/api/OpenLayers.js"></script>
<script src=
"http://www.openstreetmap.org/openlayers/OpenStreetMap.js">
```

```
    </script>
    <script>
      window.onload = function() {
        var map = new OpenLayers.Map("map");
        map.addLayer(new
          OpenLayers.Layer.OSM.Osmarender("Osmarender"));
        var lonLat = new OpenLayers.LonLat(11, 47).transform(
            new OpenLayers.Projection("EPSG:4326"),
            map.getProjectionObject()
        );
        map.setCenter (lonLat,7);
      }
    </script>
    <body>
      <div id="map" style="top: 0; left: 0; bottom: 0;
        right: 0; position: fixed;"></div>
    </body>
  </html>
```

For this example, we need to load both the JavaScript library of openlayers.org and the library of openstreetmap.org. Similar to Google Maps, an HTML `div` element is assigned to the `OpenLayers.Map` object for representation, and a layer of the type `Osmarender` is added—the standard map view of OpenStreetMap (OSM). Here, a special feature of OpenStreetMap comes into play: As mentioned in section 7.1.1, About Geographical Data, three-dimensional information must be projected to be displayed in 2D on the screen. Although Google Maps does not harass the user with these details and you simply specify the x and y coordinates in decimal degrees, OpenLayers asks you to first project data in decimal degrees into the relevant coordinate system. Internally, OpenLayers (just like Google Maps, Yahoo! Maps, and Microsoft Bing Maps) creates the map representation with a projection, the so-called *Spherical Mercator* (*EPSG* code 3785). In Spherical Mercator, coordinates are managed in meters instead of decimal degrees, which is why the degree values used here must be converted to the coordinate system used in the map (determined with the function `map.getProjectionObject()`) with the call `transform()` and specify the *EPSG* code of the desired projection (`EPSG:4326`).

WARNING

If you use DOCTYPE at the beginning of the document, as is correct with HTML5, the HTML element in which the map is displayed must contain a position of `fixed` or `absolute`. Otherwise, the OpenLayers library displays nothing. Interestingly, this limitation does not apply if no DOCTYPE is included. More information on this topic can be found in a posting on the mailing list at http://openlayers.org/pipermail/users/2009-July/012860.html.

7.2 A First Experiment: Geolocation in the Browser

To test your browser's geolocation function, you just need the JavaScript code in Listing 7.3:

Listing 7.3   Function for outputting position with "navigator.geolocation"

```
function $(id) { return document.getElementById(id); }
window.onload = function() {
  if (navigator.geolocation) {
    navigator.geolocation.getCurrentPosition(
        function(pos) {
            $("lat").innerHTML = pos.coords.latitude;
            $("lon").innerHTML = pos.coords.longitude;
            $("alt").innerHTML = pos.coords.altitude;
        },
        function() {},
        {enableHighAccuracy:true, maximumAge:600000}
    );
  } else {
    $("status").innerHTML =
      'No Geolocation support for your Browser';
  }
}
```

The first line of the listing defines an auxiliary function $, allowing for an abbreviated notation of the function document.getElementById() (similar to an alias). This trick was taken from the familiar *jQuery* library and is very convenient for our example, because the elements that need to be filled are marked with an ID attribute on the website. As in the previous examples (see Listings 7.1 and 7.2), window.onload ensures that the content of the website is fully loaded before references to HTML elements are set. The first if query checks if the browser supports the *Geolocation API*. If that is not the case, an appropriate message is written into the element with the ID status. Otherwise, the actual function for determining position is activated: navigator.geolocation.getCurrentPosition().

According to the specification, the browser has to ask when calling this function if you want it to locate your current position and share it on the website. Figure 7.1 shows the relevant dialog box in Mozilla Firefox.

Figure 7.1   Mozilla Firefox asks for permission to share your location

Three arguments are passed to the function call:

- A function to be executed after the position has successfully been determined (*success callback*)

- A function that can react to errors if the position could not be determined (*error callback*)

- Value pairs influencing how the position is determined

According to the specification, the two latter arguments are optional; the *success callback* always has to be specified. So as not to impede the JavaScript sequence, getCurrentPosition() has to be executed asynchronously in the background, and the relevant callback function can only be called once the position is known or an error has occurred.

In this very short example, both callback functions are implemented as *anonymous functions*; errors are not considered. The value pair enableHighAccuracy: true tells the browser to calculate the position as accurately as possible. On an Android cell phone, this setting causes activation of the internal GPS sensor (more on this in section 7.3, Technical Background of Determining Position). Finally, maximumAge specifies the time in milliseconds during which an already determined position can be reused. After that time, the position has to be redetermined—in our case, every ten minutes.

After successfully determining the position, the variable pos of the *success callback* in the so-called Position interface contains coordinate data (pos.coords) plus a timestamp in milliseconds since 1970 (pos.timestamp). Figure 7.2 shows the available attributes and their respective values, if present.

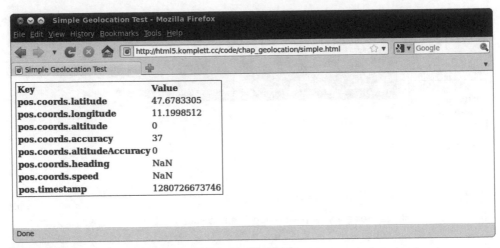

Figure 7.2 Geographic position output in Mozilla Firefox

In addition to latitude, longitude, and altitude, pos.coords also includes information about the accuracy of the position (accuracy, altitudeAccuracy) plus possible speed and direction (heading). Whereas Google Chrome is limited to the attributes required in the specification, Firefox (here, version 3.6) outputs quite a lot of additional information—even address details (see Listing 7.4), showing an extract of the result of JSON.stringify(pos):

Listing 7.4 Extract from the result of JSON.stringify(pos) for Firefox 3.6

```
{"coords":
..// ...
   "address":
     {"streetNumber":"6","street":"Postgasse",
      "premises":null,"city":"Murnau am Staffelsee",
      "county":"Garmisch-Partenkirchen","region":"Bavaria",
      "country":"Germany","countryCode":"DE",
      "postalCode":"82418","contractID":"",
      "classDescription":"wifi geo position address object",
      // ...
     },
   // ...
}
```

The browser offers a remarkable amount of information! Where it all comes from will be explained in the following section.

7.3   Technical Background of Determining Position

If you access the website http://www.google.com from abroad, you may be surprised to find that you are automatically redirected to the relevant Google domain of the country you are in. This works even if your browser is not geolocation capable: Google uses a simple trick and locates your whereabouts via the IP address.

Browsers supporting the Geolocation API can achieve a significantly greater accuracy by making use of other technical options. The following four methods are currently in use:

1.   In PCs with wired Internet connections, the position is located via the IP address. This way of determining position is rather inaccurate, as you would expect.
2.   The position can be determined much more precisely if there is a wireless LAN connection. Google has collected data worldwide from public and private WLANs.
3.   If the hardware has a mobile communications chip (for example, in a smartphone), it tries to calculate the position within the mobile communications network.
4.   If the hardware also has a GPS sensor, the position can be determined even more accurately. GPS is a satellite-based positioning system and can achieve accuracy to the meter range even with cheap sensors, provided the conditions are favorable (outside of buildings, unobstructed horizon, etc.).

Only the GPS sensor works *offline*; methods 1–3 require Internet access and are implemented through a server location service. These services are available from Google (Google Location Service, used in Firefox, Chrome, and Opera) and another American company, *Skyhook Wireless* (used in Safari and early versions of Opera).

But how do the service providers get the location information of wireless and mobile networks? In parallel with the photos taken by Google for the service *Street View*, the Google Street View vehicles also save information on public and private WLANs. The revelation, in spring 2010, that these vehicles collected not only the MAC address and SSID of the WLAN, but also user data, shed a bad light on Google, resulting in several public apologies.

But that is not all: If the browser has access to the information on a mobile network or wireless LAN router, this data is sent with every call of the service. For Google, this concerns mainly mobile communication devices with the *Android* operating system; Skyhook profits from the iPhone users. The combination of the described methods leads to a very large data set of geodata available to these two service providers and is continuously updated through *crowdsourcing* (even if the users as data providers do not know anything about it).

7.4   Display of Current Position on OpenStreetMap

In the following example, the current location is represented on a map of Open-StreetMap and indicated with a marker. You can see different layers and the OpenStreetMap navigation bar. Figure 7.3 shows the OpenStreetMap's *Mapnik* layer with the position marker in the center of the browser.

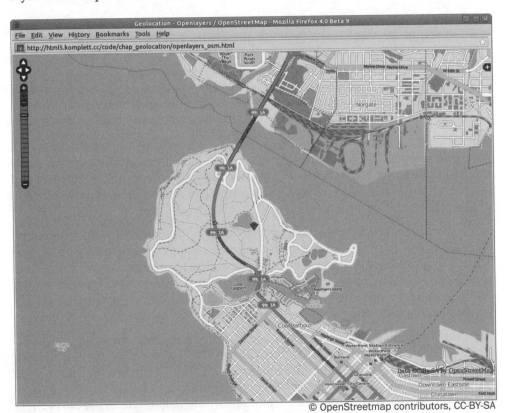

Figure 7.3   Current location using OpenLayers and OpenStreetMap

Just as in section 7.1.2, Online Map Services, the data of the OpenStreetMap project is represented using the OpenLayers library. After the two required JavaScript files are loaded, the map is initialized in this example and the desired control elements are added:

```
// Initialize map and add navigation
var map = new OpenLayers.Map ("map");
map.addControl(new OpenLayers.Control.Navigation());
map.addControl(new OpenLayers.Control.PanZoomBar());
```

In addition to the navigation element with the four arrows, we attach the zoom bar to the map variable (map). We then create the selection element for the various layers (Control.LayerSwitcher) and add several layers to the map. The function call of map.addLayers() receives an array of newly created map objects:

```
// Layer selection with four map types
map.addControl(new OpenLayers.Control.LayerSwitcher());
map.addLayers([
   new OpenLayers.Layer.OSM.Mapnik("Mapnik"),
   new OpenLayers.Layer.OSM.Osmarender("Osmarender"),
   new OpenLayers.Layer.OSM.CycleMap("CycleMap")
]);
```

To finish, the map gets a layer for the marker:

```
var markers = new OpenLayers.Layer.Markers("Markers");
map.addLayer(markers);
```

The success callback after successfully determining the position looks like this:

```
function(pos) {
   var ll = new OpenLayers.LonLat(
      pos.coords.longitude,
      pos.coords.latitude).transform(
         new OpenLayers.Projection("EPSG:4326"),
         map.getProjectionObject()
      );
   map.setCenter (ll,zoom);
   markers.addMarker(
      new OpenLayers.Marker(
      ll,new OpenLayers.Icon(
'http://www.openstreetmap.org/openlayers/img/marker.png')
      )
   );
},
```

As you already know from section 7.1.2, Online Map Services, the coordinates from the geographical coordinate system (lat/lon) must be converted to the *Spherical Mercator* system. Finally, the marker ll is placed on the determined location; the relevant icon for the marker is loaded directly off the OpenStreet-MapThe Geolocation specification includes another call, particularly suitable for moving objects: `navigator.geolocation.watchPosition()`. The next example demonstrates how a change in location can be represented graphically using the Google Maps API.

7.5 Location Tracking with Google Maps

Our quick example only makes sense if used on mobile devices. Of course, you can "get things moving" artificially for demo purposes, but you will most likely only get a real sense of achievement once you manage to determine your location accurately via GPS and using a browser while on the move. A crucial component of the following experiment was an Android smartphone showing the HTML page during a trip down the highway.

As you can see in Figure 7.4, the last five locations determined on Google Maps are marked on the map. As soon as the user leaves the map area represented on the screen, the map is centered around the next point.

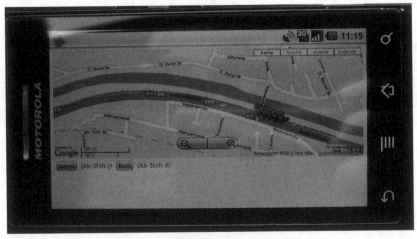

Figure 7.4   Google Maps API on an Android cell phone

Calling the Geolocation API is once again done in `window.onload` and looks like this:

```
var watchID = navigator.geolocation.watchPosition(
  moveMe, posError, {enableHighAccuracy: true}
);
```

The real work takes place in the function moveMe():

```
function moveMe(position) {
  latlng = new google.maps.LatLng(
    position.coords.latitude,
    position.coords.longitude);
  bounds = map.getBounds();
  map.setZoom(16);
  if (!bounds.contains(latlng)) {
    map.setCenter(latlng);
  }
  if (marker.length >= maxMarkers) {
    m = marker.shift();
    if (m) {
      m.setMap();
    }
  }
  marker.push(new google.maps.Marker({
    position: latlng, map: map,
    title: position.coords.accuracy+"m lat: "
      +position.coords.latitude+" lon: "+
      position.coords.longitude
  }));
}
```

The variable latlng is created as a LatLng object from the Google Maps API, and the current coordinates are passed to this object. If the current location is outside of the represented area (!bounds.contains(latlng)), the map is re-centered over the current point. Both the array marker and the variable maxMarkers at the beginning of the script are defined as global and assigned the value 5. If the array marker contains more than five elements, the first element is removed from the array with the shift function and then deleted from the map by calling setMap() without any further parameters. Finally, a new object of the type marker is added to the array in the current location.

7.6 Example: Geonotes

The idea for this example originated during a trip abroad with a new smartphone: The program is a digital travel diary that automatically adds geographical coordinates to each entry and can display all entries on a map. The high data-roaming charges in Europe soon made it necessary to integrate another technology related to HTML5—Web Storage—to keep costs down. Via the *Web Storage API*, the entries are stored locally in persistent memory, allowing the application to function even without an existing data connection. For a detailed explanation of the Web Storage API, see Chapter 8, Web Storage and Offline Web Applications.

7.6.1 Operation

The application has a very simple structure (see Figure 7.5): In the text box (top left) you can enter your diary notes. The new HTML5 placeholder attribute lets the browser show an invitation to enter a new message. If you have already entered notes, the area on the right displays a map section of Google Maps. Underneath is the list of entries, including not just the message text, but also location, time of entry, and distance to current location. You also have the option of deleting messages or displaying the location enlarged on Google Maps. As you can see in Figure 7.5, the enlarged representation indicates the location with a marker typical for Google. The circle around the location marker indicates the accuracy of the determined location.

Because you tend not to constantly change location while developing an application, the Firefox add-on *Geolocater*, introduced in section 7.3, Technical Background of Determining Position, comes in handy. You have the option of saving several locations in the add-on, allowing you to test the application while at home. Ideally though, the application would be used on a smartphone with GPS support. Both Android-based cell phones and the *iPhone* fulfill the necessary requirements.

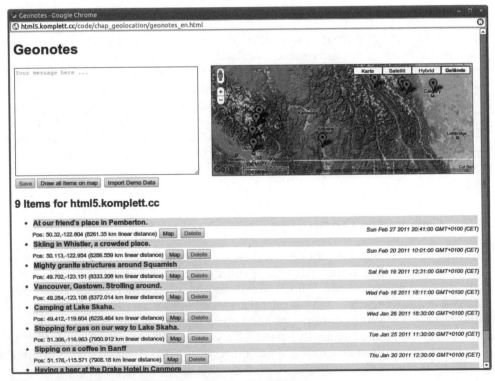

Figure 7.5 Notes with additional geographic information

To be able to test the application right away, you can use the demo data. These entries are partly made up and partly actual entries recorded by the author while developing the application.

7.6.2 Important Code Fragments

The HTML code for the application offers several div container elements, which will later house the messages (id='items') and the map (id='map'). As mentioned previously, the textarea element contains the new placeholder attribute, which can make applications much more user friendly. The relevant onclick event listener is directly assigned to the three button elements:

```
<body>
  <h1>Geonotes</h1>
  <div class='text_input'>
    <textarea style='float:left;margin-right:30px;'
      placeholder='Your message here ...'
      cols="50" rows="15" id="note"></textarea>
    <div class='map' id='map'></div>
    <div style='clear:both;' id='status'></div>
    <button style='float:left;color:green;' id='save'
      onclick='saveItem()'>Save</button>
    <button onclick='drawAllItems()'>Draw all items on
      map</button>
    <button onclick='importDemoData()'>Import Demo Data
    </button>
  </div>
  <div class='items' id='items'></div>
```

The JavaScript code is much more interesting than the few lines of HTML code. It defines an auxiliary function and three global variants:

```
function $(id) { return document.getElementById(id); }
  var map;
  var my_pos;
  var diaryItem = { id: 0, pos: 0, ts: 0, msg: '' }
```

You have already encountered the function $ in section 7.2, A First Experiment: Geolocation in the Browser. It saves you a lot of typing effort here, too, and makes the code easier to read. The variable map serves as a reference to the HTML area, which will accommodate the Google Maps representation. my_pos is required for calculating the distance and contains the current location from which the script is called. diaryItem represents the structure of the individual entries. Each diary entry is assigned an ID (id), information on the current position (pos), a time-stamp (ts) , and the message entered into the text field (msg).

As soon as the page is fully loaded, the current location is determined and existing entries are displayed:

```
window.onload = function() {
  if (navigator.geolocation) {
    navigator.geolocation.getCurrentPosition(
      function(pos) {
        my_pos = pos;
        showItems();
      },
      posError,
      { enableHighAccuracy: true, maximumAge: 60000 }
    );
  }
  showItems();
  if (localStorage.length > 0) {
    drawAllItems();
  }
}
```

The option enableHighAccuracy is activated to call getCurrentPosition(). The maximum time for reusing an already determined position is one minute. If the position is successfully determined, the previously defined global variable my_pos is assigned the values of the just determined position and then the function show-Items() is called. An error in determining the position leads to calling the function posError(), a function that outputs the corresponding error message in a dialog window. If the number of elements in the localStorage is greater than 0, the function drawAllItems() is executed as well, displaying existing entries on Google Maps.

The showItems function assembles a string of all entries and assigns it to the HTML element with the ID items:

```
function showItems() {
  var s = '<h2>'+localStorage.length+' Items for '
    +location.hostname+'</h2>';
  s+= '<ul>';
  var i_array = getAllItems();
  for (k in i_array) {
    var item = i_array[k];
    var iDate = new Date(item.ts);
    s+= '<li>';
    s+= '<p class="msg">'+item.msg+'</p>';
    s+= '<div class="footer">';
    s+= '<p class="i_date">'+iDate.toLocaleString();
      +'</p>';
    ...
  $('items').innerHTML = s+'</ul>';
```

The variable i_array is filled with the result of the function getAllItems(), which reads the localStorage, returns the contents as objects in an array, and sorts the objects by date:

```
function getAllItems() {
  var i_array = [];
  for (var i=0;i<localStorage.length;i++) {
    try {
      var item = JSON.parse(
        localStorage.getItem(localStorage.key(i))
      );
      i_array.push(item);
    } catch (err) {
      continue;    // skip this entry, no valid JSON data
    }
  }
  i_array.sort(function(a, b) {
    return b.ts - a.ts
  });
  return i_array;
}
```

The call localStorage.getItem() gets an element from the persistent memory, converting it to a JavaScript object via the function JSON.parse. The requirement is that the object be converted to a string with JSON.stringify during saving (see the following code listing). To avoid the script being aborted due to any items in local storage that are not JSON encoded, the instruction is enclosed in a try/catch block. The objects are added to the end of the array i_array with i_array.push() and sorted by date in the next step. To tell the JavaScript function sort which criteria it should sort by, it is expanded with an anonymous function. The variable ts allows temporal sorting of the objects. It contains the numbers of milliseconds since 1.1.1970, a value created via the JavaScript function new Date().getTime(). If the anonymous function returns a negative value, a is arranged after b; for a positive value, a comes before b.

We still need to answer the question about how new entries are created and saved. The function saveItem() takes care of this, initializing a local variable d to which we assign the structure diaryItem:

```
function saveItem() {
  var d = diaryItem;
  d.msg = $('note').value;
  if (d.msg == '') {
    alert("Empty message");
    return;
  }
  d.ts = new Date().getTime();
  d.id = "geonotes_"+d.ts;
```

```
if (navigator.geolocation) {
  $('status').innerHTML = '<span style="color:red">'
     +'getting current position / item unsaved</span>';
  navigator.geolocation.getCurrentPosition(
    function(pos) {
      d.pos = pos.coords;
      localStorage.setItem(d.id, JSON.stringify(d));
      $('status').innerHTML =
         '<span style="color:green">item saved. Position'
         +' is: '+pos.coords.latitude
         +','+pos.coords.longitude+'</span>';
      showItems();
    },
    posError,
    { enableHighAccuracy: true, maximumAge: 60000 }
  );
} else {
  // alert("Browser does not support Geolocation");
  localStorage.setItem(d.id, JSON.stringify(d));
  $('status').innerHTML =
     "Browser does not support Geolocation/item saved.";
}
showItems();
}
```

If the text field is empty (d.msg = ''), a corresponding dialog appears and the function is terminated with return. Otherwise, the timestamp is set to the current millisecond, and the entry's ID is assembled from the string geonotes_ and the timestamp. If several applications should access the localStorage from one server, the string prefix can help to distinguish the data. After the position has been successfully determined, the variable pos within the diaryItem object is filled with coordinates and the appropriate meta information, and then saved as a JSON string in the localStorage via JSON.stringify().

If the browser does not support the Geolocation API, the application saves the text anyway and points out that there is no support. The final call of showItems() ensures that the list of messages is updated.

7.7 Browser Support

As mentioned previously, the functions for determining location offer many new possibilities, especially for use on mobile devices. The most important mobile platforms at the time of this writing are products by Apple (*iPhone, iPad, iPod*) and Android cell phones. Both Google's browser (standard on the Android platform) and Safari (for Apple devices) support the Geolocation API.

Desktop browsers also offer a good level of support. Safari and Google Chrome include the required functions from version 5 and later; Firefox has been Geolocation-capable since version 3.5. Opera integrates the function in its browser in version 10.60 and later. Only Microsoft still fails to offer support for any kind of geolocation in the browser, and unfortunately, this even applies to the mobile platform Windows Phone 7.

Summary

In this chapter you encounter the new geolocation functions, which open amazing new possibilities, especially for mobile devices. With the rapid spread of smartphones, location-based services are becoming available to more and more people. They make it easy for users on the move to gather information, be it finding the nearest cash machine or the best public transport connection. At the moment, these tasks are still carried out by special apps that have to be developed and constantly updated separately for each mobile operating system. By implementing the Geolocation API, such functions can in the future be handled by the browser.

8
Web Storage and
Offline Web Applications

The greater complexity of web applications leads to an increase in the network bandwidth used. Although the capacity of data lines continues to increase as well, ways need to be found to optimize these transmissions by reducing them. Up until now, there was only one standardized method of storing information on the client side: cookies. Given that each cookie belonging to a website is transmitted fully from the client to the server with each call of the site, cookies should not be excessively large. In addition, web servers limit the maximum size of HTTP request fields, for example, to 8KB in the Apache server's default setting.

The solutions suggested by the WHATWG fall into two categories, which are both discussed in this chapter. On one hand, the WHATWG envisions a "Storage interface" with persistent storage for sessions and storage that is not restricted to one session. On the other hand, controlled by a central configuration, files can be defined that the browser stores locally to be able to access them even without a network connection. Both approaches are very straightforward and simple, yet robust.

8.1 Storage

A structured client-side storage that exceeds the meager cookie limit has long been requested as an extension of the World Wide Web. Adobe integrated a function for storing data locally in the Flash Player with version 6, calling this technique Local Shared Object (LSO). The default setting of LSOs is 100KB, but it can swell to 10MB if required (after confirmation by the user). The problem with LSOs, often also referred to as Flash cookies, is that they can only be used with Flash and therefore fall outside the browser's security model. Even if a user deletes all his browser cookies, a website can still track the user via Flash cookies. According to Wikipedia, more than half of the top websites on the Internet use Flash cookies to analyze user behavior.

The WHATWG has recorded its deliberations on the subject in its *Web Storage* document. Although Web Storage was removed from the core of the HTML5 specification, it is still most definitely related to it. Currently, the W3C specification is still at the *Editor's Draft* stage, but because the implementation has been stable in all common browsers for some time (see section 8.3, Browser Support), significant future changes are unlikely.

NOTE

The current version of the W3C's Web Storage specification can be found at http://dev.w3.org/html5/webstorage.

The WHATWG version is available at http://www.whatwg.org/specs/web-apps/current-work/complete/webstorage.html.

8.1.1 The "Storage" Interface

The "Storage" interface defines the common attributes and access methods of the persistent storage. Regardless of whether it is a sessionStorage or a localStorage object, both contain the methods or attributes presented in Table 8.1.

Table 8.1 Methods and attributes of the "Storage interface"

Attribute/Method	Return Value	Description
length	*integer*	Number of key/value pairs associated with this object (read-only access)
key(n)	*DOMString*	Name of the key in position *n*
getItem(key)	*data*	Value of the given *key* (a *DOMString*)
setItem(key,data)	*void*	Saves the value *data* of the *key*
removeItem(key)	*void*	Deletes the content of the *key*
clear()	*void*	Deletes all key/value pairs of this object

Similar to cookies, the Storage interface manages key/value pairs, where the key has the type DOMString. According to the W3C DOM specification, *DOMString*s are strings encoded in UTF-16, which means you could even use special characters as key values, for example the German umlauts (ü, ö, ä). You could, but usually it is advisable not to; instead, it is better to use only characters and numbers from the US-ASCII character set. Even an empty string is a legal key but is usually not chosen on purpose. If an already existing key is used in the function setItem, the existing value is replaced by the new one.

Apart from setItem() and getItem(), the *Web Storage API* also offers another access method, which is often easier to read. If you, for example, want to save the key currentTemp with the value 18 in *localStorage*, the following line is enough:

```
localStorage.currentTemp = 18;
```

Not surprisingly, the value can also be read back this way:

```
alert(localStorage.currentTemp);
```

If *localStorage* contains an unknown number of items, the "Storage interface" method key works well:

```
for (var i=0;i<localStorage.length;i++) {
  var item =
    localStorage.getItem(localStorage.key(i));
    alert("Found item "+item);
}
```

The specification states that values can be of any type, but the current browser implementations save all values as strings. To save complex data types such as arrays or objects, they have to be converted to strings first. An elegant way of doing this is via the *JSON* library:

```
JSON.stringify(itemsObject)
```

How much disk space the browser should reserve for the website is only hinted at in the specification. The recommended limit for the storage space that can be used per *origin* is 5MB (see section 8.1.3, "localStorage"). The current browser implementations adhere to this recommendation.

8.1.2 "sessionStorage"

One problem with using cookies is that the cookie is directly connected to the website and is independent of the browser window. The problem can become acute in the following example: A web shop saves the desired shopping cart in a cookie on the browser. If you open a second browser window while shopping and start shopping under a different name in that window, the products in the original window may change as well.

Although cookies can apply to several windows, the validity of *sessionStorage* is limited to the current browser window, which can be desirable in many cases. Figure 8.1 shows the difference between the two approaches using a simple example.

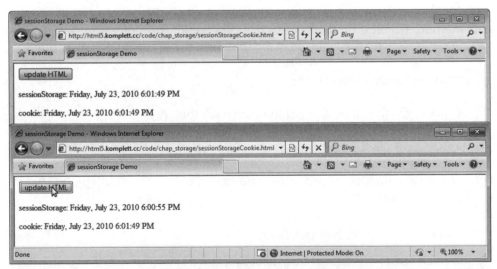

Figure 8.1   Two windows demonstrating the difference between "sessionStorage" and cookies

The central part of the JavaScript code for the example in Figure 8.1 looks like this:

```
window.onload = function() {
  var currDate = new Date();
  sessionStorage.setItem("currenttime",
    currDate.toLocaleString());
  document.cookie =
    "currenttime="+currDate.toLocaleString();
  updateHTML();
}
function updateHTML() {
  document.getElementById("currenttime").innerHTML =
    sessionStorage.getItem("currenttime");
  document.getElementById("currtimeCookie").innerHTML
    = getCookie("currenttime");
}
```

As soon as the website is loaded (`window.onload` function), the current date (including the time) is saved in both *sessionStorage* and the cookie. The `updateHTML` function inserts the relevant values in two HTML elements on the website. If the website is opened in two different browser windows, opening the second window will overwrite the cookie variable `currenttime`. If you then call the `updateHTML` function in the first window, the contents of *sessionStorage* and cookie differ.

In the specification, *sessionStorage* is assigned to the top-level browsing context. Simply put, this context can be seen as an opened browser window or an opened tab within a browser window. A nested browsing context would be, for example, an `iframe` within an HTML document. The browser also must ensure that each website has access only to its own *sessionStorage* and cannot read the contents of other websites. If this context is no longer accessible (the browser window or tab were closed), the browser can permanently delete the associated data.

8.1.3 "localStorage"

In contrast to *sessionStorage*, *localStorage* refers only to the origin of the website, not to the browser context. The origin is derived from the URL and consists of the used scheme in lowercase (for example, *http*), the server name (also in lowercase), and the port. If the port is not explicitly stated, the scheme's default port is used (for HTTP, it would be 80). The origin of the URL http://www.google.com/about consists of the three values `http`, `www.google.com`, and 80.

This means that the origin in the form mentioned in the preceding paragraph is the same for all websites on a server. Security issues ensue for web-hosting forms, which host all users under one domain, for example, Google's free service sites.google.com. Because the different homepages are all in the same directory, http://sites.google.com/site, different users have access to the same *localStorage*. The specification suggests that in such environments, *localStorage* should not be used.

8.1.4 The "storage" Event

Every data change in the storage fires a `storage` event. The `storage` event offers read access to the key, the value before and after the change, the script's URL that caused the change, and a reference to the storage object where the change was made.

The implementation of the `storage` event in current browsers can only be described as rather experimental. In Firefox 3.6, for example, the event is fired, but it does not contain the expected values. In Firefox 4 Beta 3, the *event handler* function was not started. Internet Explorer 8 does not know the standard call for attaching an event handler, `window.addEventListener`; instead, you have to use `window.onstorage`. The expected event then has to be read from the global `window.event`. The third Beta version of Internet Explorer 9 did not react to either event handler. Even Safari 5 did not show results for the `storage` event. Only Opera (version 10.60) and Google Chrome (version 6) returned the expected data for the `storage` event.

8.1.5 Debugging

While developing a web application, being able to see the current content of the persistent storage is very helpful. It is possible to fetch individual elements via `getItem()` and display them in an `alert()` window, but sometimes you just want to see the items listed as a simple table. Different browsers offer different options.

Firefox does not have its own graphic interface for displaying storage content; you need to use a free add-on. Firebug has been renowned among web developers for years as an indispensable extension of the Firefox browser and naturally also masters *localStorage* and *sessionStorage*. To look at the storage, you only need to enter the word *localStorage* or *sessionStorage* in the console, and the JavaScript object appears, containing the current values of the storage (see Figure 8.2). If you want to see the storage content without the Firebug add-on, you can also use the internal information in Firefox. The data is saved in the background in a SQLite database (version 3), which can be displayed with the command-line tool *sqlite3*. A graphic interface for SQLite is also available as a Firefox add-on: the brilliant sqlite-manager. The SQLite database file is in the Firefox profile directory and has the name `webappsstore.sqlite`.

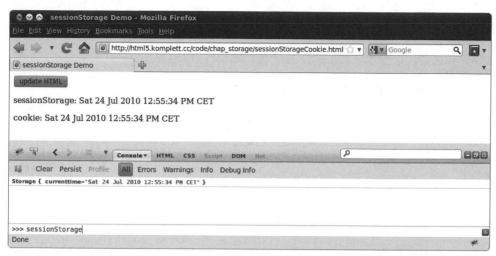

Figure 8.2   The Firefox add-on Firebug displaying "sessionStorage"

NOTE

You can download the Firefox add-ons from these Internet addresses:

- **Firebug:** http://getfirebug.com
- **sqlite-manager:** http://code.google.com/p/sqlite-manager

Apple's Safari offers an integrated debugging option, which first needs to be enabled in the Advanced Preferences. After activation, Safari shows a new Develop menu with a console that can display the storage content, just like Firebug.

Google Chrome and Opera also have integrated developer tools, allowing for very convenient access to all website elements. In both browsers, the Storage menu offers a clear and detailed list of *localStorage*, *sessionStorage*, and *Cookies*. In the table you can also add values, change them, or delete them (see Figure 8.3).

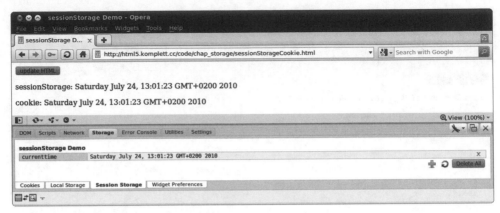

Figure 8.3 Opera displaying Developer Tools

Even Internet Explorer 9 offers *Developer Tools*. Apart from the DOM tree, CSS properties, a script debugger, and network profiling, there is a browser console that works in a similar way to that in Firebug, Safari, Chrome, and Opera.

> **NOTE**
>
> The latest browser versions really excel regarding the functions of their developer tools. Not only can cookies, *sessionStorage*, and *localStorage* be scrutinized, but these tools are also a big help in many other areas of web development.

8.2 Offline Web Applications

To make applications run completely without network access, HTML, Java-Script, and multimedia files must be reliably saved on the client machine. Up until now, all browsers had certain functions for caching content, but there was no standardized access to this content. The HTML5 specification took this problem to heart and devoted a section to *Offline Web applications*. They agreed on an independent offline memory, controllable with a simple configuration. A file with the ending .appcache contains the elements to be saved in the offline memory. It is integrated in the html tag as a manifest attribute:

```
<!DOCTYPE html>
 <html manifest="menu.appcache">
  <head>
```

The content of a *cache manifest* file can look like this:

```
CACHE MANIFEST
menu.html
menu.js
menu_data.js
```

The file structure is very simple. It does not have an XML structure, or syntax as you know it from the Windows .ini files, but is a simple text file. In the simplest case, all items listed in the file are transferred to the offline memory and only updated when the .appcache file changes. Every file referencing the manifest with the html element is automatically cached, even though the specification suggests listing the file once more explicitly. Let's have a closer look at this configuration file.

8.2.1 The Cache Manifest File

The cache manifest file must be a text file encoded with the character set *UTF-8*, and the first line must contain the string CACHE MANIFEST. The web server also has to use the MIME type *text/cache-manifest* when it outputs the file.

If required, three special keywords can appear in the .appcache file, each introducing a separate section. Here is a quick example:

```
CACHE MANIFEST
menu.html
menu.js

# login requires network connection
NETWORK:
login.php

FALLBACK:
/ /menu.html

CACHE:
style/innbar.css
```

After the already familiar beginning of the file is a comment line starting with the symbol #. The string NETWORK: marks the beginning of a new section. Data in this section is put on a *whitelist* and always has to be fetched from the network. In the preceding example, it is the file login.php, because we want the login check in our example to be possible only online.

The FALLBACK section is applied if the browser is offline and the desired item cannot be accessed because it is not present in the *offline cache*. In this example, the desired item is defined with the lowest level of the web server (/) and therefore applies to all files on this server simultaneously. Instead of an inaccessible resource, we want to display the file menu.html.

Finally, the configuration file also contains the entry CACHE:, introducing another section of content to be saved. In this example, the stylesheet style/innbar.css could just as well be listed at the very top of the configuration file, and we could omit the CACHE section altogether.

The specification describes an interesting special case in which the cache manifest file contains the following:

```
CACHE MANIFEST
FALLBACK:
/ /offline.html
NETWORK:
*
```

With this trick, you can construct something like a complete *offline cache* of HTML pages on a web server: Each file referencing the cache manifest is saved locally when first loaded and only fetched from the server if the manifest changes. The FALLBACK section redirects all queries about HTML pages not found in the cache to the page /offline.html. The section NETWORK with the joker symbol (*) is required to display the page correctly even if the browser is online.

8.2.2 Offline Status and Events

Via the application programming interface (API) for *Offline Web applications*, web developers have the option of checking the status of the offline storage and can change it manually if necessary. The status queries refer to the constant status assigned to the object window.applicationCache. Its numeric content relates to the meanings presented in Table 8.2.

Table 8.2 Meaning of constants for application cache status

Value	Name	Meaning
0	UNCACHED	The page is not in the cache. This can be due to the fact that the page is not meant to be saved offline or has not yet been downloaded.
1	IDLE	The browser has downloaded the latest version of the offline storage.
2	CHECKING	The browser is checking whether the cache manifest has changed.

Value	Name	Meaning
3	DOWNLOADING	After a changed cache manifest was found, the browser downloads the new cache content.
4	UPDATEREADY	The browser has downloaded all necessary content for the cache but is not yet using the new cache.
5	OBSOLETE	The cache is marked as *obsolete* if the cache manifest file cannot be loaded. The browser should then delete the cache.

To retrieve the current values of the constant, you just need to enter its name in the browser console: `window.applicationCache.status`. This outputs the corresponding numeric value, similar to Figure 8.2. To be able to control application cache behavior, the browser triggers certain *events*, which can be retrieved in the programming:

```
window.applicationCache.addEventListener("progress",
    function(e) {
      alert("New file downloaded");
    }, false);
```

The progress event, for example, is fired for each newly loaded file. In that case, an alert window appears for every downloaded file. Table 8.3 shows a list of all events.

Table 8.3 The events for "Offline Web applications"

Name	Description
checking	The browser is checking whether there is a new version of the cache manifest.
noupdate	There is no new cache manifest on the server.
downloading	The browser is downloading a version of the files to be saved. The event is also fired when the files are downloaded the first time.
progress	The event is called for each file to be downloaded.
cached	All elements for the cache have been downloaded.
updateready	All elements for the cache have been redownloaded (the cache manifest file was changed).
obsolete	The cache manifest file could not be loaded.
error	An error occurred on downloading the elements for the cache. The error can occur for several reasons, for example, a faulty entry in the cache manifest file.

The error event can be especially useful when trying to locate errors. A file listed in the cache manifest that cannot be found fires this event in the browser. The browser aborts any script execution from this point on, a situation in which you probably would not think of first during debugging. More on debugging can be found in section 8.2.3, Debugging.

The JavaScript API offers two additional methods for the cache: update() and swapCache(). With these methods you can update the cache without reloading the page, for example, via an Update button. The following HTML fragment creates the button:

```
<button onclick="window.applicationCache.update();">
  update applicationCache</button>
```

We handle the updateready event in the JavaScript code:

```
window.applicationCache.addEventListener("updateready",
    function(e) {
       window.applicationCache.swapCache();
       alert("New Cache in action");
    }, false);
```

As soon as the update has been successfully downloaded, the function swap-Cache() overwrites the old cache with the updated version. The update function first checks the cache manifest file. If it has not changed, no update takes place regardless of whether individual files for the cache have changed or not. The same result as clicking the button with the mouse can be achieved by reloading the page.

There can be situations in which manual or automatic control of the cache can be appropriate, for example, for a monitor without user interaction displaying current news in a public space. The cache can be updated in the background via a continuously repeating function (setInterval()). The system can then display HTML pages reliably with or without network access.

The specification prescribes another attribute that indicates whether the browser is online or offline. window.navigator.onLine is meant to return the value *false* if the browser is set to not access the network or is sure that network access will fail. In all other cases, the variable returns *true*.

NOTE

Even if the value of window.navigator.onLine is *true*, this does not automatically mean that the browser has access to the Internet. The browser can also be *online* in private networks without necessarily being connected to the public Internet.

Modern browsers have a function for changing to offline mode. In Mozilla Firefox, for example, this function can be found in the File menu as Work Offline. If the browser changes from online to offline mode, the event offline is fired; vice versa, the event is online is fired:

```
window.addEventListener("online", function() {
  alert("You are now online");
}, false);
window.addEventListener("offline", function() {
  alert("You are now OFFLINE");
}, false);
```

This brief example creates an alert window as soon as the browser changes its online state. Offline-capable applications can use these events to load updated data from the server or copy locally saved data to the server.

8.2.3 Debugging

You have probably had the same problem as many web developers at one stage or another: You spend ages changing line by line of source code, but although the page is reloaded in the browser each time, the result remains unchanged. On the way from server to browser are many places where the web content can be stored temporarily. This is a desirable improvement in many cases and helps to conserve bandwidth but is also the cause of many lost hours of sleep for web developers.

The bad news is that *Offline Web applications* make this problem even more complicated. By adding an additional cache component, there are now even more places where elements can be updated or not updated. A structured approach to solving this problem is essential and can save you a lot of time.

You first need to ensure that the web server really does output the cache manifest in the current version. Look at the server log files, as in this example of the Apache web server:

```
::1 - - [26/Jul/2010:14:50:46 +0200] "GET
/code/chap_storage/menu.appcache HTTP/1.1" 200 491
"-" "Mozilla/5.0 (X11; U; Linux x86_64; en-US)
AppleWebKit/534.3 (KHTML, like Gecko) Chrome/6.0.472.0
Safari/534.3"
::1 - - [26/Jul/2010:14:50:46 +0200] "GET
/code/chap_storage/menu.appcache HTTP/1.1" 304 253
"-" "Mozilla/5.0 (X11; U; Linux x86_64; en-US)
AppleWebKit/534.3 (KHTML, like Gecko) Chrome/6.0.472.0
Safari/534.3"
```

The HTTP status code 200 means that the file was fully processed; 304, however, means that the file remains unmodified and is not reprocessed.

The next debugging options are integrated in the browsers. Here, the status is different in each browser; the most convenient tools can currently be found in Firefox and Google Chrome.

Google Chrome tracks the current state of the *applicationCache* object in the Developer Tools console. Figure 8.4 shows a first call of the page during which the browser creates the offline storage. Then, all related documents are downloaded, with the `progress` event being fired each time (see also, section 8.2.2, Offline Status and Events). Reloading the page creates the `noupdate` event because the cache manifest file has not been modified. Chrome lists the events very clearly in order.

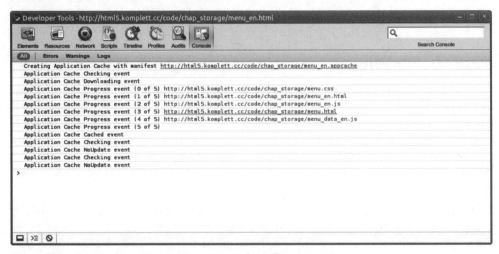

Figure 8.4 Google Chrome status messages for offline storage

The developers of Mozilla Firefox integrated information about the cache directly in the browser. Under the address `about:cache?device=offline`, Firefox displays all elements in this cache as a list. If the browser is in offline mode, you can get even more detailed info on each element, such as the location of the file on the hard disk (see Figure 8.5).

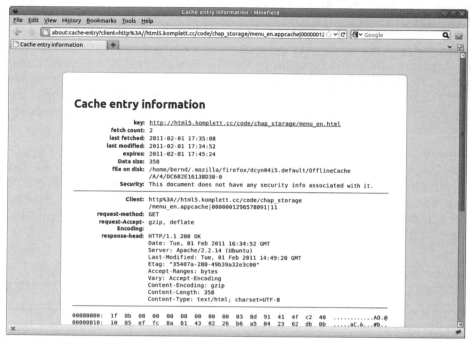

Figure 8.5   Firefox information on an element in the offline cache

For the browser to reload the cache manifest, its content first needs to be modified. It is not enough to resave the file with the same content or update the date of the last modification with the UNIX command touch. When developing applications, this leads to developers adding a character in a commented out line only to then delete it again for a repeated reload request—a situation justifiable during developing, but the question remains how this could be automated in a productive environment.

If you use version control, such as *Subversion*, for your web applications, you may have just thought of keywords, such as *ID* or *revision*, which Subversion automatically replaces in case of a modification. But such a keyword is also only changed in the cache manifest file if its content has changed—so that's another dead end. One possible aid would be a script that reads the version of the directory when distributing the new application version and writes it into the cache manifest. The prerequisite would be that all contents in the directory belong to the cache. A shell command for UNIX could look like this:

```
SVNV=$(svnversion -n) && \
 sed -e "s/^## svn.*/## svn repo version $SVNV/" \
 -i menu.appcache
```

It replaces an existing comment line with the Subversion version of the current directory.

8.3 Browser Support

Support for Web Storage is present in all current browsers. Even Internet Explorer offers this function in version 8 and later. If you need to support older versions of Internet Explorer, you can use an Open Source JavaScript library for *sessionStorage*; it emulates the session storage using a trick. For further information and the download, see http://code.google.com/p/ sessionstorage.

Unfortunately, Internet Explorer does not have any support for offline applications. Even in the upcoming version 9 these functions are not provided. Table 8.4 offers an overview of browser versions implementing Web Storage and offline apps. To see the connection between browser version and date, look at the Timeline at the end of the Introduction chapter, or go to the companion website at http://html5.komplett.cc/code/chap_intro/timeline.html?lang=en.

Table 8.4 Web Storage and offline web applications support in different browsers

	Firefox	Opera	Chrome	Safari	IE
Web Storage	3.0	10.50	3.0	4.0	8.0
Offline Apps	3.5	10.60	4.0	4.0	

8.4 Example: *Click to tick!*

To finish the chapter, we will use an example to illustrate the two techniques introduced here in combination. *Click to tick!* is a learning game that finds places or other geographical features using an unlabeled map. On this map, the player tries to mark a target as accurately as possible by clicking on the map with the mouse. The more hits per round, the more points the player will score in the final scoring.

To allow children to play the game on the *iPad* during a long car journey, the required resources, such as images, JavaScript, and HTML files, are saved in the cache for offline use (see section 8.2, Offline Web Applications). The list with top scores is saved in *localStorage* (section 8.1, Storage) to ensure that this information is not lost, even when the computer is switched off. Once the computer can reconnect to the Internet, the new score can be uploaded to the server, a function discussed in section 8.4.4, Expansion Options. Via an interface, the browser also checks if there are new game objectives and downloads these to the computer if necessary.

By applying the new techniques associated with HTML5, we created an independent program that uses the browser as a kind of runtime environment. Hardware as well as software and the operating system of the device become secondary; the browser is the central component for executing the program. Modern operating systems, such as Google's *ChromeOS* or Palm's *webOS*, count on this technique. By using the offline storage and the .appcache file, the program is equipped with an automatic update function—a true joy for developers.

Figure 8.6 shows the game in action: In this round, six out of eight places were successfully located in downtown Paris. Not bad!

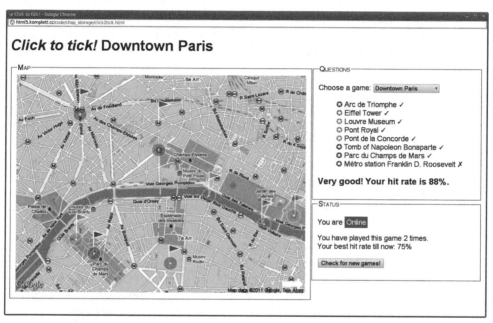

Figure 8.6 The program "Click to tick!" during a game

8.4.1 Using the Application: As a Player

When starting the application, the browser loads the playing area on the left with an interactive map section containing the targets to be located. On the right, the browser displays a selection list with the available games and the current score. If the user has played the game before, he or she can also see the maximum percentage scored and the number of games played. As you can see in Figure 8.6, the game also shows whether the browser is currently connected to the Internet or not. If Internet access is possible, a button for updating the game is visible (Check for new games!).

In the course of the game, the user is asked to find specific places and can click on the map to guess the location of the desired place. In response to each mouse click, a little flag appears on the map, marking the location the user clicked on. At the same time, a circle marks the correct target location. The flag and the circle have the same color and are drawn transparently onto the map. If both symbols overlap, the target was correctly marked and the task was solved. The target is added to the list of targets found and ticked off with a check mark for a correct answer or an *X* symbol for an incorrect answer. This list also uses the same colors as on the map (refer to Figure 8.6).

Once all questions have been answered, the program rewards the user with praise or encourages the user to do better next time. The comments are based on the percentage of correct answers scored. The user can then choose a new game from the selection menu or reload the page to try the current game again.

8.4.2 Using the Application: As an Administrator

As mentioned previously, the game has a mode where you can define new targets (click2tick_creator.html). This admin interface loads the familiar map view of Google Maps and allows you to set the zoom factor, choose a map section, and then define several points on the map. Before you can start placing the points, you need to fixate the map section via the Record button. For each point, a line of JavaScript code is displayed on the right side of the browser, listing the coordinates in pixels and an identifier for the relevant point.

This part of the page is declared as contenteditable, so the identifiers can be modified directly in the HTML page (see Figure 8.7, the bordered area on the right). After all points have been marked and the identifiers adapted, the administrator has to copy the JavaScript code and save it in a JavaScript file, which is then referenced in the game's HTML code in the head area. More details on how this works can be found in the introductory text of the admin site.

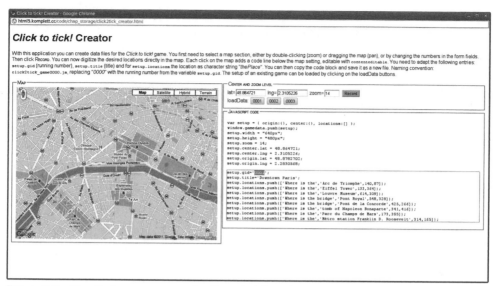

Figure 8.7   Creating a new game using the administration interface

The last step for making the new game offline-capable is to enter the created JavaScript file into the appcache file. To find the correct address for the static Google Maps map, you need to call the game once with the debug option. This is easily done by adding the following string to the URL of the administration site: ?debug=1. In this mode, the URL of the active image is displayed below the playing area.

If you are interested in finding out more about the fascinating interplay between Google Maps API, Canvas, and JavaScript in the administration interface, look at the source code at http://html5.komplett.cc/code/chap_storage/click2tick_creator.html.

8.4.3   Important Code Fragments

The following sections explain the most important parts of the *Click to tick!* game. We begin with the HTML code, move on to the manifest instructions, and finally work out the JavaScript part.

8.4.3.1   *The HTML Code for the Game*

The HTML code for the game *Click to tick!* is rather clear. Less than 50 lines of well-formatted code form the basic structure of the application, as shown in Listing 8.1. Of course, the application logic resides not in the HTML code, but in the approximately 300-line long JavaScript file. It is primarily the placeholders for the elements to be filled that are encoded in HTML:

Listing 8.1   Extract of the HTML code for the game "Click to tick!"

```
<!DOCTYPE html>
 <html manifest=click2tick.appcache>
  <head>
    <meta charset="utf-8">
    <title>Click to tick!</title>
    <link rel="stylesheet" media="all"
      href="click2tick.css">
  <script src="click2tick.js"></script>
  <script src="click2tick_game0001.js"></script>
  <script src="click2tick_game0002.js"></script>
  ...
 <div id="map">
  <fieldset>
    <legend>Map</legend>
    <canvas>This game requires a canvas capable browser/canvas>
  </fieldset>
  <p id=mapUrl></p>
 </div>
 <div id="controls">
  <fieldset>
    <legend>Questions</legend>
    <p>Choose a game:
      <select id=selGame name=games></select></p>
    <ul id="gameResults"></ul>
    <h3 id="curQuestion"></h3>
  </fieldset>
  <fieldset>
    <legend>Status</legend>
    <p>You are <span id="onlineStatus" class=online></span></p>
    <p id="localStorage"></p>
    <p id="updateButton"><input type=button onclick="location.reload();"
      value="Check for new games!"></p>
  </fieldset>
 </div>
```

The listing starts with the familiar DOCTYPE definition and the subsequent reference to the appcache file where the content to be saved is referenced. For each game, a dedicated JavaScript file is loaded—here, for example, the file named click2tick_game0001.js.

In the second part of the listing you see a canvas element, a strong indication that this is the interactive playing area. The select element with the ID selGame is still empty but will contain the list of all active games when the game is started. The other HTML elements with the IDs gameResults, curQuestion, onlineStatus, and localStorage are placeholders, which will also later be filled by JavaScript functions. The button labeled Check for new games! reloads the website via `location.reload` and automatically checks if the manifest file has been modified.

8.4.3.2   The Manifest File

After the obligatory first line, the cache manifest contains references to the HTML code, the JavaScript file, and the stylesheet. Then, the corresponding JavaScript file and the static map of Google Maps are referenced for each game:

```
CACHE MANIFEST

# application files
click2tick.html
click2tick.js
click2tick.css

# gamedata
# Downtown Paris
click2tick_game0001.js
http://maps.google.com/maps/api/staticmap?sensor=false&maptype=satellite
&size=640x480&center=48.864721,2.3105226&zoom=14
```

Although the map call for the Google Maps map consists of a dynamic URL, the resulting image is saved in offline storage and correctly loaded even without network access if called. Figure 8.8 shows successful loading of three games into the application cache.

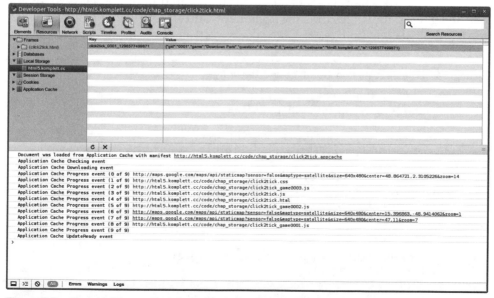

Figure 8.8   Google Chrome Developer Tools loading the offline cache

8.4.3.3   JavaScript Functions of the Game

The HTML part of our example was not very exciting, but the JavaScript part of the game is much more interesting. The previously mentioned `window.onload` function initializes a new object game with the type `click2tick` and then calls the init function of this object:

```
window.onload = function() {
  var game = new click2tick();
  game.init();
};
```

To keep the JavaScript code as flexible as possible, the entire game function is wrapped in a library (`GameLib`), made accessible with all functions as global object:

```
(function () {
  var GameLib = function () {
    var elem = {};
    var image, canvas, context;
  ...
  };
  // expose object
  window.click2tick = GameLib;
}());
```

In the second-to-last line of the listing, the `window` object is assigned the `GameLib` class with the new name `click2tick`. The `init` function of this class loads the existing games, initializes the canvas element, and starts the first game (see Listing 8.2):

Listing 8.2   The init function for the `GameLib` library

```
this.init = function() {
  // build game-selection pulldown
  var o = '';
  for (var i=0; i<gamedata.length; i++) {
    o += addOpt(i,gamedata[i].title);
  }
  _get('selGame').innerHTML = o;
  _get('selGame').options.selectedIndex = 0;
  _get('selGame').onchange = function() {
    startGame(this.value);
  };

  // define empty image used for map later
  image = new Image();

  canvas = document.querySelector("CANVAS");
  context = canvas.getContext('2d');
```

```
    canvas.onclick = function(evt) {
        checkPosition(evt);
    };
...
    startGame(0);
};
```

The functions addOpt() and _get() will probably be new to you. These are two auxiliary functions; addOpt() serves to assemble the string for a new option element, and _get() allows efficient access to the elements in the DOM tree (via their ID). The HTML element with the ID selGame is the selection list of all games. This list is set to the first element with selectedIndex = 0. If another item in this list is selected, the startGame function is activated with this new value.

An event handler for the mouse click event is assigned to the canvas element and calls the checkPosition function. Then the first game is started.

Because many functions of the GameLib are designed to ensure that the game runs properly and are not directly connected with Web Storage or the offline cache, we will not describe them in great detail here. If you are curious, you can peek at the source code for the JavaScript library *click2tick.js*. But more relevant for our offline chapter is the JavaScript code involving the Storage interface with *localStorage*: We will use it when saving a game:

```
// store basic data in localStorage, add hostname
// and timestamp
var ts = new Date().getTime();
var id = "click2tick_"+game.store.gid+"_"+ts;
game.store.hostname = location.hostname;
game.store.ts = ts;
localStorage.setItem(id, JSON.stringify(game.store));
```

To ensure the keys in *localStorage* are unique, they are created by combining a prefix string (click2tick), a game ID (game.store.gid), and a timestamp (ts) connected by an underline (_).

The game.store structure is saved as a value with all results in the form of a JSON string. The following listing shows the value after five out of eight questions have been correctly answered at the end of the game. The key for the following entry is click2tick_0001_1281026695083 (see also Figure 8.8):

```
{ "gid":"0001","game":"Downtown Paris",
  "questions":8,"correct":5,"percent":63,
  "hostname":"html5.komplett.cc", "ts":1281026695083
}
```

The timestamp `ts` is the time in milliseconds since 1.1.1970. Now that the values are saved in *localStorage*, you can give appropriate feedback to the user if the user tries the game again:

```
// get collected data
var games_done = [];
var max_percent = 0;
for (var i=0;i<localStorage.length;i++) {
  var key = localStorage.key(i);
  if (key.substring(0, 9) == "click2tick") {
    var item = JSON.parse(localStorage.getItem(key));
    if (item.gid == game.store.gid) {
      games_done.push(item);
      max_percent = Math.max(max_percent, item.percent);
    }
  }
}

// show collected data
var s = '';
if (games_done.length == 0) {
  s += 'You have not played this game before.';
}
else {
  s += 'You have played this game '+
      (games_done.length+1)+' times<br>';
  s += 'Your best hit rate till now: '+
      max_percent+"%\n";
}
_get('localStorage').innerHTML = s;
```

The `for` loop runs over all items found in `localStorage`. For each element, the key is determined and checked if it starts with the string `click2tick`. This check ensures that any elements saved by another application of this website are skipped in *localStorage*.

We then use the `JSON.parse` function to convert valid elements into JavaScript objects. If the game ID matches the ID of the current game (`item.gid == game.store.gid`), the object is added to the array `games_done` and checked if its hit rate is higher than the highest previous one (`Math.max`). A string `s` is then assembled, giving details on the number of games played and the maximum percentage. As you can see in Figure 8.5, the game also indicates whether the browser is online or offline. This is relevant for our application because the player cannot look for new games and updates while in offline mode:

```
var setOnlineStatus = function() {
  if (navigator.onLine) {
    _get('onlineStatus').innerHTML = 'Online';
    _get('onlineStatus').className = 'online';
```

```
      _get('updateButton').style.visibility = 'visible';
    }
    else {
      _get('onlineStatus').innerHTML = 'Offline';
      _get('onlineStatus').className = 'offline';
      _get('updateButton').style.visibility = 'hidden';
    }
}
```

A check of the variable navigator.online (see section 8.2.2, Offline Status and Events) decides if the button for updating the application will be displayed. To ensure the online status is always up-to-date, event listeners are defined for both switching to and from offline mode:

```
// control online-status
window.addEventListener("online", function() {
  setOnlineStatus();
}, false);
window.addEventListener("offline", function() {
  setOnlineStatus();
}, false);
```

8.4.4 Expansion Options

To make the game more attractive, you could try adding the following optional expansions:

- **Select difficulty level.** The valid area of objects is defined in pixels in the image. The default setting of 15 pixels is suitable for average difficulty. You could make this area variable via an input field using the new HTML5 form element range. The level of difficulty would of course have to be taken into account in the high score list.

- **Incorporate variable sizes/shapes of target.** Because the objects to be located often have different sizes, an additional parameter for each target object might be conceivable, specifying the radius of the area to be searched. If a circle is not accurate enough as a target object, you could integrate other geometric forms as targets.

- **Include score by distance.** You could incorporate the distance to the target into the scoring: the closer a player's mouse click was to the desired target on the map, the higher the score the player gets for being right.

- **Add online high score.** An extension in connection to *offlineStorage* would be integrating the application into an online high score list. You would require an application with access to the database on the web server.

- **Combine with Geolocation API.** This expansion takes our example a bit further: After locating the player's current position with sufficient accuracy (see Chapter 7, Geolocation), a corresponding Google Maps map section could be loaded. The player's task would then be to find his own location on the map as accurately as possible. In this variation, the game is no longer offline-capable but is definitely suitable for mobile devices.

Summary

In this chapter you encountered two different types of client-side storage: web storage, a structured storage for reading and writing web applications, and offline storage, temporarily saving entire web applications or parts of them on the client side.

The chapter concluded with a programming example, the game *Click to tick!*, demonstrating the strengths of the offline cache and *localStorage*. By using the two new techniques, we created an application that could run on the web browser but was still fully functional without Internet access. The automatic update function was the icing on the cake. The user did not have to worry about installation, nor did the user need administrator rights.

9
WebSockets

The *Hypertext Transfer Protocol (HTTP)* is just great. Together with FTP, SMTP, IMAP, and many others, it is part of the large family of text-based protocols executed in the TCP/IP Application Layer. In these protocols, client and server communicate via messages in text form. The following listing demonstrates how easy it is to "speak" HTTP with a web server:

```
user@host:~> telnet www.google.com 80
Trying 209.85.135.103...
Connected to www.l.google.com.
Escape character is ,^]'.
GET /search?q=html5 HTTP/1.0
```

To run a Google search for the term *html5*, we first connect to www.google.com on the port reserved for HTTP, port 80. The request has three parts: In the first part

GET determines the method for the request; in this case we want to get information from the server. The second part is the URI; here, we call the script search with the parameter q=html5. In the third part we specify the protocol version 1.0.

The server promptly replies with the following information:

```
HTTP/1.0 200 OK
Cache-Control: private, max-age=0
Date: Fri, 28 Jan 2011 08:29:43 GMT
Expires: -1
Content-Type: text/html; charset=ISO-8859-1
...

<!doctype html><head><title>html5 - Google Search</title>
....
```

The first block of the message, the header, contains meta information separated by an empty line from the following payload data (note how Google is already using the new DOCTYPE). This gives us almost everything we need to program our very own browser. Joking aside, the simplicity of the protocol is decisive for the quick success and widespread use of HTTP. The header lines are nearly endlessly expandable, making the protocol future-proof.

Each request is a closed issue after it has been answered. So, an HTML page referencing a stylesheet and five images needs seven connections to load. This means that a connection is established seven times, and each time metadata and payload is transmitted. In version 1.1 of HTTP, this behavior was somewhat improved by the keepalive function (new TCP connections do not need to be created every time), but the meta information for each object is transmitted separately. To track a user's session, you need to resort to other tools (sessions, cookies), because HTTP has not integrated this function.

These considerations provide the starting points for developing a new protocol, which is by no means meant to replace HTTP but can complement it. The *WebSockets protocol* transports data without meta information in a constant stream, simultaneously from the server to the client and vice versa (full duplex).

Web applications that promptly show small changes in the browser can especially profit from this new method. Examples of such applications are a chat program, the display of stock exchange prices, or online games. What was previously only possible via proprietary plug-ins or unpleasant JavaScript tricks is now codified in a standardized protocol (as an IETF draft) and an associated API (currently as an Editor's Draft with the W3C). Both were still in a very early stage at the time of this writing; however, both the WebKit engine (and thus Google Chrome and Safari) and the Beta version of Mozilla Firefox contain a functioning implementation.

We do not want to penetrate the depths of the WebSocket protocol, because the communication on the protocol level is taken care of by the browser anyway.

However, we will provide a few comments to clarify: Although an HTTP request involves sending several header lines back and forth, WebSockets only use two bytes for this. The first byte shows the start of a message; the second contains the length of the message. This is a saving (of bytes transferred and bandwidth) with dramatic consequences when you have to manage many users accessing the site at short intervals.

> **NOTE**
>
> If you want to know more about the details of the WebSocket protocol, read the relevant *Internet Draft* on the WHATWG website at http://www.whatwg.org/specs/web-socket-protocol.

Interesting statistics regarding the advantages of WebSockets in different applications can be found in the article at http://soa.sys-con.com/node/1315473: The authors even go so far as to refer to WebSockets as a quantum leap in scalability for the web.

9.1   The WebSocket Server

Client-side support for WebSockets is integrated in modern browsers. But we are still missing one component: the WebSocket server. Although the protocol specification is not set in stone at the moment, there is already a surprising selection of software products available. You can choose a server depending on your preference, be it Java, PHP, Perl, or Python (of course, all products are still in the test stage).

For this book, we chose a special solution. With *node.js* is a JavaScript interpreter capable of running without a browser. The code developed by Google under the name *V8* is working in the background. Because we used JavaScript exclusively for all previous programming in this book, it made sense to write the server using JavaScript as well.

There are currently no finished binary packets of *node.js*, so the installation requires some manual work. With UNIX-type operating systems, the installation is usually straightforward; for Windows, you still have to resort to the UNIX emulation *cygwin*.

> **NOTE**
>
> For a more detailed description regarding the installation of *node.js*, see the project's website at http://nodejs.org.

node.js does not yet contain a WebSocket server, but help is available on the Internet. At http://github.com/miksago/node-websocket-server, you will find a small library implementing the current specification of the WebSocket protocol for the server. The three JavaScript files of the node-websocket-server are simply copied into a subdirectory and loaded with the following lines:

```
var ws = require(__dirname + '/lib/ws'),
    server = ws.createServer();
```

From this point on, the variable server contains a reference to the WebSocket server object. We still need to specify a port for the server:

```
server.listen(8887);
```

To start the server, we call the JavaScript file with the *node.js* interpreter:

```
node mini_server.js
```

Our minimal WebSocket server is now running and accepts connections at port 8887. But that is all our server can do for the moment. A more sensible application is developed in the following example, which we will use to investigate the individual components in more detail.

9.2 Example: A Broadcast Server

For our first little example, we want to communicate with a WebSocket that transmits entered text to all clients with an active connection to the socket. This is not a real Internet chat application but is well suited to the purpose of testing the interactivity of WebSockets. Figure 9.1 shows how four interconnected clients exchange messages with each other.

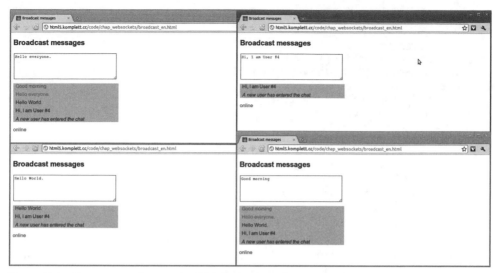

Figure 9.1   Four connections to the WebSocket broadcast server

9.2.1   The Broadcast Client

In the HTML code we just need a text field for entering the message to be sent. To demonstrate the capabilities of WebSocket, we want every character to be sent to all connected users immediately. To achieve this, we use the oninput event of the text field and call the sendmsg() function for each keystroke, which we will analyze later on:

```
<h2>Broadcast messages</h2>
<textarea accesskey=t oninput="sendmsg();"
  onfocus="select()" rows=5 cols=40 id=ta
  placeholder="Please insert your message">
</textarea>
<div id=broadcast></div>
<p id=status><p id=debug>
```

The JavaScript section starts with a definition of the previously encountered $() function, loaned from the jQuery library. As soon as the whole document is loaded, the WebSocket is initialized and assigned to the variable ws. In our example, we use the server html5.komplett.cc on the special port 8887. The server is specified via a URL, and the protocol is abbreviated with ws://. Similar to the SSL encoded HTTPS, there is also an encoded channel for WebSockets, called with wss:// as the protocol. For our example, we stick with the uncoded variation. The path specified in the URL (/bc) is not relevant for our WebSocket server, because the server on this port has the sole purpose of serving this example (more about the server in section 9.2.2, The Broadcast Server):

```
function $(a) { return document.getElementById(a); }

var ws, currentUser, ele;
window.onload = function() {
ws = new WebSocket("ws://html5.komplett.cc:8887/bc");
ws.onopen = function() {
  $("status").innerHTML = 'online';
  $("status").style.color = 'green';
  ws.onmessage = function(e) {
    var msg;
    try {
      msg = JSON.parse(e.data);
    } catch (SyntaxError) {
      $("debug").innerHTML = "invalid message";
      return false;
    }
```

If the connection is successfully established, the WebSocket's onopen event is activated. The anonymous function in our example writes the string *online* in green into a status line at the end of the HTML document. For each message received by the WebSocket, it activates the onmessage event. The data attribute of the variable e available for this function contains the payload sent by the server. In our example, the data is converted into a JavaScript object via JSON.parse, which means that the server has to send a *JSON* string (details on this will follow later in this section). If the conversion is unsuccessful, the function is terminated and an appropriate error message appears on the HTML page.

A valid message contains a JavaScript object with user name (user), message text (text) , and the color in which the message is to be displayed (color). As you can see in Figure 9.1, each user is writing on his own line and in his own color. The server assigns colors to users; assigning a new line is implemented on the client. The subsequent if query checks if the last message is from the same user as the previously received message. If that is the case, the innerHTML value of the variable ele is assigned the received text. If it is a different user or this is the first message, a new paragraph with the name ele is created and added to the div element with the ID broadcast. The variable currentUser is then set to the value of the current user:

```
    if (currentUser == msg.user) {
      ele.innerHTML = msg.text;
    } else {
      ele = document.createElement("p");
      $("broadcast").appendChild(ele);
      ele.style.color = msg.color;
      ele.innerHTML = msg.text;
      currentUser = msg.user;
    }
  };
};
```

```
function sendmsg() {
  ws.send($("ta").value);
}
ws.onclose = function(e){
  $("status").innerHTML = 'offline';
  $("status").style.color = 'red';
};
window.onunload = function(){
  ws.close();
};
```

The sendmsg() function fired with every keystroke within the text field sends the entire content of the text field to the WebSocket.

If the connection to the WebSocket is terminated for any reason (for example, due to an absent network connection or server problems), the WebSocket object fires the *close* event and consequently the onclose function. In our example, we set the status line to offline in red. When leaving the site (window.onunload), we explicitly close the WebSocket, logging out of the server.

9.2.2   The Broadcast Server

To complete the example, we still need the server component. As mentioned earlier, we use the *node.js* runtime and the node-websocket-server for the Web-Socket examples in this book. This makes sense didactically because we do not need to switch to another programming language. After all, the server code is meant to be easily understandable for you as well.

Similar to the client, the server works based on *events*. Each established connection and each received message fires a connection or message event, respectively, to which we react in the JavaScript code. At the beginning of the script, we load the node-websocket-server library, located in the directory lib/ under the name ws.js. A new WebSocket object is assigned to the variable server:

```
var ws = require(__dirname + '/lib/ws'),
    server = ws.createServer();
var user_cols = {};
server.addListener("connection", function(conn) {
  var h = conn._server.manager.length*70;
  user_cols[conn.id] = "hsl("+h+",100%,30%)";
  var msg = {};
  msg.user = conn.id;
  msg.color = user_cols[conn.id];
  msg.text = "<em>A new user has entered the chat</em>";
  conn.broadcast(JSON.stringify(msg));
```

The first event handler (`connection`) handles the new connections. As in Chapter 8 in the section 8.5, Example: Click to tick!, we assign the color for the user step by step in HSL, jumping ahead for each new user by 70 degrees (the number of users can be retrieved via the array `conn._server.manager`). The colors are saved in the variable `user_cols` with the connection ID (`conn.id`) as an index. The variable `msg` is furnished with the created color and the notification that a new user has entered; then it is sent as a JSON string via the method `conn.broadcast`. This method is a function of the node-websocket-server and broadcasts messages to all clients except the one who fired the current event, which is exactly what we want in this case: All users are informed that a new user has entered the chat:

```
conn.addListener("message", function(message) {
    var msg = {};
    message = message.replace(/</g, "&lt;");
    message = message.replace(/>/g, "&gt;");
    msg.text = message;
    msg.user = conn.id;
    msg.color = user_cols[conn.id];
    conn.write(JSON.stringify(msg));
    conn.broadcast(JSON.stringify(msg));
  });
});
```

The second function reacting to the `message` event replaces the start and end characters for HTML tags in the passed string (`message`) to ensure that no script code or similar tricks can be smuggled in. A reliable application would have to check input even more thoroughly to protect against possible attacks. After all, the message is broadcast to all clients and displayed in their browsers, a nearly ideal attack scenario. As in the `connection` event, a local variable `msg` is filled with the desired content and sent as a JSON string. But here, it happens twice: first with the `write()` method to the actual user and then with the `broadcast()`method to all other users.

The WebSocket server is almost finished. We are still missing an event handler for closed connections and the actual start of the server:

```
server.addListener("close", function(conn) {
   var msg = {};
   msg.user = conn.id;
   msg.color = user_cols[conn.id];
   msg.text = "<em>A user has left the chat</em>";
   conn.broadcast(JSON.stringify(msg));
});
server.listen(8887);
```

As with the `connection` event, all users receive a message in the `close` event as well. In this case, they are told that a user has left the conference. Then the server is bound to port 8887 and receives queries from that point on.

That was an initial, very brief example. In the next section we will develop a game that makes even better use of the advantages of WebSockets.

9.3 Example: Battleships!

A more detailed `websocket` example is devoted to a popular strategy game for which you would normally only need paper and pencil—Battleships! The rules are easy to explain: Each player places ten ships of different sizes on a play area sized ten-by-ten spaces. The ships are not allowed to be touching, can be arranged horizontally or vertically, and are two to five spaces long. You distribute them following the rule: 1×5, 2×4, 3×3, and 4×2 spaces per ship. The player who is first to finish arranging his or her ships can start the game by choosing one of the opponent's spaces. If the space chosen contains only water, it's the opponent's turn next; if that space contains a ship or part of a ship, the player can keep guessing. You continue in this way until all parts of all ships have been hit, and the ships have been sunk.

For converting Battleships! to HTML5, we require an HTML file on the client with a JavaScript library and a CSS stylesheet; on the server we use `node-web-socket-server`, which we already mentioned in section 9.1, The WebSocket Server. All files relevant for the application can be found on the companion website at these links:

- http://html5.komplett.cc/code/chap_websockets/game_en.html
- http://html5.komplett.cc/code/chap_websockets/game_en.js
- http://html5.komplett.cc/code/chap_websockets/game.css
- http://html5.komplett.cc/code/chap_websockets/ws/game_server.js

The game is shown in Figure 9.2.

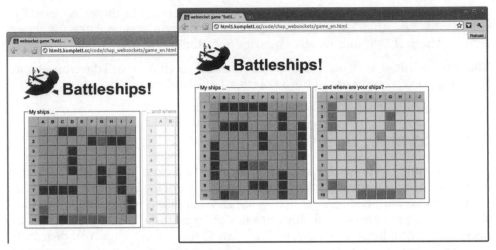

Figure 9.2 The game "Battleships!" in action

In the HTML code, control elements and game dialogs are defined as `form` elements, visible or hidden depending on the game phase. Four of them are message windows, displayed centered with `position:fixed` as an invitation to play, rejection of the invitation, and congratulations or commiserations at the end of the game. The other forms contain the login mask, two game areas for the player's own and the opponent's ships, a digitalization component for placing the ships in the desired orientation, plus a list of currently logged-in users and their status.

On loading the page, the login mask appears and you are asked to enter your *nickname* (see Figure 9.3). Two special users are available for testing the application, *test1* and *test2*, for which the ships are positioned automatically, and player *test1* can always start the game. The auxiliary page `test_game.html` is a good way to observe the game from both players' viewpoints. Here you can log in under two different user names via embedded `iframe` elements, so you can play against yourself, as it were. The advantage is that you always win and are able to follow the application's game logic more easily. This testing page can be found at http://html5.komplett.cc/code/chap_websockets/game_test_en.html.

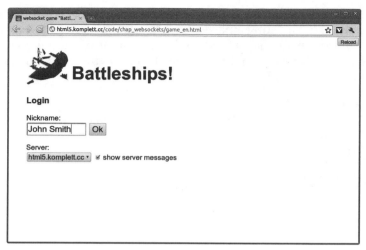

Figure 9.3   Start page of the "Battleships!" game

If you click OK after logging in, the connection to the WebSocket server is created. Its tasks are limited to exchanging messages between players and updating the user list. The user list shows each user with a connection ID, nickname, and current game status.

All messages are sent as JSON strings and fall roughly into two categories: The first one comprises messages sent to all users, concerning changes in the game status of individual players. The second category comprises private messages exchanged only between users currently playing a game together. For this purpose, we had to add the additional method `writeclient()` to the connection library of the `node-websocket-server`, passing messages only to the desired user.

Immediately after login, your own game area appears. Just as the opponent's game area, it consists of ten-by-ten `button` elements whose `value` attributes reflect the grid position and have values between `1,1` (top left) and `10,10` (bottom right). Each button has a `class` attribute that can be changed several times in the course of the game. The CSS stylesheet contains the classes presented in Table 9.1 (relevant to the gameplay).

Table 9.1   Gameplay-related CSS classes in the game area

Class	CSS Formatting
.empty	*background-color: #EEE*
.ship	*background-color: slategray*
.water	*background-color: lightblue*
.hit	*background-color: salmon; pointer-events: none*
.destroyed	*background-color: darkseagreen; pointer-events: none*

Before we can start digitalizing the ships, we need to find a partner so we can play. This is done by selecting a player from the list of logged-in users and clicking the button Invite Player to send that user an invitation to play. The callback function of this button locates the player ID and sends an invitation message to the WebSocket server:

```
this.invitePlayer = function() {
  var opts = document.forms.loggedin.users.options;
  if (opts.selectedIndex != -1) {
    wsMessage({
      task : 'private',
      request : 'invite',
      client : opts[opts.selectedIndex].value
    });
  }
};
```

The called function `wsMessage()` directs the message in JSON format to the server. It can also contain additional steps, such as checking the validity of the message or similar steps:

```
var wsMessage = function(msg) {
  game.websocket.send(JSON.stringify(msg));
};
```

The variable game in this code listing represents the central game object, and contains all variables relevant to the game. On the server, the invitation is identified as a private message, the sender's data is added, and then the message is sent to the selected player.

With the server in `game_server.js`, it would look like this:

```
else if (msg.task == 'private') {
  msg.from = USERS[conn.id];
  conn.writeclient(JSON.stringify(msg),msg.client);
}
```

This user is presented with a little window asking to play a game with you (see Figure 9.4). If the user declines, you receive the answer *No thanks, not now*; if the user accepts, the user list is hidden and the digitalization component for placing the ships is displayed. Let's first look at the code for inviting someone to play. On the client, we see it as part of the onmessage callback function for all server messages:

```
game.websocket.onmessage = function(e) {
  var msg = JSON.parse(e.data);
  if (msg.request == 'invite') {
    var frm = document.forms.inviteConfirm;
```

```
      var txt = '<strong>'+msg.from.nick+'</strong>';
      txt += 'wants to play a game with you.';
      txt += 'Accept?';
      frm.sender.previousSibling.innerHTML = txt;
      frm.sender.value = msg.from.id;
      frm.sendernick.value = msg.from.nick;
      frm.style.display = 'inline';
   }
};
```

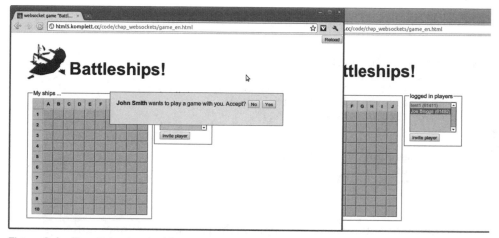

Figure 9.4   The dialog box inviting you to a new game

So the ID and nickname of the person who sends the invite are contained in the form inviteConfirm, and the message window can be displayed. When the other player clicks on Yes or No, the appropriate response is sent back to the inviter via the server and once again lands in the onmessage callback:

```
else if (msg.request == 'confirm') {
   if (msg.choice == true) {
      wsMessage({
         task : 'setPlaying',
         client : msg.from.id
      });
      prepareGame(msg.from.id,msg.from.nick);
      document.forms.loggedin.style.display = 'none';
   }
   else {
      show('nothanks');
      window.setTimeout(function() {
         hide('nothanks');
         document.forms.users.style.display = 'inline';
      }, 2000);
   }
}
```

If the invitation to play was answered with Yes, the server is informed that the two players are now playing together, the game is prepared, and the selection list of logged-in players is hidden. If the answer was No, only the message *No thanks, not now* is displayed for two seconds.

As a direct consequence of the server message *We are now playing together*, other steps follow, such as the update of the player status object on the server, which then informs all users that the two players involved are not currently available for other games.

For the server in game_server.js, it would look as follows:

```
var setBusy = function(id) {.
  USERS[id].busy = true;
  var msg = {task:'isPlaying',user:USERS[id]};
  conn.broadcast(JSON.stringify(msg));
  conn.write(JSON.stringify(msg));
};
...
else if (msg.task == 'setPlaying') {
  setBusy(conn.id);
  setBusy(msg.client);
}
```

Back in the client, this message is caught in the onmessage callback and the locally kept list of logged-in players is updated. The result of this update is that both players can no longer be selected, because their option elements are deactivated via a disabled attribute:

```
else if (msg.task == 'isPlaying') {
  var opts = document.forms.loggedin.users.options;
  for (var i=0; i<opts.length; i++) {
    if (opts[i].value == msg.user.id) {
      opts[i].disabled = 'disabled';
    }
  }
}
```

If both players agree that they want to play together, they can start placing the ships. If you are logged in as user *test1* or *test2*, your ships are already prepared for you; if not, a pull-down menu pops up, allowing you to digitalize your flotilla via five buttons. Select whether to arrange each ship in a *horizontal* or *vertical* orientation, and then click on the desired ship type and place the ship onto the play area in the desired place by clicking once more.

The relevant fields are formatted to represent ships via a CSS class ship and are recorded in three JavaScript variables. The variable game.ships.isShip remembers the designated positions, and the variable game.ships.parts records the fields belonging to each ship as an array of arrays. A copy of these arrays is worked through successively in the variable game.ships.partsTodo during the game and only contains ten empty arrays at the end of the game for the losing player, because the relevant position is deleted for each hit.

With each newly placed ship, the label of the relevant button is updated as well, showing how many ships of this type are still available. It disappears once all ships of this type have been placed. Once all ships are placed, the entire form disappears and a message is sent to the opponent: Ready to start the game!

```
if (game.ships.parts.length == 10) {
  document.forms.digitize.style.display = 'none';
  game.me.grid['1-1'].parentNode.style.pointerEvents =
    'none';
  wsMessage({
    task : 'private',
    request : 'ready',
    client : game.you.id
  });
  game.me.ready = true;
}
```

Who comes first, goes first is the motto, so the player who is the quickest to place all his ships can begin the game. The slower player has to bite the bullet and suffer the first attack on his fleet. To allow each player to attack the opponent's ships, a second play area is displayed after both players have placed their ships.

The game logic for attacking and sinking ships is implemented fully on the client side. The server only distributes the game moves as private messages to both players involved. Each click on an active play field calls the reveal function:

```
this.reveal = function(evt) {
  wsMessage({
    task : 'private',
    request : 'challenge',
    field : evt.target.value,
    client : game.you.id
  });
};
```

The server transmits the message to the opponent's side, which then checks whether the field the other player clicked on contains part of a ship or not:

```
else if (msg.request == 'challenge') {
  var destroyed = 0;
  if (game.ships.isShip[msg.field]) {
    game.me.grid[msg.field].setAttribute("class","hit");
```

Figure 9.5 shows the game in demo mode.

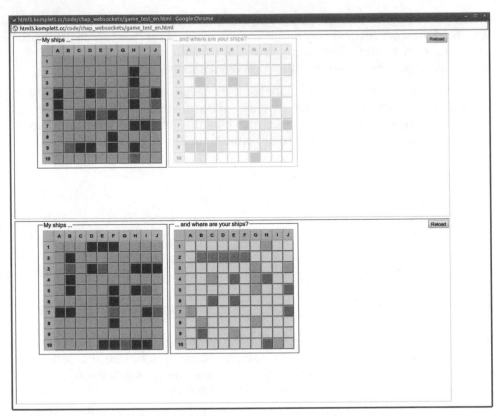

Figure 9.5   "Battleships!" in demo mode

In case of a hit (isShip is *true*) , the relevant button on the player's own play area is assigned the class hit, coloring it red according to the stylesheet instruction. If a ship is hit but is not yet completely destroyed, the opponent receives an appropriate message:

```
wsMessage({
    task : 'private',
    request : 'thisFieldIs',
    result : 'hit',
    field : msg.field,
    client : game.you.id
});
```

If the request part of the message is thisFieldIs, the field is treated accordingly for the opponent:

```
else if (msg.request == 'thisFieldIs') {
    if (msg.result == 'water') {
```

```
    game.you.grid[msg.field].setAttribute("class",
        msg.result);
    deactivateField();
  }
  else if (msg.result == 'hit') {
    game.you.grid[msg.field].setAttribute("class",
        msg.result);
  }
...
```

From the attacker's point of view, the answer *hit* marks the field he clicked on in red. If the answer is *destroyed*, all fields belonging to that ship are turned from red to green to show it was hit and destroyed. At the same time, in the play area of the attacked player, his *hit* position is marked in red. In the case of *destroyed*, all previously red ship sections are turned blue to show that the attacked ship was destroyed and has been replaced by blue blocks, or *water*. So, the more blue you can see on your play area, the worse the situation; the more green in the opponent's play area, the better the chance of victory.

If the answer is *water*, it is now the attacked player's turn to retaliate (the deactivateField() function prevents further actions). The game continues back and forth until one of the two players has destroyed all of the opponent's ships and is declared the winner. Marking the status of your own and enemy ships is done via CSS formats for each button element, as mentioned previously. The turn-taking between players is possible because the opposing game area for the currently inactive player is deactivated with pointer-events:none and opacity:0.2.

After the end of the game, both players are separated again; their status is reset to *Available to play*, and the next invitation can be issued. In the current version, *Battleships!* does not yet allow for playing several consecutive games with the same player; perhaps you would like to try implementing this new feature? Another good idea might be a Logout button, and if you are feeling really brave, you could implement a *multiplayer mode*. There are many options for developing this application further. You are only limited by your imagination!

The example demonstrates in an impressive way the new options offered by the WebSocket protocol for developing interactive applications. Our examples dealt with interaction between users. But a feature you could easily implement would be the WebSocket server getting information from the Internet, processing it, and then sending it to the connected users. The previously mentioned application for broadcasting current stock market prices would be a good example of this. Another possible scenario would be displaying new messages received in Twitter. The advantages are obvious: The client is notified of news via the mes-sage event, and the data stream between client and server is very lean, conserving network bandwidth.

Summary

With WebSockets, a new protocol has stepped onto the WWW stage. By no means does this spell the end of the Hypertext Transfer Protocol. The WebSocket protocol was developed for special applications where bidirectional communication between client and server with little overhead is required.

Both the server-side and the client APIs are very easy to program, as you can see from our first example of a rudimentary chat application. A full-blown, multiuser, online game is presented in our final example, *Battleships!*. Here, too, the communication between client and server can be programmed with a few lines of JavaScript code, and less code always means less risk of errors.

The introduction of WebSockets makes it easy to program web applications that previously could only be realized very laboriously via XMLHttpRequests or by constantly reloading web pages. Large amounts of rapidly changing data can then be monitored through one website; stock exchange data is just one example.

10

Web Workers

If you have already been experimenting a bit with JavaScript, you may have come across a browser message similar to this: *A script on this page may be busy, or it may have stopped responding.* This could be the result of a programming error, perhaps an endless loop. But what should you do if your JavaScript does not have an error and the calculation is just taking a bit longer than usual? This is where web workers come in.

10.1   Introduction to Web Workers

To ensure that long calculations on the client side do not block the browser, a *worker* can work in the background and inform the calling script about the status of its calculations via messages. Workers have no access to DOM APIs, the `window` object, and the document object. What at first seems like a great limitation is in fact very sensible on closer inspection. If scripts running in parallel access the same resources and change them, very complex situations can arise as a result. The strict isolation of the workers and their communication via messages makes the JavaScript code more secure.

The start of a new worker is relatively labor intensive for the operating system, and each worker takes up more memory space than executing the same functions without workers. The advantages are obvious nevertheless: The browser remains able to react, and complicated calculations can be carried out in parallel, leading to a potential increase in speed for modern hardware.

When created, each worker receives the script containing the code for the worker:

```
var w = new Worker("calc.js");
```

The script, in this case `calc.js`, contains JavaScript code that is executed when the worker is called. Optionally, the worker contains an event handler for the `message` event, reacting to requests by the calling script. In practice, this supplies the worker with data for calculations and triggers the computing process:

```
addEventListener('message', function(evt) {
  // evt.data contains the data passed
```

The data transfer from the calling script to the worker and vice versa takes place via the `postMessage()` function. To supply the worker `w` with data, the following call is suitable:

```
w.postMessage(imgData);
```

JavaScript objects can be passed to the `postMessage()` call and converted to JSON strings internally by the browser. The important point is that this data is copied with every call, which can mean a considerable loss of speed in the case of large amounts of data.

As mentioned earlier, workers have no access to the `window` object. Exceptions are the functions of the WindowTimers interface: `setTimeout()`/`clearTimeout()` and `setInterval()`/`clearInterval()` can also be used within a worker. And workers can load external scripts, which is why the `importScripts()` function was introduced. One or more JavaScript files can be passed to this function (separated by commas), which the worker loads and can then use.

The worker also has read access to the `location` object, where the `href` attribute returns an absolute URL to the running worker. Via the XMLHttpRequest, workers can communicate with web services.

For web workers, the specification distinguishes between Dedicated Workers and Shared Workers; the second category, Shared Workers, is able to receive messages from different scripts and send their own messages to various scripts. In this chapter, we will only address the first variety, *Dedicated Workers*; for information on *Shared Workers*, please refer to the relevant sections in the specification at

http://dev.w3.org/html5/workers/#shared-workers-introduction.

Because this specification on web workers is still in an early stage and the existing implementations in WebKit and Firefox are still incomplete, we will omit a detailed description of the API and instead present you with two introductory examples of the way web workers function.

10.2 Search for Leap Years

Both prime numbers and the Fibonacci sequence have already been calculated sufficiently with web workers (you can easily find the relevant examples via Google). We want to turn to another, similarly exciting, task. In the first example, we will search for leap years since 1.1.1970. Because this task would only take a few fractions of a second on modern hardware and would not demonstrate the capabilities of web workers, we will make it difficult for our program. It is supposed to check for very short time spans (seconds or minutes) if it is February 29 and therefore a leap year. A selection for the step size of the time span is required, because different hardware will execute the program at different speeds. Figure 10.1 shows the output on a weak CPU after several seconds.

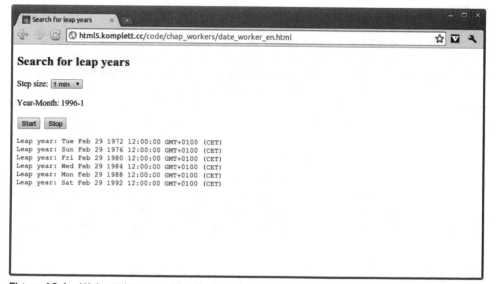

Figure 10.1 Web worker searching for leap years

Clicking the Start button executes the startCalc() function. This reads the step value set in the option field and then initializes the web worker worker with the script date_worker.js:

```
var opts = document.forms.stepForm.step.options;
startCalc = function() {
   var step = opts[opts.selectedIndex].value;
   var w = new Worker('date_worker.js');
   w.postMessage(step);
```

The call of the postMessage() function to which the selected step size is passed communicates with the event listener for the message event in the script date_worker.js. Now the worker starts working:

```
addEventListener('message', function(evt) {
   var today = new Date();
   var oldMonth = -1;
   for (var i=0; i<today; i+=Number(evt.data)*1000) {
     var d = new Date(i);
     if (d.getDate() == 29 && d.getMonth() == 1
       && d.getHours() == 12 && d.getMinutes() == 0) {
       postMessage(d.toLocaleString());
     }
     if (d.getMonth() != oldMonth) {
       postMessage("y "+d.getFullYear()+"-"
         +(d.getMonth()+1));
       oldMonth = d.getMonth();
     }
   }
}, false);
```

A for loop in the worker runs from the second 0 to the current date (today), converting the value passed by postMessage() to a number via the Number() function and then multiplying it by 1000 to get the step size. Access to the postMessage() data takes place via the data attribute, which you have already encountered in the previous chapter about WebSockets. Multiplying by 1000 is necessary because the variable today contains the current value in milliseconds, not in seconds. If a date in the loop is recognized as February 29, the worker sends a message to the calling script and passes the day as a formatted string.

To indicate the current progress of the calculation, the program sends another message as soon as the loop reaches a new month. This message starts with the string "y " and also contains the year and the month. The following listing shows how the calling script distinguishes this message from a leap year notification:

```
w.onmessage = function(evt) {
   if (evt.data.substr(0,2) == "y ") {
```

```
      $("y").innerHTML = evt.data.substr(2);
    } else {
      $("cnt").innerHTML += "Leap year: "+evt.data+"\n";
    }
}
```

The substr() function extracts the first two characters of the variable evt.data and compares them to the value "y ". In the case of a match, the field for displaying the date is updated; otherwise, the date is added as a new line to the field with the ID cnt. As in many other examples, we use the $() function as an abbreviation for the document.getElementById() call.

If the worker takes too long to run (for example, if your computer does not compute fast enough), you can force the process to end by clicking the Stop button. This stops the worker via the terminate() function; thereafter, the Start button is reactivated after being inactive during the computation:

```
stopCalc = function() {
  w.terminate();
  $("start").removeAttribute("disabled");
}
```

The next, more extensive example shows how several workers can work in parallel and carry out a more practical computation than the previous one.

10.3   Calculate Altitude Profiles with Canvas

Among the areas where web workers are particularly useful is undoubtedly the client-side analysis of audio, video, and image files. In our example, we use a PNG file showing the area of Tyrol, Austria, with a special feature: The image's alpha channel contains the altitude information of the area. You can find this image online at

http://html5.komplett.cc/code/chap_workers/images/topo_elevation_alpha.png.

Via canvas we can not only read the color values, but also the alpha channel values (see Chapter 5, Canvas), allowing us to carry out computations regarding the region. One simple example for such a computation is an altitude profile, extracting the altitude value for each point along a certain line.

The profiles in our example consist of several sections, and we can set both the number of the sections and the number of profiles via text fields on the website. This is necessary to be able to adapt the computation to computers of different speeds. The individual profile sections result from randomly chosen points within the picture. We want the program to display a progress bar during the computation and to output the calculated minimum and maximum altitude along the profile. Once all sections have been calculated, the program returns the number of points found. The website displays the number of points as well as the time it took to calculate the profile. It would make sense to send the entire altitude profile back to the calling program as a result, but if many sections are used, the profile takes up a lot of memory space and slows down the program considerably. This would not achieve the desired demo effect. Figure 10.2 shows two profiles being calculated in parallel using web workers.

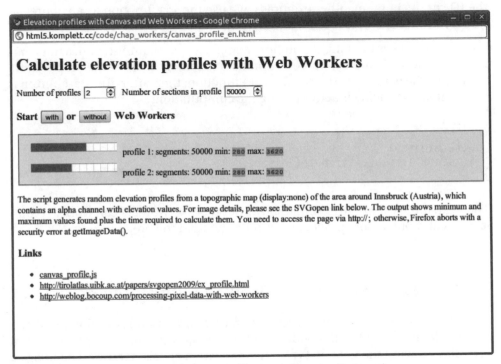

Figure 10.2   Web workers calculating two altitude profiles simultaneously

If we are creating more than one profile, we can let the web workers carry out the calculations in parallel, whereas an analysis without web workers always has to be done sequentially. On modern hardware, where the operating system has multiple core processors available on the CPU, this means that the browser can divvy up the workload between the different cores. Figure 10.3 shows this situation on a system with four CPU cores. Although the call with web workers uses two cores to 100 percent capacity (at about 30 seconds), we can see in the second case that without web workers only one CPU core is used to its full capacity (at 15 seconds). The result is a marginally faster computation with web workers, with the browser reacting to input during the computation and continually updating the progress bar.

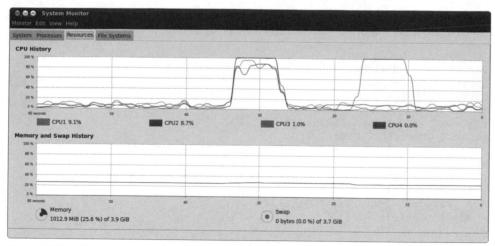

Figure 10.3 CPU usage in calculations with and without web workers

10.3.1   Important Code Fragments

To compare how the script behaves with and without web workers, you can call the program with both methods. You first need to integrate the external Java-Script file containing the code for the worker (canvas_profile.js) into the head of the calling website. From that point on, the onmessage function is globally available—but more on the worker code shortly. Let's start with the HTML code for the program:

```
<script src="canvas_profile.js"></script>
...
<h1>Calculate elevation profiles with Web Workers</h1>
<p>Number of profiles <input type=number id=profiles
  size=2 oninput="updateProgressBars();" value=2>
Number of sections in profile
<input type=number id=parts value=500 size=4
  oninput="updateProgressBars();">
</p>
<h3>Start
<input type=button onclick="calcProfiles(true)"
    value="with"> or
<input type=button onclick="calcProfiles(false)"
    value="without"> Web Workers
</h3>
```

Each time the content of the two input fields of the type number are changed, they cause the function updateProgressBars() to be called. In it, the progress bar and the placeholders for the results output are created. The two buttons with and without start the calculation of the altitude profiles.

In the JavaScript code, we first extract the altitude values from the PNG image. To do this, we load the image into a new canvas element:

```
var canvas = document.createElement("CANVAS");
canvas.width = 300;
canvas.height = 300;
var context = canvas.getContext('2d');
var image = document.querySelector("IMG");
context.drawImage(image,0,0);
// document.querySelector("BODY").appendChild(canvas);
var elev =
context.getImageData(0,0,canvas.width,canvas.height).data;
var alpha = [];
for (var i=0; i<elev.length; i+=4) {
  alpha.push(elev[i+3]);
}
```

In the variable image, the only img element on the website is loaded and then drawn onto the newly created canvas element. Neither the image nor the canvas is visible on the website, because the img element is marked with display:none and the canvas is never attached to the DOM tree. If you activate the commented-out line in the preceding code, you can see the canvas at the end of the page. As you know from Chapter 5, Canvas, the getImageData() function produces an array with the color and alpha channel values of the canvas (in each case four entries per pixel). Because only the alpha channel values are relevant for our example, we extract them from the array via the for loop. This data reduction is sensible because each worker receives a copy of the array. If we are starting four workers in parallel, the memory usage increases linearly with each worker.

The calcProfiles() function then starts the calculation with or without workers, depending on whether *true* or *false* is passed to the function:

```
calcProfiles = function(useWorker) {
  USE_WORKER = useWorker;
  startTime = new Date();
  for (var i=0; i<PROFILES; i++) {
    var imgData = {
      id : i,
      alpha: alpha,
      parts : PARTS,
      height : canvas.height,
      width : canvas.width
    }
```

The variable PROFILES contains the value of the relevant input field and controls how often the central for loop is run. The imgData variable is created with the altitude values of the image (alpha), the number of sections (PARTS), the canvas height (height), and canvas width (width), plus an ID (id), with the latter being required as reference for the profiles. Then the program logic divides itself into the part working with web workers and the part without web workers:

```
if (USE_WORKER) {
  imgData.useWorker = true;
  var worker = new Worker('canvas_profile.js');
  worker.postMessage(imgData);
  worker.onmessage = function(evt){
    if (evt.data.task == 'update') {
      progress.item(evt.data.id).value = evt.data.status*i;
    } else if (evt.data.task == 'newMin') {
      $('progDivMin'+evt.data.id).innerHTML = evt.data.min;
    } else if (evt.data.task == 'newMax') {
      $('progDivMax'+evt.data.id).innerHTML = evt.data.max;
    } else {
      showResults(evt);
    }
  };
}
else {
  imgData.useWorker = false;
  showResults(
    onmessage({data:imgData})
  );
  progress.item(i).value = PARTS;
}
```

In the first case, a new worker is created and activated with postMessage(). The entire data structure of the imgData variable is passed to it. Then an event listener is defined, which receives four different message types. Messages of the type update will update the progress bar, and newMin and newMax reset the relevant altitude values on the website. All other messages call the showResult() function, which works out the time of the calculation and displays it with the number of points on the altitude profile.

If the call is to be started without workers, the onmessage() function of the external JavaScript file is started, with the imgData variable wrapped into the data attribute of a JavaScript object. This is useful because the postMessage() call in the worker also wraps data into such a structure, and we therefore do not need to further adapt the external code.

The external JavaScript file canvas_profile.js starts with the onmessage() function. In the notation shown here, this function has a double purpose: as an event handler for the worker's message event and also as a global function, which we can call without a worker. In it, the random points for the individual sections are created:

```
onmessage = function(evt) {
...
  var p1 = [Math.round(Math.random()*(evt.data.width-1)),
```

```
             Math.round(Math.random()*(evt.data.height-1))];
    for (var i=1; i<evt.data.parts; i++) {
      var p2 = [Math.round(Math.random()*(evt.data.width-1)),
             Math.round(Math.random()*(evt.data.height-1))];
      var len = Math.sqrt((Math.pow(p2[0]-p1[0],2)
        +Math.pow(p2[1]-p1[1],2)));
      var profile = [];
      for (var j=0; j<len-1; j++) {
...
      var h = getHeight([x,y]);
```

The length in pixels (len) between the two random points (p1 and p2) is calculated via the *Pythagorean theorem*, using the JavaScript function Math.sqrt() (for the square root) and Math.pow() (for squaring). Then a second loop runs over all pixels along this route and extracts the altitude value from the array:

```
var getHeight = function(p) {
  var pos = ((parseInt(p[1])*evt.data.width) +
             parseInt(p[0]));
  return evt.data.alpha[pos] * equidistance;
};
```

To determine the desired position within the one-dimensional array of alpha channel values, we need to multiply the y-value by the canvas width and then add the x-value. The attentive reader will have noticed another detail: Before returning the determined value, it is multiplied by the variable equidistance. The reason is that we can only save 256 different values per channel in an 8-bit image file. But the area around Innsbruck, Austria, has an altitude difference of more than 256 meters, so the altitude in this PNG image is specified in steps of 20 meters.

If a new minimum value along a profile line is found, the calling script is notified accordingly:

```
if (h < min) {
  min = h;
  if (evt.data.useWorker) {
    postMessage({task:'newMin',min:min,id: evt.data.id});
  }
}
```

The same applies of course for new maximum values. At the end of each loop over all sections, the progress bar is updated, and as soon as all sections have been calculated, the result, wrapped in the variable d, is sent back to the main script. If the script is executed as a worker, the data is sent with postMessage(), without a worker, the result is returned to the calling function with return:

```
if (evt.data.useWorker) {
  postMessage({task:'update', status:i, id:evt.data.id});
}
...
if (evt.data.useWorker) {
  postMessage(d);
}
else {
  return {data:d};
}
```

The client-side analysis of image data conserves server capacity and network bandwidth. Provided there is suitable hardware equipment on the client side, this could give users the option of digitalizing altitude profiles on an image with an alpha channel and then graphically representing these in realtime.

If this has whet your appetite for web workers, please do not forget that using workers requires more resources than scripts working without workers. Data transfer with messages between a worker and the calling script is especially slower than in a script with direct access to the resources.

Summary

This chapter introduced the concept of scripts running parallel in the browser. In desktop applications these are known as threads; in the browser they are called web workers. Access to the elements of the website is subject to certain restrictions, but information can comfortably be exchanged between the calling script and the individual workers through the concept of message passing.

Web workers are particularly useful for large web applications where processes are running in the background and should not block user input. Think for example of automatic saving while you are working on a document or coloring source code while you create it, as demonstrated by Mozilla's Web Editor *Ace*.

11

Microdata

Saturday, October 9th 2010, just before half past eight in the evening. Pat Metheny steps onto the stage of the sold-out Community Theater in Morristown, NJ. The stage is decorated with a Persian rug and heavy red drapes. In the background we spot a piano, two vibraphones, various small instruments, and several strange objects resembling organ pipes, pharmaceutical jars, or rocket launchers.

The setting seems rather strange, because the long-time companions of the ingenious guitarist are missing: no Antonio Sanchez on the drums, no Steve Rodby on the bass, and no Lyle Mays on the piano. Instead of the Pat Metheny Group in flesh and blood, we now see an army of machines, small hammers, and LEDs which are activated in turn to bring the surrogate human artists to life. By the time we have listened to the obligatory solo on the 42-string guitar, just as the red curtain is lifting, the whole dimension of the enterprise Orchestrion hits home: This will be a fascinating evening full of awe and wonder.

This could be the beginning of a fictitious review of a concert in an equally fictitious blog: two paragraphs full of information, filtered and combined automatically by the reader whilst reading. The event is defined in terms of time and location; objects, instruments, and events on stage are recognized and people mentioned in the text are identified as a matter of course as musicians with their respective instruments. The human brain is trained to filter information efficiently. Computers are not and require help to filter information. This help basically boils down to marking and correlating the relevant information.

Which information is relevant depends entirely on what we want to filter out of the text. For a diary it would be the name of the event, its time, and place; for an address book, the contact details of the musicians; and for searching for new CDs to add to your music collection, you need the names of the artists and bands. One option for offering the quintessence of a text in the relevant context and in machine-readable form is *microdata*—a very young and emotionally debated feature of HTML5.

In the eyes of many critics, microdata stands in direct competition with RDFa, the Resource Description Framework, another option of embedding metadata. Its close connection to XHTML makes it especially difficult to fit in with the concept of HTML5, which lacks the *namespaces* used abundantly in RDFa. The result of the tug-of-war between the two approaches is, not surprisingly, two specifications, with microdata present both as an integrated WHATWG version and as a W3C *stand-alone* version, whereas RDFa can only be found in the W3C. The links to the specifications are

- http://www.w3.org/TR/microdata
- http://www.whatwg.org/specs/web-apps/current-work/multipage/links. html#microdata
- http://www.w3.org/TR/rdfa-in-html

The *a* in RDFa stands for *attributes*, which brings us to the feature both techniques have in common. Both RDFa and microdata use a set of attributes to define metadata. In RDFa, this metadata is present as a triple of subject, predicate, and object. As explained in Wikipedia with regard to the Resource Description Framework, the subject denotes the resource (*Pat Metheny*), the predicate denotes traits or aspects of the resource (*musician*), and the object expresses a relationship between the subject and the object (*Orchestrion*). With microdata, the information ends up as name-value pairs, such as *Pat Metheny : musician* or *Pat Metheny : Orchestrion*. Which of the two approaches will ultimately prevail is uncertain. Both techniques have advantages and disadvantages, and could also co-exist. But because microdata can already be integrated seamlessly into HTML5, we will concentrate on microdata in this chapter.

11.1   The Syntax of Microdata

If we take the text at the beginning of the chapter and add a few links, an image, and the signature of the blog author, we end up with a complete, fictitious blog entry, as shown in Figure 11.1. It will accompany us through an explanation of the microdata syntax.

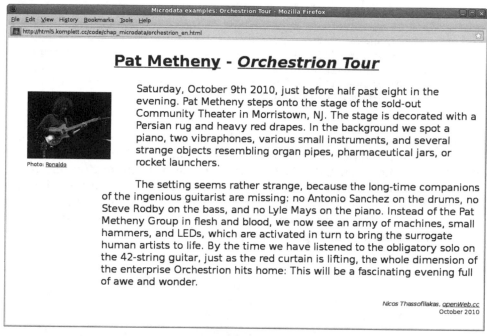

Figure 11.1   Screen shot of fictitious blog entry about Pat Metheny's Orchestrion Tour

11.1.1   The Attributes "itemscope" and "itemprop"

We first need to define the area relevant for microdata. Structuring elements are suitable, as are container elements, such as div or p. In our example, we chose an article element, which encloses the entire blog entry. The required attribute for defining the scope starts with *item*—just as the other four microdata attributes—has the type *boolean*, and is called, rather logically, itemscope:

```
<article itemscope>
...
</article>
```

The itemscope defines a new group of name-value pairs, also called *items* in the specification. The corresponding values are supplied by itemprop attributes, where *prop* means *properties*. If we want to mark all musicians in the text as musicians, we therefore require four `itemprop` attributes, which we insert in a suitable place. If no suitable elements are readily available, we first need to create them as a span or div element. So "Pat Metheny" becomes "Pat Metheny" in the HTML code, an addition that does not affect the text layout and allows us to specify an `itemprop` attribute for the span element. Unlike `itemscope`, `itemprop` is not a *boolean* attribute, but defines the name of the corresponding property via its attribute value:

```
<article itemscope>
... <span itemprop=musician>Pat Metheny</span> steps onto the stage ...
... <span itemprop=musician>Antonio Sanchez</span> on the drums ...
... <span itemprop=musician>Steve Rodby</span> on the  bass ...
... <span itemprop=musician>Lyle Mays</span> on the piano ...
</article>
```

Our first microdata example is now complete, and the question arises as to how this metadata could be interpreted by a search engine spider that indexes the blog entry. Philip Jägenstedt's Live Microdata viewer, from now on referred to as *microdata viewer*, helps us visualize the data structure. This is an online application where we can copy code fragments with microdata content into a text field, making hidden microdata visible in JSON notation. You should probably save the link http://foolip.org/microdatajs/live as a bookmark: You will need it for testing all code examples.

TIP

To avoid having to painstakingly retype the example texts, all HTML code fragments in this chapter are available as a plain text file online so they can easily be copied into the microdata viewer. The individual fragments are listed in the same order as they appear in the chapter. The link to the file is http://html5.komplett.cc/code/chap_microdata/fragments_en.txt.

If we copy the second HTML fragment from the file `fragments_en.txt` into Philip Jägenstedt's microdata viewer, the JSON notation shows the following structure:

```
{
  "items":[{
      "properties":{
        "musician":["Pat Metheny",
          "Antonio Sanchez",
          "Steve Rodby",
          "Lyle Mays"
        ]
      }
    }
  ]
}
```

At first glance, the many curly and square brackets may seem confusing, but they disclose the metadata structure very clearly if you look closer. Each entry (*"items"*) consists of an array of properties (*"properties"*), which are in turn made up of name-value pairs with the name of the property (*"musician"*) and the corresponding values (*"Pat Metheny," "Antonio Sanchez," "Steve Rodby," "Lyle Mays"*) as an array.

Some HTML elements automatically define the value of the specified property as soon as an itemprop attribute is assigned to them. Let's use the blog entry's descriptive picture to test the microdata viewer and give it an itemprop attribute *image*:

```
<article itemscope>
  <img itemprop=image src=icons/orchestrion.jpg alt=...>
</article>
```

This automatically gives us the value of the src attribute as the value for the property *image*. In addition to the img element, there are a number of other elements to which this behavior applies. You can see them in Table 11.1.

Table 11.1 Elements with special "itemprop" values

Attribute	Element(s)
src	audio, embed, iframe, img, source, video
href	a, area, link
datetime	time
content	meta
data	object

Let's turn back to the spider, which is now indexing our microdata-filled blog. It won't know what to make of the items *musician* and *image*. The reason is because we have defined our own microdata terms that have meaning only to us. To be able to use microdata sensibly, we need standardized dialects that can be comprehended by our spider, just as by an intelligent mail program that automatically extracts e-mail addresses encoded as microdata if you drag a URL into its address book, or by a diary able to recognize diary dates by the same method.

11.1.2 The "itemtype" Attribute

We do not have far to go during our search for standardized dialects. The WHAT-WG's Microdata specification already contains three of them: *vCard* for contact information, *vEvents* for dates of events, and a third one for specifying licenses of a work. A multitude of other dialects can be found in the microformats *community* at http://microformats.org. But in contrast to microdata, these dialects are defined in the microformats scheme, making lavish use of class and rel attributes for determining metadata structure.

With the attribute itemtype, you determine that the existing microdata follows a standardized vocabulary. As an attribute value, itemtype expects a URL for the corresponding standard. vCard and vEvent reflect the close link between microdata and microformats, because both profiles in the specification refer directly to microformats.org:

- http://microformats.org/profile/hcard
- http://microformats.org/profile/hcalendar#vevent

Let's try to code a vEvent for the concert in our blog entry. We need to add the correct itemtype and then specify the itemprop attributes in accordance with the hCalendar specification:

```
<article itemscope
 itemtype=http://microformats.org/profile/hcalendar#vevent>
 <time itemprop=dtstart
   datetime="2010-10-09T20:30:00-04:00">
   Saturday, October 9th 2010, just before half past eight in the
evening
 </time> ...
 <span itemprop=location>Community Theater</span> in
 <span itemprop=location>Morristown, NJ</span>...
 <span itemprop=summary>Orchestrion</span> ...
</article>
```

If we copy this microdata fragment into the microdata viewer, we can see another output option next to the JSON notation, this time in *iCal* format, which could be seamlessly imported into your own calendar:

```
BEGIN:VCALENDAR
PRODID:jQuery Microdata
VERSION:2.0
BEGIN:VEVENT
DTSTAMP;VALUE=DATE-TIME:20101227T205755Z
DTSTART;VALUE=DATE-TIME:20101009T2030000400
LOCATION:Community Theater
LOCATION:Morristown\, NJ
```

```
SUMMARY:Orchestrion
END:VEVENT
END:VCALENDAR
```

The conversion of microdata to the iCal format is based on Philip Jägenstedt's JavaScript library *microdatajs,* which is also the core of the microdata viewer. You can download it from http://gitorious.org/microdatajs.

On this occasion we can also write the license for this library as a microdata structure. The rules for the vocabulary are in the WHATWG version of the microdata specification in the section *Licensing works* and require as an itemtype the URL *http://n.whatwg.org/work* plus the keywords work, title, author, and license as *itemprop* attributes:

```
<div itemscope itemtype=http://n.whatwg.org/work>
<a itemprop=work
 href="http://gitorious.org/microdatajs">
 <span itemprop=title>microdatajs</span></a> by
<span itemprop=author>Philip Jägenstedt</span>
<a itemprop=license
 href=http://creativecommons.org/licenses/publicdomain/>
 (<span>Public Domain</span>)</a>
</div>
```

The next example shows how microdata dialects can be used in combination. As part of a concert review, it makes sense to code the event as vEvent and the author of the review as vCard. The technique for nesting dialects is quite simple. If we want to define the itemProp attribute reviewer in the hReview dialect as vCard, we just have to add an itemScope attribute with the itemType of the vCard dialect to the same element and then add the desired entries of the vCard. The same applies for embedding vEvent into hReview and can be tested with the following code fragment in the microdata viewer:

```
<article itemscope
 itemtype=http://microformats.org/wiki/hreview>
 <div
  itemprop=item itemscope
  itemtype=http://microformats.org/profile/hcalendar#vevent>
  <span itemprop=summary>Orchestrion</span>,
  <time itemprop=dtstart
   datetime="2010-10-09T20:30:00-04:00">October 9th 2010
  </time>:
 </div>
 <span itemprop="summary">A fascinating evening</span>
 rated with <span itemprop="rating">5</span> stars out of 5 stars.
 <div itemprop=reviewer itemscope
  itemtype=http://microformats.org/profile/hcard>
  <span itemprop=fn>Nicos Thassofilakas</span>,
```

```
    <a href=http://openweb.cc itemprop=url>openWeb.cc</a>
  </div>
</article>
```

11.1.3   The "itemid" Attribute

As soon as a microdata structure has an itemtype attribute, items in the dialect used can be tagged with unique IDs via the itemid attribute. Examples of such IDs are the ISBN (*International Standard Book Number*) for books, the EAN (*European Article Number*) for identifying products, and the ASIN (*Amazon Standard Identification Number*) for orders within Amazon.

Valid values for the itemid attribute are URLs, including Uniform Resource Names (URN) with the prefix urn:. Using a fictitious vocabulary for describing books, the tablature of Pat Metheny's solo album *One Quiet Night* could be identified via its unique ISBN number:

```
<div itemscope
     itemtype=http://vocab.example.net/book
     itemid="urn:isbn:978-0634066634">
<span itemprop=album>One Quiet Night</span> by
<span itemprop=artist>Pat Metheny</span>
(<time itemprop=pubdate datetime=2005-04-01>2005</time>,
<span itemprop=pages>88</span> pages)
</div>
```

11.1.4   The "itemref" Attribute

Often, it is not possible to accommodate all desired microdata information within one container element. With our blog entry, the itemscope attribute goes with the surrounding article element, and all associated itemProp attributes are within the article. If you want to include itemProp attributes outside of the article elements, you can use itemref attributes. Separated by commas, they contain a list of IDs of elements also to be searched for microdata contents. The connection between the itemscope attribute and a container element can then be removed completely:

```
<article>
  <div id=location>
    <span itemprop=member>Pat Metheny</span>
  </div>
  <div id=intro>
    <span itemprop=member>Antonio Sanchez</span>
    <span itemprop=member>Steve Rodby</span>
```

```
    <span itemprop=member>Lyle Mays</span>
    <span itemprop=band>Pat Metheny Group</span>
  </div>
</article>
<div itemscope itemref="location intro"></div>
```

In this example, the two paragraphs of the blog entry are divided into two div elements with the IDs *location* and *intro*. Within these div elements, the individual musicians are identified as members of the band *Pat Metheny Group* via itemprop attributes. The itemscope attribute is outside of the article and refers via the itemref attribute to the IDs of those areas where the actual information can be found. In complicated microdata structures, this option can be very useful.

11.2 The Microdata DOM API

As you would expect, the microdata structure of a document can also be explored via JavaScript via the *microdata DOM API*.

Accessing all *top-level* microdata items (that is, those items that have an itemscope attribute and are not part of another item) takes place via the method document.getItems(). It returns as a result a *DOM-NodeList* of elements found in the order in which they appear in the DOM tree. If we are only after items of a particular type, we could pass a list of desired itemtype attributes, separated by commas, in the getItems() call:

```
var allNodes = document.getItems();
var vCards = document.getItems(
  'http://microformats.org/profile/hcard'
);
```

Each element of the resulting *NodeList* allows access to the additional microdata attributes present for each element. Table 11.2 lists the attribute names and their content.

Table 11.2 Attributes of a top-level microdata item

Attribute	Content
itemScope	Value of itemscope attribute
itemType	Value of itemtype attribute, if present
itemId	Value of itemid attribute, if present
itemRef	Value of itemref attribute, if present

Starting from the relevant *top-level* item, we can then work towards the properties defined with `itemprop`. We find these in `item.properties`, the so-called `HTMLPropertiesCollection`, which allows access to the name-value pairs of each property via additional interfaces. The elements are sorted according to their position in the DOM tree. Table 11.3 shows the required attributes and methods, and their content.

Table 11.3   Attributes and methods of "HTMLPropertiesCollection"

Attribute/Method	Content
length	Number of elements in a collection
item(index)	Element in a collection at position *index*
namedItem(name)	Collection consisting of the elements whose `itemprop` attribute has the value *name*
namedItem(name).values	Array with the contents of all `itemprop` attributes whose value is *name*
names	`DOMStringList` of all `itemprop` attribute values in the collection
names.length	Number of `itemprop` attribute values
names.item(index)	Name of `itemprop` attribute value at position *index*
names.contains(name)	*Boolean* attribute for testing if the string *name* is present as an `itemprop` attribute value

The last attribute in the microdata DOM API is `itemValue`. It allows access to the content of elements that have an `itemprop` attribute. If an element in a variable `elem` is a container—for example, `article`, `div`, or `span`—then `elem.itemValue` represents the text content that can also be changed.

You need to be careful if nested items are involved, because then the element concerned also has an `itemscope` attribute and the content of the element has to be interpreted independently, almost as a *top-level* item. The specification takes this into account and requires that in this case `elem.itemValue` makes a new item object available.

A second and last special case concerns HTML elements, which you have already encountered as elements with special status in the section on `itemprop` attributes. `a`, `src`, `time`, `meta`, and `object` belong to this category and assign their `href`, `src`, `datetime`, `content`, or `data` attribute to `elem.itemValue`, in contrast to the usual practice. The list of all representatives in this category are found in Table 11.1.

Summary

In this chapter we take a closer look at the syntax of microdata, a mechanism to add semantic markup to documents using a variety of global attributes. Starting with the *boolean* attribute `itemscope` that marks the area relevant for microdata and defines a new, empty group of name-value pairs— the so-called items—we then move on to the `itemprop` attribute that actually defines the name of the corresponding property via its attribute value.

We use the `itemtype` attributes to denote standardized vocabularies like `vCard` for contact information or `vEvents` for dates of events and `itemid` attributes to tag items in these dialects with unique IDs, such as ISBN or EAN numbers. Last but not least we finish the topic of microdata attributes with `itemref`, enabling us to specify a comma-separated list of element IDs also to be searched for microdata contents. A walk through the Microdata DOM API concludes this chapter and shows how you can easily access your microdata structure via JavaScript.

Unfortunately, no browser supports microdata at the time of this writing, so the only way to explore the many examples shown in this chapter is with Philip Jägenstedt's Live Microdata viewer, which is available at http://foolip.org/microdatajs/live. We can only wait and see if and when microdata will eventually become established.

12

Finishing Touches:
Some Global Attributes

In this last chapter, we will look at some seemingly insignificant global attributes of the HTMLElement interface. Our leitmotif in this chapter will be the development of a simple game that requires putting terms in a particular order following given criteria, similar to the preliminary round of the popular TV show *Who Wants to Be a Millionaire*. We call our game *1- 2-3-4!* It involves the capital cities of the 27 EU member states. Can you put the capital cities in order by number of inhabitants? Do you know which city is farther north, south, west, or east? If not, you probably will by the end of this chapter.

12.1   News for the "class" Attribute

We first turn to a new DOM method of the `HTMLElement` interface, which allows us easy access to elements by the content of their respective `class` attribute: `document.getElementsByClassName()`. Its use could hardly be simpler and looks like this:

```
var questions = document.getElementsByClassName('q');
```

This gives us a list ordered by position in the DOM tree of all elements whose `class` attribute contains the value q. If this list happens to consist of `li` elements with the names of the capital cities, the first step toward implementing our game is done: A live reference to the game objects is set in the variable `questions`. It reflects the current status of the individual `li` elements:

```
<li id=de class=q>Berlin</li>
<li id=at class=q>Vienna</li>
<!-- and 25 others -->
```

Access to the individual `li` elements can happen in two ways: either via the offset in the list or via a name, by which we do not mean the node content but the value of the existing id or name attribute:

```
questions.item(1).innerHTML          => Vienna
questions.namedItem('de').innerHTML  => Berlin
```

The length of the list can be found in `questions.length`, which means the offset for `item(i)` values can be between 0 and `questions.length-1`. Instead of an id attribute, elements with `name` attributes, for example `form`, can also be searched via `namedItem(str)` for values in this attribute.

If you want to search for several classes, you only need to pass the desired values during the method call, separated by spaces. Using the fictitious example of a fruit shop, searching for fruit defined as *red* or *apple* as their *I like* criteria could be successful with the following instruction:

```
var mmm = document.getElementsByClassName('red apple');
```

This helps us find all red fruit, all apples, and of course also a red apple.

12.2 Defining Custom Attributes with "data-*"

Previously, it was not possible in HTML to freely define custom attributes within your application, but now the HTML specification offers a mechanism to achieve exactly that: the data-* attribute. Its use could not be simpler and only requires that the desired attribute has the prefix data-. There are few limitations for naming the attribute: It must be at least one character long and may not contain any uppercase letters. Using the data entry of one of the 27 capital cities of our game as an example, the data attributes for number of inhabitants, geographical location, and associated country could look like this:

```
<li id=at class=q
    data-pop=1705080
    data-geo-lat=48.20833
    data-geo-lng=16.373064
    data-country='Austria'>Vienna</li>
```

So how can you access your custom attributes? One option would be the classical method with getAttribute() and setAttribute(), but the specification has something better to offer: the dataset property. It allows for retrieving and setting all data attributes of an element via element.dataset:

```
var el  = q.namedItem('at');
var pop = el.dataset.pop;       // 1705080
var lat = el.dataset.geoLat;    // 48.208
var lng = el.dataset.geoLng;    // 16.373
var ctr = el.dataset.country;   // Austria
// and two years later perhaps ...
el.dataset.pop = 1717034;
```

By the time you read the third line, which contains el.dataset.geoLat, it will have become clear that hyphens have a special significance with data attributes; why else would data-geo-lat suddenly turn into dataset.geoLat. Hyphens are replaced by the next letter converted to uppercase—the special term for this way of capitalizing is called *CamelCase*. Now you know why no uppercase letters are allowed in data attributes: They could result in unexpected problems when replacing hyphens.

Unfortunately, support for element.dataset has not progressed well as yet. At the time of this writing, only WebKit had implemented the dataset DOM property in its *Nightly builds*. The game uses Remy Sharp's *html5-data.js* as a workaround for this shortcoming, a JavaScript *shim* that at least enables the reading of data attributes. For setting, we must resort to the good old setAttribute() method.

12.3 The "hidden" Attribute

In the *HTML Working Group*, the hidden attribute caused a great stir. It managed to reach *ISSUE* status with a following *Straw Poll for Objections* and only got its final blessing through a decision of the HTML Working Group chairmen. The critics mainly claimed that hidden is superfluous. We will shortly demonstrate that the hidden attribute can indeed be useful, because selecting the questions for our game will be done via hidden. The algorithm is quickly explained: We first hide all items with hidden and then reveal four randomly selected items again. The relevant JavaScript code looks like this:

```
var showRandomNItems = function(q,n) {
  var show = [];
  for (var i=0; i<q.length; i++) {
    q.item(i).hidden = true;
    show.push(i);
  }
  show.sort(function() {return 0.5 - Math.random()});
  for (var i=0; i<n; i++) {
    q.item(show[i]).hidden = false;
  }
};
```

As arguments, we pass the list with li elements in the variable q and the desired number of elements to be shown in n to the function showRandomNItems(). We then hide all items with hidden=true and fill a new array with the indices of 0 – q.length. This array is then put in random order, and the desired number n of capital cities is revealed again.

12.4 The "classList" Interface

With getElementsByClassName(), we have already encountered the first option of working with the global class attribute. The classList interface is another one, allowing us to manage all values of a class attribute in a so-called DOMTokenList via the methods item(), contains(), add(), remove(), and toggle(). Let's again use the example of the class attribute of a product in our fictitious fruit shop:

```
<li class="red apple">
```

Via li.classList, we then have the following properties:

```
li.classList.length          => 2
li.classList.item(0)         => red
```

```
li.classList.item(1)            => apple
li.classList.contains('red')    => true
li.classList.contains('apple')  => true
li.classList.contains('organic') => false
```

If we forgot to attach the organic label during pricing, we can assign it afterward to our red organic apple:

```
li.classlist.add('organic')
li.classList.item(2) => organic
```

The banana on the next shelf that traveled all the way from Ecuador has wrongly been categorized as organic; we can easily fix that mistake:

```
banana.classList.remove('organic')
```

For bread, fresh in the morning and not quite as fresh in the evening, we could insert toggle() for showing the relevant state:

```
// freshly baked in the morning
bread.classlist.add('fresh')
// late afternoon
bread.classList.toggle('fresh')
bread.classList.contains('fresh')   => false
// and the next morning after the new delivery
bread.classList.toggle('fresh')
bread.classList.contains('fresh')   => true
```

In the *1-2-3-4!* game we will use classList for displaying *correct* or *wrong* for the selected order. Before turning to the core of the game, the drag-and-drop function, we will quickly adapt the game's layout and add four areas to the left of the city list where the cities can be sorted. All four li elements get the class a for *answer* during the selection, analog to q for *question*, and Unicode symbols for numbering in the range ૘ to ૛—so-called *DINGBAT NEGATIVE CIRCLED DIGITS:*

```
<ol>
<li class=a>&#x2776;</li>
<li class=a>&#x2777;</li>
<li class=a>&#x2778;</li>
<li class=a>&#x2779;</li>
</ol>
```

With a few additional CSS formats, we finalize the static basic version of the game. Figure 12.1 shows the basic layout. The online version can be found at http://html5.komplett.cc/code/chap_global/1234_static_en.html.

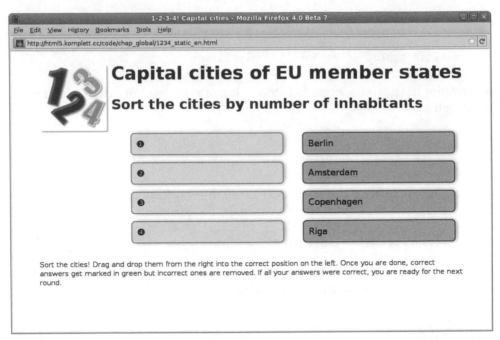

Figure 12.1 Static basic layout of the 1-2-3-4! game

As you can see in the title bar in Figure 12.1, the screen shot was created with a beta version of Firefox 4, because only that browser version meets the requirements of the game. With the exception of data-*, for which we use Remy Sharp's JavaScript *shim* as mentioned earlier, all necessary attributes and methods are implemented in this version.

12.5 Drag and Drop with the "draggable" Attribute

Drag and drop in the browser is really nothing new. This function has been present in Internet Explorer (IE) since 1999, in version 5.0 at that time. Based on the IE implementation, drag and drop was then included in the specification in 2005 and is now available in all common browsers, with the exception of Opera.

The checklist for the implementation of a classic drag-and-drop operation, as used in the game for sorting the cities by number of inhabitants, involves the following tasks:

1. Selecting elements that can be dragged
2. Determining data to be dragged along in the background as soon as the drag-and-drop operation is started

3. Deciding where the dragged element can be dropped
4. Extracting the data as soon as the user ends the drag-and-drop operation on a valid target object

We can fulfill the first task with the global draggable attribute. Via draggable=true it marks the relevant element as a candidate for dragging to another position. Two HTML elements are by default defined as draggable: the img element and the a element, provided it has an href attribute, which made it possible previously to drag links or images on the desktop and save them easily. If we wanted to prevent drag and drop in these elements, we could use draggable=false.

To prepare an entry in the city list for drag and drop, we first need to add the draggable attribute and set it to *true*:

```
<li id=be draggable=true>Brussels</li>
```

Drag-and-drop operations are not an end unto themselves but a means to an end: Their purpose is to transfer information from one place to another. Which information this is must be determined at the start of the *drag* operation in question, which is why we add a dragstart event handler to each item in our city list. It calls the callback function startDrag() and passes it the so-called DragEvent in the argument event:

```
<li id=be draggable=true
    ondragstart="startDrag(event)">Brussels</li>
```

This DragEvent plays a central role in drag and drop, because its *readonly* attribute dataTransfer gives us access to the DataTransfer interface of the drag-and-drop API, where all necessary methods and attributes of drag and drop are available. One of these methods is setData(format, data). This determines which data is to be dragged along in the background when dragging from A to B. In our case, it is the ID in the format *text*. With this we will later be able to access the original data:

```
var dragStart = function(evt) {
   evt.dataTransfer.setData('text',evt.target.id);
};
```

From this point on, the list item can be dragged—where we will drop it remains open. It would be helpful to have a droppable attribute available in parallel to the draggable attribute, but this is not the case, which is why we require no less than three events for successful dropping: dragenter, dragover, and drop. Strangely enough, two of them must be aborted in order for the third and most important event to be fired. The HTML code for one of the list items on the left of the game, where the cities are arranged, shows us which ones they are

```
<li ondragenter="return false;"
    ondragover="return false;"
    ondrop="drop(event)">&#x2776;</li>
```

The two events dragenter and dragover exist primarily to signal: *You can drop here!* In our case, they are immediately aborted with return false. If we were to use two callback functions, we could offer additional user feedback, for example: *You can drop here!* for dragenter or *Are you sure you got it right?* for dragover. To abort the event in the callback function, we do not use return false, but instead use evt.preventDefault(). The effect is the same; it fires the drop event.

This brings us to the last task of the checklist, extracting previously set data and implementing the game logic with the ondrop event. We again pass the DragEvent in the argument event to the callback function drop() and then use getData() to access the ID saved at dragstart:

```
var drop = function(evt) {
  var id = evt.dataTransfer.getData('text');
  var elemQ = questions.namedItem(id);
  var elemA = evt.target;
  elemA.setAttribute("data-id",id);
  elemA.setAttribute("data-pop",elemQ.dataset.pop);
  elemA.innerHTML = elemQ.innerHTML;
  // continue game logic
};
```

Via the ID, we can use questions.namedItem(id) to directly access the source object, store its number of inhabitants as a data attribute in the target object, and use its city name as a label. The two variables elemQ and elemA are *shortcuts* for the two li elements involved. Remember that Remy Sharp's JavaScript *shim* for data attributes unfortunately works only for read access, so we use the familiar elamA.setAttribute("data-id",id) for saving the values instead of the more elegant elemA.dataset.id=id.

As part of the game logic, the two buttons concerned are also deactivated at this point and visual feedback is given—in both cases via CSS classes, which we can conveniently add via classList.add(). The additional items in the function drop() are

```
elemQ.classList.add('qInactive');
elemA.classList.add('aInactive');
```

The corresponding formats in the CSS stylesheet are as follows:

```
.qInactive {
  pointer-events: none;
```

```
    color: #AAA;
    background-color: #EEE;
    border-color: #AAA;
}
.aInactive {
    pointer-events: none;
    background-color: hsl(60,100%,85%);
    border-color: hsl(60,100%,40%);
}
```

At this point in the game, we check whether all cities have been assigned in the order of their number of inhabitants. Correct answers are highlighted in green. Incorrect answers are removed and can then be arranged once more. For the color change in correct answers, we again use classList.add(); the corresponding CSS format looks like this:

```
.aCorrect {
    background-color: hsl(75,100%,85%);
    border-color: hsl(75,100%,40%);
}
```

As soon as all answers are correct, the player is congratulated on his or her success, and if the player clicks the RESTART button, four other randomly selected cities are offered for another game. If a user finds numbers of inhabitants too tedious, the user can select two other game modes from the pull-down menu: arranging the cities by geographical location from *North to South* or *East to West*. For details on the JavaScript and CSS implementation, see these links:

- http://html5.komplett.cc/code/chap_global/1234.js

- http://html5.komplett.cc/code/chap_global/1234.css

You can see the completed game in action in Figure 12.2. If you would like to expand the game, you can go right ahead and implement an expansion *Select number of cities!* The static list on the left should then be generated dynamically. *Have fun!*

Let's get back to our original topic, drag and drop. After this simple and practical example, several details are still open—for example, three other events available for drag and drop operations: drag, dragend, and dragleave. During dragging, a drag event is created at an interval of 350 ms (±200 ms); dropping creates a dragend event. The third event, dragleave, concerns the target object and occurs when leaving a potential drop zone.

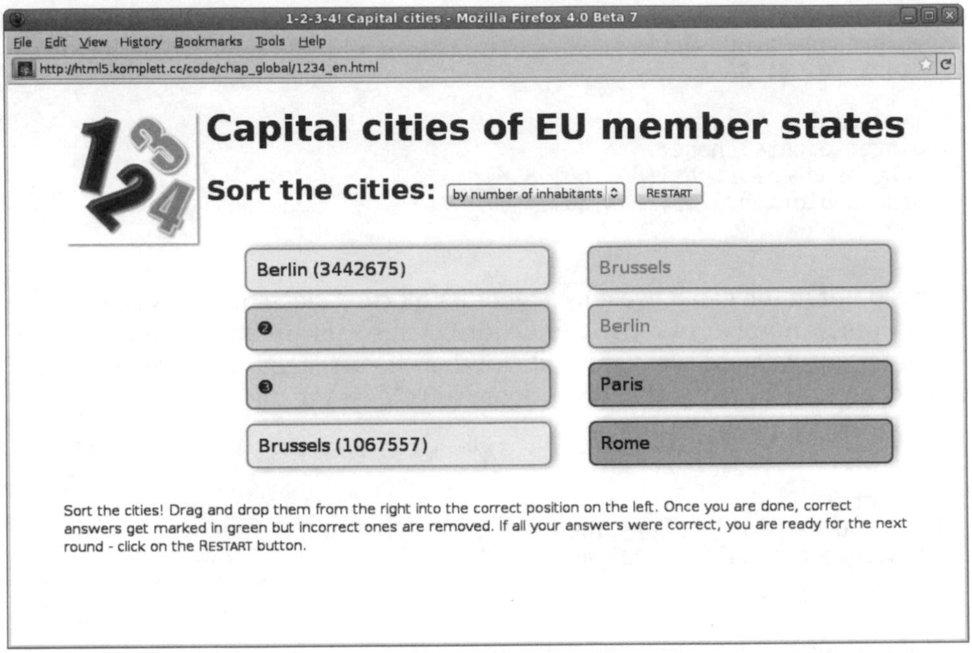

Figure 12.2   The game "1-2-3-4!" in action

The DataTransfer object also provides interesting methods and attributes—for example, the method setDragImage(element, x, y) with which we can display a custom image during dragging to provide feedback. A similar effect can be achieved with addElement(element), but this time we can drag along not just an image, but whole sections of a page as a feedback indicator.

With dataTransfer.types, we can return a DOMStringList of all formats and their values that were assigned with setData() at the startdrag event. In our game this list was short and contained only one item with the ID in the format *text*, interpreted automatically by the browser as text/plain. The format is not completely restricted to using MIME types; the specification also allows formats that do not correspond to a MIME type. So we could have used all data attributes with *speaking* names as a format. Using the example of the ID and the number of inhabitants, this would look as follows:

```
evt.dataTransfer.setData('id',evt.target.id);
evt.dataTransfer.setData('pop',evt.target.dataset.pop);
```

Retrieving them at a later time would then have been easier via getData('id') or getData('pop').

TIP

When dragging elements with *microdata* attributes, all values are automatically taken along as a *JSON* character string. You can access them easily via getData('application/microdata+json').

If we decide to remove certain formats from the list during the drag-and-drop operation, we can use the method clearData(format) to delete the specified format. If we omit format altogether, all existing formats are deleted.

The two DataTransfer attributes effectAllow and dropEffect sound promising, hinting at appealing optical effects during dragging and dropping. On closer inspection it becomes clear that they only serve to control the appearance of the cursor while entering the drop zone. Permitted keywords for dropEffect are copy, link, move, and none. They add a plus symbol, link symbol, arrow, or nothing (if none is selected) to the cursor during the dragenter event. With a small application (see Figure 12.3), you can test the behavior of your browser online at http://html5.komplett.cc/code/chap_global/dropEffect_en.html.

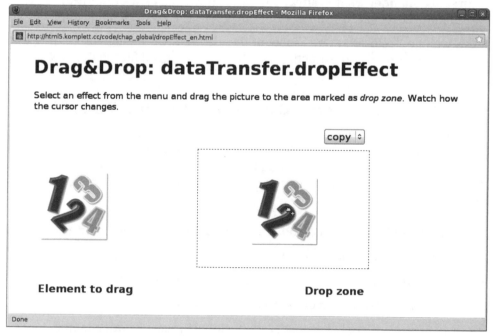

Figure 12.3   Test application of the "dataTransfer.dropEffect"

The value of the dropEffect attribute can be changed in any phase of the drag-and-drop action, but it must always correspond to the value specified previously in effectAllow. In addition to copy, link, move, and none, effectAllow also permits combinations, such as copyLink, copyMove, or linkMove, marking both components as valid. Via the keyword all, you can also allow all effects.

Before we move on to the next section, here are a few closing thoughts on security issues with drag and drop: Data in the DataTransfer object is only made available to the script again at the drop event. So, while dragging a document from A to B, data is prevented from being intercepted by a *malicious* document C. For the same reason, the drop event must be explicitly triggered by the user by dropping the object, not automatically by the script. Even the script-controlled moving of the window underneath the mouse position must not fire a dragStart event; otherwise, sensitive data could be dragged into malicious third-party documents against the user's will.

Drag and drop in the browser opens a wealth of new possibilities. If you are looking for an impressive example of combining drag and drop with *Canvas, localStorage, offline cache,* and other techniques associated with HTML5, such as XMLHttpRequest or the FileAPI, do not miss Paul Rouget's blog, *an HTML5 offline image editor and uploader application,* with its four-minute video. Even though it is only meant to be a *showcase* for features in Firefox 3.6, it does show in an impressive manner what is already possible now. Check it out at http://hacks. mozilla.org/2010/02/an-html5-offline-image-editor-and-uploader-application.

Now, we'll look closer at one aspect of this demo, introducing you to drag and drop in a document and extracting data from the dragged file via the FileAPI.

12.5.1   Drag and Drop in Combination with the "FileAPI"

Figure 12.4 shows a screen shot of the application we will develop in this section based on drag and drop and the FileAPI. It allows us to drag locally saved images taken with a digital camera or a mobile device directly into the browser and then make parts of their EXIF information visible. The necessary files are again available online at:

- http://html5.komplett.cc/code/chap_global/extract_exif_en.html
- http://html5.komplett.cc/code/chap_global/extract_exif.js
- http://html5.komplett.cc/code/chap_global/extract_exif.css
- http://html5.komplett.cc/code/chap_global/lib/exif.js
- http://html5.komplett.cc/code/chap_global/images/senderstal.jpg

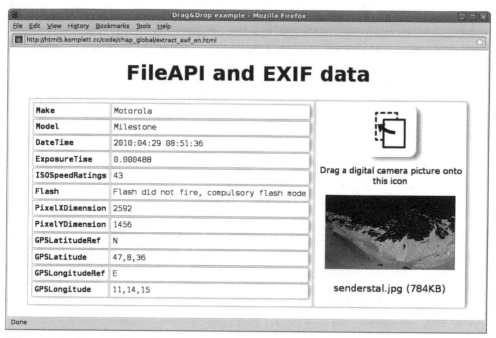

Figure 12.4   Drag and drop in combination with "FileAPI"

Let's begin by preparing the drop zone. You can see it on the right in the screen shot of Figure 12.4. It consists of the Unicode symbol *PREVIOUS PAGE* (⎗), some CSS instructions, and the event listener attributes required for drag and drop:

```
<div ondragenter="return false;"
     ondragover="return false;"
     ondrop="drop(event)">&#x2397;</div>
```

As soon as an image is dragged from the desktop to this area, the dropped image can be accessed in the callback function drop() via the dataTransfer object:

```
var drop = function(evt) {
  var file = evt.dataTransfer.files[0];
};
```

From now on we are within the FileAPI, because the attribute files represents a so-called FileList object that is an array of all file objects involved in the current drag-and-drop operation. Although the demo by Paul Rouget allows the loading of several images simultaneously, you can only drop one image at a time into the drop zone in our example. So the reference to this file is always to be found in files[0].

For the thumbnail of the image, we use a `data:` URI as a `src` attribute, created via the `FileAPI`, as discussed in Chapter 5, Canvas (see section 5.12, Base64 encoding with "canvas.toDataURL()"). We first define a new `FileReader` object, and then load the image *asynchronously* into the memory via `readAsDataURL()`. At the end of the loading process, we assign the resulting `data:` URI to the image as a `src` attribute. The relevant JavaScript code is short and clear:

```
var dataURLReader = new FileReader();
dataURLReader.onloadend = function() {
  imgElem.src = dataURLReader.result;
  imgInfo.innerHTML = file.name+' ('+_inKb(file.size)+')';
}
dataURLReader.readAsDataURL(file);
```

The width of the thumbnail is specified in the CSS stylesheet as `width: 250px`; the height is adjusted automatically by the browser. The text below the image reflects the `FileAPI` attributes `file.name` and `file.size`. The byte information in `file.size` must be divided by *1024* to convert the file size to kilobytes. The auxiliary function `_inKb()` does this for us and also adds the characters *KB* at the end of the calculated value.

For reading the EXIF information, the file must be in binary form. Similar to `readAsDataURL()`, we now use `readAsBinaryString()` and get our desired result in the `onload` callback. This does not yet allow us to access the EXIF data, because the data is hiding somewhere in the binary code and needs to be extracted first. We want to thank Jacob Seidelin for his JavaScript implementation for reading EXIF data, which made this example possible.

NOTE

The version of exif.js used in this example is not the original version by Jacob Seidelin, but instead is a slightly adapted version by Paul Rouget. You can find both versions online in the relevant demos at these URLs:

- http://www.nihilogic.dk/labs/exif
- http://demos.hacks.mozilla.org/openweb/FileAPI

A single line is now sufficient to find the existing EXIF information as key-value pairs via the function `findEXIFinJPEG()`. In a for loop, this list is then processed and converted into table rows with the auxiliary function `_asRow()`, and the result is added to the result table in the variable `exifInfo`:

```
var binaryReader = new FileReader();
binaryReader.onload = function() {
  var exif = findEXIFinJPEG(binaryReader.result);
```

```
  for (var key in exif) {
    exifInfo.innerHTML += _asRow(key,exif[key]);
  }
};
binaryReader.readAsBinaryString(file);
```

As you can see in the screen shot in Figure 12.4, only selected EXIF info is listed in our example. Apart from information about camera type, date and time, exposure time, ISO speed, use of flash, or image dimensions, there are even GPS coordinates that were recorded by the camera when taking the picture. A glance at the coordinates and the image name reveals the location: the *Senderstal* valley near the *Kalkkögel* in the *Stubai Alps* (southwest of Innsbruck, Tyrol, Austria). The prominent peak in the center of the image is called *Schwarzhorn*.

> **TIP**
>
> If you want to display all EXIF information of your own images while testing the application shown in Figure 12.4, you simply need to remove the comment characters from the item //showTags = '*' in the file extract_exif.js!

Although the FileAPI specification is rather short, it offers several interesting features. In addition to the already familiar methods for reading files in binary mode or as data: URI, you have the option of reading text files via readAsText(). The onprogress event serves as user feedback for implementing a progress display during loading, and if loading takes too long, you can also abort it with abort(). Additionally, the FileAPI can also be used for forms via <input type=file>.

The same applies here as for drag and drop: If you want to implement more complex applications, you will have to study the details in the specification. The relevant contents for the FileAPI and drag and drop can be found at these links:

- http://www.w3.org/TR/FileAPI
- http://www.w3.org/TR/html5/dnd.html

After this excursion into the world of the FileAPI, there are still two interesting global attributes that we want to mention in this chapter. Similar to drag and drop, they open up a new and unknown world, only encountered previously through word-processing programs. Who would have thought a few years ago that the content of an HTML page could be edited directly in the browser and the spelling checked immediately?

12.6   The Attributes "contenteditable" and "spellcheck"

HTML pages can be made editable via the `contenteditable` attribute, but of course the changes occur only in memory. For filling in an online form before printing it, this can be very useful, and there are surely fields of application within the intranet as well, especially if amended content is written back with scripts. We do not want to go quite that far in this section; instead, we will merely demonstrate how `contenteditable` can be activated. The syntax in the HTML code is simple:

```
<p contenteditable=true>
  Text to be edited ...
</p>
```

The editable area is highlighted by clicking on the paragraph, and a flashing cursor appears in the text. You can then use hotkeys or the context menu to cut, paste, copy, or delete content, just as in a text editor, and all actions can also be undone step by step. If we want to also activate the spell check, we need to add the attribute `spellcheck` and set it to *true*:

```
<p contenteditable=true spellcheck=true>
    Text to be edited ...
</p>
```

The specification does not define how the spell check should be carried out in detail; this is up to the individual browser. Using the example of Firefox 3.6, Figure 12.5 shows what such an implementation could look like. The example is of course also available for testing online at http://html5.komplett.cc/code/chap_global/edit_page_en.html.

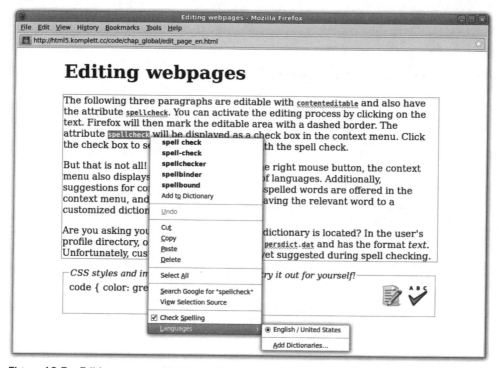

Figure 12.5   Editing a page with the spell checker in Firefox 3.6

The screen shot in Figure 12.5 shows how misspelled words as well as unknown words are indicated with red wavy lines. The context menu allows you to switch to another language, install new dictionaries, and even correct mistakes by choosing from suggestions. Unknown words can also be added to a personal dictionary.

In Firefox, personal dictionaries are located in the user's profile folder and are named persdict.dat. Even though the file extension suggests otherwise, these files are pure text documents with one word per line. Unfortunately, entries from personal dictionaries are not yet listed during correction, at least with Firefox 3.6.

At the time of this writing, no browser had implemented the spellcheck attribute without errors. It seems that browsers view all text areas of a page as natural candidates for spell checking and always allow checking in the context menu without taking into account the spellcheck attribute. The attempt to exclude the CSS code from spell checking via spellcheck=false was unsuccessful in all of the browsers tested.

Figure 12.6 shows that not only text components, but also CSS styles and even images can be made editable.

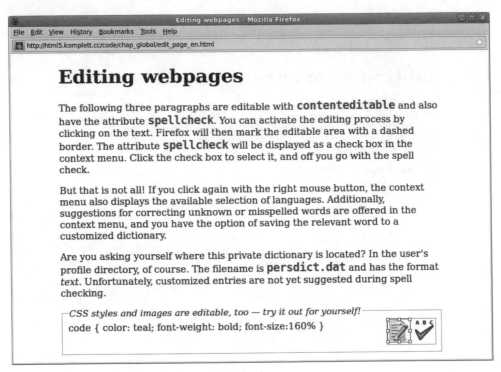

Figure 12.6   "Live" editing of styles and image sizes

The editing options for images are as yet not very impressive. Firefox allows for at least changing the image size by dragging eight available anchor points. The idea of changing styles *live* within a style element is more exciting. This idea comes from Anne van Kesteren who first demonstrated this effect via a simple trick (see http://bit.ly/dtnyIJ). As with Anne van Kesteren's example, the style element in our application is first made visible with display:block and then editable with contenteditable=true. The result is astonishing. Changes become effective immediately. In our case, after changing the CSS instruction for the code element, the corresponding objects appear in the named color *teal* with font-size 180%. Try it out!

Summary

Seven selected global attributes, some of them new, and their JavaScript APIs are the focus of the final chapter of this book. We encounter five of them in more detail while developing our 1-2-3-4! game. The starting point is a new method for the class attribute: the classList interface. It drastically simplifies manipulating the individual class components. The same applies to the dataset property, enabling easier management of custom, user-defined attributes that are marked with the special prefix data-*.

Our game incorporates the highly controversial hidden attribute, plus one of the key features of HTML5: drag and drop. The draggable attribute, a handful of events, and the DataTransfer interface enable not only dragging and dropping elements within a browser, but also interaction with the underlying operating system. The impressive example for reading EXIF information of digital images uses this feature and introduces the FileAPI.

The final section of the chapter demonstrates that text content and even CSS formats of an HTML5 page can be directly edited in the browser. To avoid spelling errors during editing, the spellcheck attribute can be used to activate spell checking in the browser, complete with a dictionary. Could HTML5 be on its way to turning into a full-blown office package?

Afterword

The development of HTML5 is progressing rapidly. The specification is amended and improved daily, angles and corners are smoothed, superfluous components are removed, and if necessary, new features are added. The driving force behind this process is an active community of representatives of WHATWG, W3C, the browser manufacturers, interested individuals, and of course Ian Hickson, the disputatious editor of the specification, whose decisions quite often lead to heated debates.

If he has his way, the HTML standard of the future will be developed as a "living standard" continuously and without a version number. Instead of descriptions, such as *HTML5*, *HTML6*, or *HTML-Next*, we would then simply use the term *HTML*. The implementation of the specification should take place in parallel to its development—a wish that has already been fulfilled in practice, because although the specification is not yet completely final, many of its components are already implemented in the main browsers.

If the guidelines of the *HTML Working Group* of the W3C are fulfilled, HTML5 will probably reach *Last Call* status in May 2011, by which time it should be clearer which features become part of the final web standard in the eyes of the W3C and which do not. Nevertheless, experimental features of the WHATWG specification could potentially find their way into the final version of the standard, primarily the track element for video subtitles or audio with WebVTT (Web Video Text Tracks) as a format for specifying these. The device element, too, allowing websites access to input devices such as microphones or video cameras, is a potential candidate for being incorporated into the specification at some time in the future.

A solution is urgently required to the unsolved questions regarding accessibility in Canvas, audio, and video, and a decision must be made whether microdata, RDFa, or even both have a place in the final version of the specification. Harmonizing the various versions of the specification at W3C and WHATWG is also long overdue.

HTML—with or without the 5 at the end—is most definitely a *work in progress* and comes one step closer each day to achieving its goal of becoming the *de facto* standard for the Internet of the future. If during your journey through this book you should stumble across any inconsistencies or even errors, please let us know. The companion website to this book at http://html5.komplett.cc/ welcome offers plenty of space for comments, feedback, and ideas, in accordance with the *join-in* spirit of the HTML specification. We look forward to your visit!

Index

FREE Online Edition

Your purchase of **HTML5 Guidelines for Web Developers** includes access to a free online edition for 45 days through the Safari Books Online subscription service. Nearly every Addison-Wesley Professional book is available online through Safari Books Online, along with more than 5,000 other technical books and videos from publishers such as Cisco Press, Exam Cram, IBM Press, O'Reilly, Prentice Hall, Que, and Sams.

SAFARI BOOKS ONLINE allows you to search for a specific answer, cut and paste code, download chapters, and stay current with emerging technologies.

Activate your FREE Online Edition at
www.informit.com/safarifree

> **STEP 1:** Enter the coupon code: QZBJPXA.

> **STEP 2:** New Safari users, complete the brief registration form.
> Safari subscribers, just log in.

If you have difficulty registering on Safari or accessing the online edition, please e-mail customer-service@safaribooksonline.com

WEB PROGRAMMING/HTML

HTML5 › GUIDELINES for WEB DEVELOPERS

In *HTML5 Guidelines for Web Developers,* two pioneering web developers provide a comprehensive guide to HTML5's powerful new elements and techniques through compact, practical, easy-to-understand examples. You'll discover just how much you can do with HTML5—from programming audio/video playback to integrating geographical data into pages and applications.

This concise, friendly reference is packed with tips, tricks, and samples for making the most of HTML5 with JavaScript and the DOM. The authors present "pure HTML5" examples that are supported by browsers right now, and they share realistic insights into the challenges of leading-edge HTML5 development. All examples are available for download, with links to web resources for new information and specification updates. Topics covered include

> Browser support: What you can (and can't) do with HTML5 today
> HTML5 document structure and semantics
> Intelligent forms, including new input types, elements, and client-side validation
> The "video" and "audio" elements, and scripting media solutions
> Advanced graphics with Canvas and SVG
> Geolocation in the browser, including location tracking via Google Maps
> Web storage, offline web applications, We... and Web Workers
> Embedding sematic markup with Microdata and the Microdata DOM API
> Implementing drag-and-drop with the "draggable" attribute
> New global attributes: "data-*," "hidden," "contenteditable," "spellcheck," and more

If you're a web developer or designer with at least basic knowledge of HTML, JavaScript, and CSS, this book is all you need to master HTML5—and get to the cutting edge of web development.

informit.com/aw
html5.komplett.cc/welcome

Cover Design by Chuti Prasertsith
Cover illustration by Marco Lindenbeck, webwo GmbH
Text printed on recycled paper

Addison-Wesley
Pearson Education

ABOUT the AUTHORS

Klaus Förster, an open source enthusiast, works at the Department of Geography at the University of Innsbruck, Austria. He has attended numerous SVG Open conferences as speaker, reviewer, and workshop leader, and contributed SVG modules to the free software projects PostGIS, GRASS GIS, and SpatiaLite.

Bernd Öggl, lecturer and system administrator at the University of Innsbruck, is coauthor of books on PHP and MySQL. He has programmed web applications for many years.

HTML N°5

ISBN-13: 978-0-321-77274-9
ISBN-10:   0-321-77274-1

$34.99 U.S. | $36.99 CANADA